Trade theories and empirical evidence

MANCHESTER
UNIVERSITY PRESS

Trade theories and empirical evidence

NICHOLAS PERDIKIS

and

WILLIAM A. KERR

Manchester University Press

Manchester and New York

distributed exclusively in the USA by St. Martin's Press

Copyright © Nicholas Perdikis and William A. Kerr

Published by Manchester University Press
Oxford Road, Manchester M13 9NR, UK
and Room 400, 175 Fifth Avenue, New York, NY 10010, USA

Distributed exclusively in Canada by
UBC Press, University of British Columbia, 6344 Memorial Road, Vancouver, BC,
Canada V6T 1Z2

Distributed exclusively in the USA by
St. Martin's Press, Inc., 175 Fifth Avenue, New York, NY 10010, USA

British Library Cataloguing-in-Publication Data
A catalogue record is available from the British Library

Library of Congress Cataloguing-in-Publication Data

Perdikis, Nicholas
　　Trade theories and empirical evidence / Nicholas Perdikis and William Kerr.
　　p.　　cm.
　　Includes bibliographical references and index.
　　ISBN 0-7190-5409-5 (cloth)
　　1. International trade.　　I. Kerr, William A. (William Alexander)
　II. Title.
　HF1379.P47　　1998
　382′.104–dc21　　　　　　　　　　　　　　　　　　　　　97-48662

ISBN 0 7190 5409 5 *hardback*

First published 1998

05 04 03 02 01 00 99 98　　　　　　　　　10 9 8 7 6 5 4 3 2 1

Typeset in Great Britain
by Special Edition Pre-Press Services, London
Printed in Great Britain
by Bookcraft (Bath) Ltd, Midsomer Norton

This book is dedicated to the memory of
Violetta and Lazaros Perdikis

and is for

Adrienne, Jill, Kara, Kevin, Leonie, May and Rhiannon – friends and former students who all studied at both the University of Wales – Aberystwyth, and the University of Calgary and are compelling evidence of the benefits of international education and cooperation.

Contents

Tables

Preface

One of the central concerns in the study of international economics has been the development of theoretical models that explain the pattern of world trade. While advances in trade theory continue to be made, empirical testing – and, hence, the important step of validating the hypotheses posed by theorists – has often taken place much later and the reports of such studies are widely dispersed in the literature. Even with the oldest of trade theories empirical testing is probably never finished. The aim of this book is to trace the development of the various theories and to document the empirical evidence that has been used to support or contest them, and the interplay between theoretical effort and empirical testing provides its focus. New theories provide new opportunities for empirical testing. When difficulties are encountered in the empirical validation of trade theories, theorists are spurred on to new efforts. We think it is a compelling story that illustrates the process – often slow and tortuous – by which progress is made in economics. It is hoped that this volume will act in part as a reference source, enabling those embarking on empirical work to see what was done and how and when it was done. The book is, thus, targeted primarily at final-year undergraduates, postgraduates and those who completed their formal education in international economics a few years ago and wish to bring themselves up to date.

The approach that has been taken is roughly chronological. A reviewer of our proposed manuscript suggested that an alternative, more thematic structure might be more appropriate. We gave the suggestion much consideration. We thought it was a valid point; chronologies can often be turgid to read and are not friendly to readers who are interested in quickly locating the evidence concerning a specific theory or finding out when a particular test has been applied. In the end we rejected the thematic approach – primarily because we believe that the chronology of the interplay between those who devise trade theories and those who develop empirical tests for them explains so much of the current state of trade theory. Divorcing trade theory from its historical development would be a disservice to the reader and would leave him or her with an incomplete picture of either trade theory or empirical evaluation.

We have purposely avoided commenting on the validity of the empirical techniques used in the various studies. Econometric theory and practice have come a long way in recent decades – and will continue to make progress. Judging the methods used in the past by those of today is both unfair to the original authors and of transient value. In all likelihood, by the time the book has gone to press the standard may well have moved. Most of the studies examined were published in the very best journals of the discipline and, hence, were subject to the scrutiny of review by the authors' contemporaries. The reader who is equipped with current econometric methods will, we are convinced, find that there are a large number of questions that can be better answered with such techniques. Hopefully, new questions will also be suggested to readers, and they can join in the process from which progress in the explanation of patterns of trade arises.

Acknowledgements

No project such as this book arises in isolation. Many hands (and minds) have a part. Nick Perdikis would like to thank Professor L. J. Williams and David Law for reading earlier drafts of some of the chapters. He is also grateful to Professor G. L. Rees, who provided him with the opportunity to teach international economics and to research the subject.

We would like to thank Laurie Stephens and Moira Jensen, who typed successive iterations of the manuscript. Both of us wish to thank Nicola Viinikka of Manchester University Press for shepherding the manuscript through to publication.

CHAPTER 1

The issues

Paul Samuelson[1] tells the story of how he was constantly challenged by his colleagues in mathematics and science at the Massachusetts Institute of Technology (MIT) to produce a proposition from economics that was not either trivial or banal or both. At the time, he says, he always failed this test. Only later did he realise that there was a decisive answer – the law of comparative advantage. This most fundamental proposition of international economics demonstrates that although one country may be more efficient than another in producing all tradeable goods, they will nonetheless both gain from trading with each other, and that trading will, moreover, maximise their joint output. This proposition is neither trivial, since it provides the theoretical justification for a sizeable part of international commerce, nor is it banal in the sense of being self-evident or simply common sense. For example, when first introduced to comparative advantage most students find the proposition counterintuitive. Convincing students of the validity of the examples provided to 'prove' comparative advantage requires considerably more class time than almost any other basic proposition in economics.

The logical arguments of the law of comparative advantage were fully developed in the early nineteenth century and, although subjected to considerable intellectual scrutiny, have remained a central pillar of international trade theory. It is the objective of this book to trace, over the last two centuries, the refinements that have been made to the economic theory which has at its heart the law of comparative advantage, along with the ways in which empirical findings have led to modifications and restatements of its hypotheses or the propounding of alternative theories.

The classical treatment of international trade, whose evolution dates from the late eighteenth century, was based on the assumption of a two-country world in which each country produced the same two commodities with one homogeneous factor, labour. The productivity of labour was assumed to differ between countries and industries were characterised as having constant returns to scale.

This theory was originally developed to explain trade in agricultural products and simple manufactures where the major inputs were based on natural resources. Differences in the quality of climate and soil would give rise to differences in the productivity of labour. Differences in labour productivity would, in turn, determine a country's comparative advantage and, hence, the goods it would export and import.

There were two major limitations to the classical – or Ricardian,[2] as it is sometimes called – explanation of trade patterns. The first was its assumption of one factor of production when it was obvious that many factors were used in actual production processes. The second limitation was the difficulty the model had in explaining how comparative advantage could come about in a world where knowledge and skills – in addition to natural resources – were becoming economically important. These limitations were addressed by the factor proportions, neoclassical or Heckscher–Ohlin model, which sought to explain comparative advantage on the basis of a country's relative factor endowments. A country with abundant endowments of capital relative to its labour supply would find that the price of capital was relatively lower than the price of labour. As a result of this difference in relative prices, a capital-abundant country would have a comparative advantage in the production of goods that used this abundant factor intensively. To put it starkly, cheap capital gave a country a comparative advantage in the production of capital-intensive goods. It would, therefore, export capital-intensive goods and import labour-intensive goods. Rigorous empirical tests of the neoclassical model were seldom attempted until the costs – in terms of both calculation effort and ensuring a reasonable degree of accuracy – of using statistical methods fell with the advent of widely available computers. This did not happen until the early 1960s.

The factor endowments or Heckscher–Ohlin theory was unquestionably the predominant paradigm in the literature on international trade until it was tested empirically. Empirical examination of the trade patterns of the US, a country considered to be the world's most capital-abundant, found that its exports were labour-intensive while its imports were capital-intensive. This result was contrary to the prediction of the factor endowments model and became one of the foremost paradoxes of modern economics. Subsequent tests on the US and other countries also produced results that were contrary to theoretical expectations and appeared to confirm the paradox.

A number of explanations were put forward to reconcile trade theory with the evidence. Two – the inclusion of land (shorthand for resources) and human capital, measured by a number of indicators of skill and education, as additional inputs into production – were the most successful. There were, nevertheless, instances when the paradoxes could not be resolved either for US trade or for that of other countries. While some economists were happy to accept a modified Heckscher–Ohlin model, others were not and sought to develop alternative theories. These theories were largely based on assumptions opposite to those of the neoclassical theory.

Explanations based on increasing returns to scale, as opposed to constant returns, were advanced to describe trade patterns in manufactures. Whereas Heckscher–Ohlin related an economy's trade pattern to its underlying physical characteristics, economies of scale introduced a degree of arbitrariness into the analysis. Allowing for economies of scale meant that observed trade patterns could be determined simply by historical accident. Export success depended on which country had established an early lead over its rivals – and so was able to take advantage of economies of scale – in one or a range of particular industries. By gaining a lead a country could achieve lower costs and would, therefore, make it difficult for rival countries to compete successfully. Hence, it became theoretically possible for a country to export a good or goods that would be contrary to those expected from examination of its factor endowments.

The economies of scale argument implied that large countries would be in a better position to exploit the potential benefits of trade than small countries. It was suggested, however, that even small countries could achieve economies of scale, and thereby comparative advantage, if they concentrated their production on standard goods that did not rely on national characteristics as a selling feature.

Another important step in the evolution of alternative trade theories was the *availability thesis*, which tried to incorporate the effects of technology on trade patterns. Neoclassical theory assumes that all countries are able to use the same (currently most productive) technology. The availability thesis accepted that a country's endowments could affect its trade pattern but also supposed that trade patterns could be influenced by factors that were specific to each country. For example, an oil- or diamond-rich country would be an exporter of those products because they were not available elsewhere. This argument could also be applied to technologically advanced products. All countries could produce them if they undertook the appropriate investment, but the cost of doing so might well be prohibitive except in a small number of countries. As a result, only a few countries are likely to have technology-intensive products available for export.

Subsequent trade theories based on differences in technological capability emphasised that the lead one country possessed over another was finite. As the product and the production process became standardised, costs of acquiring and using the technology would fall, allowing other countries' firms to enter the market. In the interim, however, the inventing country would have a comparative advantage in the production of the new good and would export it in return for other goods.

Differing technological capabilities have been used to explain two types of international exchange: trade between technologically advanced countries and trade between advanced and developing countries. The first case arises even if two countries are equally inventive but they have specialised in the development of different types of goods. This specialisation provides a basis for the exchange of one good for another. Invention and innovation are assumed to be random processes. In the second case it is assumed that the technologically advanced country maintains its innovativeness, exporting new goods to developing countries in return for standardised products. Over time, these new goods become standardised and are eventually produced in developing countries. In the meantime, however, the advanced countries develop a whole new range of goods. As long as the technological lead is self-perpetuating the fundamental trading pattern is maintained.

Trade models based on sustained differences in technological capability (or a 'technology gap') assume that there is a link between high income levels and innovativeness or dynamism. A large potential market for relatively expensive goods incorporating sophisticated technology is required so that firms can recoup their development costs. Otherwise, expensive research and development will not be undertaken. Although a link between income and dynamism or innovativeness can be established, it is not so clear why the production of new goods should be located in technologically advanced countries. One answer is provided by examining the changes in a good's characteristics as it matures. In the initial phases of a product's development there are major uncertainties with regard to its shape and style and the appropriate production process. These uncertainties can be reduced if changes in the market's mood can be translated quickly into alterations in the product or production process. The need to alter a product can be acted upon if production is carried out close to the market, while improvements to production processes can be achieved if skilled, and hence flexible, labour is substituted for fixed capital equipment. As the product matures and becomes more standardised, marketing and production uncertainties are reduced and competitive pressures increase. Firms seek out cheaper locations for their production facilities and the comparative advantage moves from the innovating countries to those with lower production costs.

As well as encouraging the development of new goods, income can also be looked upon as influencing tastes and, hence, demand patterns. National differences in consumers' tastes were put forward as an explanation for the increasing volume of trade between developed countries with similar factor endowments. Initially, entrepreneurs gear their production to supplying local needs. But as their firms grow and their local market becomes saturated they seek new outlets abroad. Firms searching for new markets will be attracted to those countries whose consumers share similar wants and tastes. As income levels are a major determinant of demand, trade will be greatest in intensity between countries with similar per capita national incomes.

Empirical work progressed almost concurrently with these later theoretical developments as the computer and econometric methods had become a standard part of the economist's tool kit. Initially, the testing of the technological theories was concentrated around case studies, but this approach was soon replaced by more formal statistical tests that became increasingly sophisticated over time. By and large, the empirical tests gave a measure of support to each theory taken individually. Work involving the simultaneous testing of neoclassical theories and the new, alternative theories also progressed apace. The results of this work were generally supportive of all the theories – although some fared better under empirical scrutiny than others. One of the main difficulties experienced by empirical researchers was in trying to find adequate proxies with which to test their theoretical propositions. The theoretical debate was often clouded by discussion of the appropriateness of the data used in the tests.

During the late 1950s and early 1960s it became increasingly obvious that the trade patterns of the developed countries had come to be dominated by trade among themselves in similar but differentiated goods. This phenomenon, known as intra-industry trade, required a new theoretical explanation because the existing theories could not account for it. The Ricardian, neoclassical and alternative theories all predicted that countries would export the goods in which they possessed a comparative advantage and import different goods in which they had a comparative disadvantage. The goods of one industry were exported while goods from another industry were imported and, hence, the same good could not be simultaneously imported and exported.

Initially, a number of economists felt that intra-industry trade was nothing more than a statistical artifact. Given the difficulties associated with defining an industry, any intra-industry trade observed might simply have been due to the misclassification of products into overly broad industry groups. Two arguments were put forward to dispel this view – one theoretical, the other pragmatic. The first argument suggested that to eliminate the phenomenon of intra-industry trade in an industry group such as automobiles, one might need to designate each make of car as a unique industry. This suggestion, however, was not very helpful. It did, however, force proponents of intra-industry trade to be more precise in the use of the industry classifications on which they based their empirical measurements. The pragmatic argument arose directly out of the classification discussion as, when the statistics were reworked or examined at lower levels of industry aggregation, a significant amount of intra-industry trade still existed. In other words, intra-industry trade could not be explained away by improved classification and measurement.

The debate surrounding intra-industry trade quickly segmented the types of goods traded into homogeneous and differentiated goods. Studies soon established that intra-industry trade in the former was accounted for by entrepôt trade,[3] seasonality in the production of goods and the existence of transport costs. The empirical evidence also suggested that intra-industry trade can occur in both competitive and oligopolistic market structures.

In the case of differentiated goods, it was suggested that intra-industry trade arose as a result of consumers demanding variety. Under autarky,[4] domestic producers would concentrate their production on those varieties of goods that had the largest domestic market share. Once trade was opened up, consumers would have more varieties to choose from and those with high incomes would demand varieties which were produced abroad. As a result, two-way trade would arise in similar but differentiated products. Demand for variety was expected to be greater at higher rather than lower levels of income because only rich consumers would be willing to pay for the more costly imported products. At low levels of income the opportunity cost of consuming variety was assumed to be greater and, therefore, poorer consumers refrained from this activity.

Although demand for differentiated products could suggest why intra-industry trade might arise and why it appeared to increase at a faster rate than income, it did not account for the distribution of production activity among countries or which goods a country would produce. One explanation was that each variety required different factor proportions in production. Each country would then concentrate on the varieties most suited to its own endowments in line with the Heckscher–Ohlin model. The problem with this view, it was argued, was that it was difficult to believe that *similar* goods required such different technologies.

Another, and possibly more realistic, explanation of intra-industry trade utilised the concept of economies of scale. This approach began with the proposition that although firms are technically able to produce a number of varieties, the cost of producing additional lines of product has to be balanced against the benefits derived from specialisation. Thus, it was suggested, when trade is opened up between countries, the production of some varieties is concentrated in one country while others are concentrated in the other in order to reap the benefits of economies of scale. Which varieties are produced where is determined by chance, the competitive process and the long-term strategies of the companies concerned.

As with inter-industry trade, those undertaking empirical tests of the various hypotheses of intra-industry trade ran into difficulties over the appropriateness of various proxies. Concepts such as product heterogeneity and differentiation, brand imaging, research and development, economies of scale, industrial structure and tariff levels were all measured in a variety of ways. Again, the empirical evidence supported the principal theories but no single hypothesis predominated.

With the empirical evidence providing support for a number of the major hypotheses, the development of a general theory of trade incorporating some aspects of each theory suggested itself as an appealing avenue for research. The form that this synthesis should take, however, was not clear. The inclusion of human capital within the Heckscher–Ohlin framework, although fairly straightforward, did not overcome a suspicion felt by many economists that technological factors were not being fully taken into account. A more successful synthesis was an amalgamation of the demand patterns hypothesis and the Heckscher–Ohlin model. The influence of factor endowments on research and development has also been investigated. An integration of the Heckscher–Ohlin model with intra-industry trade models has also been used to account simultaneously for the patterns of trade between developed economies and between developed countries as a group and developing countries.

Another, more eclectic, approach has been taken by some economists. No attempt was made to build a general theory of trade. Instead, the strengths of each individual theory are recognised. Trade in a specific group of products is explained by the most appropriate theory – almost on a case study basis. This approach implies that the Ricardian theory can be used to analyse the trade patterns of natural resource industries or those manufactures which are produced using simple processes and incorporating basic materials. For industries with standardised products and manufacturing processes and, hence, where the reduction of input costs is the most important consideration, the Heckscher–Ohlin model would be appropriate. For industries that utilise sophisticated technology to produce non-standardised goods for rapidly changing consumer tastes, theories based on differences in technological sophistication would be useful in explaining trade patterns. Insofar as the goods found in intra-industry trade are either standardised or technologically advanced, their trade can be explained by either Heckscher–Ohlin or technology-gap models.

The validity of this eclectic approach depends on whether one can categorise products fairly easily. A number of authors have taken this approach and their results are, by and large, encouraging. It must be said, however, that other researchers have suggested that the observed trade patterns are the result of the existence of tariffs and quotas rather than the factors suggested by various theories. Analyses based on data from markets not subject to distortions caused by trade policy measures tend to rehabilitate the traditional Heckscher–Ohlin model.

Notwithstanding the limited evidence from undistorted markets, the central question remains: why, with so much evidence against it, has the Heckscher–Ohlin model survived as the main contender for the position of a general theory of international trade? The answer must lie in its intuitive appeal and its analytical power. Further, the narrowness of the alternative theories and weak empirical support for them have made it difficult to dislodge. This is particularly true given the philosophical acceptability of the model within the broader neoclassical paradigm. As the contentious empirical issues surrounding the methodologies that are used to test theories have not been resolved, no defining judgement of a theory's validity can be made. As a result, the Heckscher–Ohlin model continues to be the ruling paradigm for theoretical work on international trade.

The reader should by now have gained some insight into the issues surrounding the development of trade theories and their empirical testing. Chapter 2 outlines the classical and neoclassical trade theories, while Chapter 3 deals with the empirical tests that have been applied to them. Chapter 4 traces the development of alternative theories, concentrating mainly on the technology-based theories and their extensions. In Chapter 5 the empirical evidence for each of these alternatives is discussed in full. Chapter 6 expands the discussion to include intra-industry trade theories and the empirical work that has been undertaken to test them. Simultaneous testing of the Heckscher–Ohlin model and the alternative theories is discussed in Chapter 7, along with some of the theoretical developments that it engendered. The final chapter provides a summary and closes by examining the question of the use of empirical evidence and its effect on the current state of the study of international trade.

Notes

1 Paul Samuelson is a Nobel laureate in economics who is considered to be one of the most influential economists of the latter half of the twentieth century. This is for two reasons. First, his scholarly activity has been immense, of high quality and very wide ranging – including forays into international trade topics. Second, he authored an extremely popular textbook that has been used to provide an introduction to economics for hundreds of thousands of students in many countries.
2 Named after David Ricardo (1772–1823), who fully articulated the law of comparative advantage in his book *Principles of Political Economy and Taxation*, first published in 1817.
3 Entrepôt trade takes place when a country imports and subsequently exports the same goods. An entrepôt, therefore, is a place of transhipment. Hong Kong is probably the best known, acting as a major channel of trade between China and the West.
4 i.e. where no trade is allowed.

CHAPTER 2

Classical and neoclassical trade theory

2.1 Introduction

This chapter outlines the development of what have come to be known as the classical and neoclassical theories of international trade. Although the major focus of the chapter is theoretical explanations of trade patterns, it is impossible to avoid discussing the gains arising from trade. This is because the writings of Adam Smith,[1] David Ricardo[2] and other classical economists were very much concerned with the benefits international trade could bring to a nation's economy. Classical economists writing on trade topics were responding to the existing mercantilist views of how strategic management of trade could enhance a country's economic wellbeing. Once we have laid out the basics of classical trade theory, two major subsequent developments in the theory will be explored: (1) the extension of the model from an assumption that there is only one productive resource to a model based on two resources (as well as two goods and two countries); and (2) the abandonment of the labour theory of value in favour of the opportunity cost approach (Haberler, 1936). The neoclassical, or factor endowments, model proposed by Ohlin (1933) is then explored. The neoclassical model attempted to explain more completely the underlying determinants of trade flows between countries. The major assumptions underlying the formal neoclassical model and its evolution are discussed. Empirical tests of the models will be examined and their results discussed in Chapter 3. Hence, when reading this chapter it is important to identify the testable hypotheses that are suggested by the theoretical models presented.

2.2 Mercantilist views of trade

Mercantilism was the dominant view of international commerce in Western Europe from approximately 1500 to 1800. The objective of mercantilist trade policy was that exports should exceed imports (or to run a surplus on a nation's balance of trade). At that time foreign transactions had to be settled in gold or silver; hence, a surplus would lead to the accumulation of precious metals, which could then be used to finance larger armies and navies. In turn, these military forces could be deployed to conquer lands overseas, expanding the nation's colonial empire and adding to its political power. Further, a trade surplus would mean that more gold and other precious metals would go into circulation in the domestic market, which would enhance business activity. However, if individuals were allowed to trade freely they would exchange gold or silver for foreign-made consumer and capital goods. As a result, the nation would use up its reserves of exchangeable precious metals and become less militarily and politically powerful (although consumers would be better off). With the world stock of precious metals fixed at any one time and as all nations could not simultaneously run trade surpluses, one nation could only gain at the expense of others. To achieve the goal of a trade surplus, countries were advised by the mercantilists to place strict limits on their imports from other countries and to produce domestic substitutes to the greatest degree possible. Exports were to be maximised.

The value premise of those who criticised mercantilist thought (and who subsequently became known as classical economists) was in complete contrast to the national economic power orientation of the mercantilists. They equated the nation's welfare with the sum of the welfare of individual citizens or, as David Ricardo phrased it, 'the sum of enjoyments'. Thus, what benefited individuals benefited the country as a whole. Working from this assumption, classical trade economists produced a theory that arrived at radically different conclusions to those of the mercantilists. Their theory has survived considerable intellectual scrutiny and remains to this day the basis of the trade theory which is taught in introductory university economics courses.

2.3 Classical trade theory

Classical economics, of which classical trade theory is a part, refers to an era of economic thought covering the period 1750–1870. The two central concepts of classical trade theory are 'absolute advantage' and 'comparative advantage'.

2.3.1 Absolute advantage

Adam Smith's proposition concerning international trade was simple. He argued that if two nations traded with each other voluntarily, both must gain. Otherwise trade would not take place. Mutually beneficial trade would come about if each country specialised in the production and export of the good in which it had an absolute advantage. By absolute advantage Smith meant that, in a two-country, two-good world, one country could be more efficient than the other in producing one good while being less efficient in producing the second good. For the other country the opposite could be the case. If each country concentrated on producing and exporting the good in which it possessed an absolute advantage, the resources of each country would be used in the most efficient way. The output of each commodity would increase and part of this increase could be used to import the good in which the country had an absolute disadvantage. A key feature of classical absolute advantage is its assumption that a single resource is available for use in production.

Absolute advantage can be illustrated using the numerical example provided in Table 2.1. It is usual to prove absolute advantage numerically using the simplest case possible. This is an example where there are only two countries, only two goods and a single resource or productive input. While the real world is clearly far more complex, the results derived from the simple case can be applied to more complex cases (i.e. can be generalised) by adding countries and/or goods. In Table 2.1 there are two countries, I and II, and two goods, A and B. There is one productive input – labour. By expending one unit of labour (per hour/week/month, etc.) country I can produce one unit of A or five units of B. For the same outlay of labour, country II can produce six units of A or four units of B. Thus, country I is more efficient in the production of good B and therefore has an absolute advantage in its production. It has an absolute disadvantage in the production of good A.

Table 2.1 Absolute advantage: output per unit of labour

| | Goods | |
	A	B
Country I	1	5
Country II	6	4

With unrestricted trade, country I would specialise in the production of B while country II would specialise in good A. If country II exchanges six units of A for six units of B with country I, it will gain two units of B and save itself one-third of the labour time required to produce an equivalent amount of B domestically. This can be seen if one considers the situation of autarky (when a country does not trade). If country II wishes to increase its consumption of B by moving a unit of labour out of the production of A and into the production of B, it can effectively exchange six units of A for only four of B.

The six units of A that country I receives would have required it to expend six units of labour time if it had produced these domestically. If it had used the labour time in the production of B, it could have produced thirty (six units of labour times five) units of B. By exchanging six units of B for six units of A, country I can gain twenty-four units of B or save five labour units. In this example we can see that country I gains more than country II; nevertheless, it is also clear that both countries have gained from specialisation and trade.

2.3.2 Comparative advantage

The logic of absolute advantage is straightforward and the conclusions reached are intrinsically intuitive. The question that arose, however, was: what if one country has an absolute advantage in the production of all commodities? Would countries cease to trade since the more efficient country could produce the goods it needed more cheaply in terms of real resources? In attempting to answer these questions, the concept of comparative advantage was developed first by Robert Torrens[3] in the early years of the nineteenth century and was subsequently stated rigorously by Ricardo (see Sraffa, 1951–1973).

Comparative advantage concentrates not on the absolute differences in countries' efficiencies in producing goods but on the differences between their relative efficiencies. As long as their relative efficiencies differ, trade will take place and be beneficial to both countries.

The theory of comparative advantage states that the nation with the absolute advantage in both goods should specialise in the production and export of the good in which its absolute advantage is greatest. Consumption of the other good could be satisfied by importing it from the other country, which in turn should specialise in the good in which its absolute disadvantage is the least. Comparative advantage can be illustrated by examining the numerical example in Table 2.2.

Table 2.2 Comparative advantage: output per unit of labour

| | Goods | |
	A	B
Country I	1	2
Country II	6	4

Again, assume the simplest case of two countries, I and II, each producing two goods, A and B, with only one productive input – labour. In this example, country I has an absolute disadvantage in the production of both good A and B and, of course, country II is more efficient at producing both of them. Country II is six times more efficient at producing good A and twice as efficient at producing good B. Hence, country II's major advantage lies in the production of good A, and so it can be said that its comparative advantage lies in the production of A. Compared to country II, country I is least inefficient in the production of good B, producing only half of the output of B per unit of labour $(2:4)$ compared to one-sixth in the case of A $(1:6)$. Thus, country I can be said to have a comparative advantage in the production of good B. If both nations specialise in and export the good in which they have a comparative advantage, they will both benefit from trade.

To illustrate the gain from trade, let us assume as in our previous example that country II can exchange six units of A for six units of B produced in country I.

Country II would gain two units of B compared to its autarkic position or save itself half of the labour time expended in the production of B. Country I would also gain in that the six units of A it would receive in exchange for its B would have taken it six units of labour time to produce. Country I could now use that labour to produce twelve units of B and exchange six of these for six units of A. Under autarky, country I could only produce six units of A with six units of labour time, so by trading it has gained six units of A or saved itself three units of labour time. Country I gains more than country II, but they have both gained by specialising and entering into trade with one another.

It should not be assumed that mutually beneficial trade only arises when six units of A are exchanged for six units of B. Rates of exchange other than one of A for one of B (1:1) also lead to gains. As long as country II can achieve more than four units of B by giving up six units of A, it will gain. Similarly, if country I can give up less than twelve units of B for six units of A, then it too will gain. Thus, the range within which advantageous trade can take place lies between 6A being exchanged for 4B and 6A being exchanged for 12B (4B < 6A < 12B). When the two countries trade six units of A for six units of B country II gains two units of A and country I gains six units of A, a gain of eight units in total. As the ratio of the exchange moves closer to six units of A for four units of B, the smaller is the share of the gain accruing to country II. Conversely, the closer the exchange rate approaches six units of A for twelve units of B, the greater is the gain for country II. For example, if country II exchanged six units of A for eight units of B, both countries would gain eight units of B. If country II exchanges six units of A for 10 units of B, it would gain six units of B but country I would only gain two units of B. Thus, differences in the ratio of the exchange determine the actual as opposed to the possible gains from trade and, more relevant to the topic of this book, predictions of the type and quantity of goods traded – i.e. the pattern and volume of international trade.

Since its inception more than 180 years ago, the rather counterintuitive conclusion that a country which is more efficient at producing both goods can gain from trading has formed the basis of the argument for trade liberalisation. The simple elegance of the logic of comparative advantage has withstood close intellectual scrutiny by both disinterested academics and protectionists with vested interests. It has stood the test of time so well that it is often called the 'law of comparative advantage'. However, although the logic of comparative advantage has stood the test of time, empirical verification of its predicted trading patterns has been less successful. This problem is discussed in Chapter 3.

The determination of the rate at which goods are exchanged is not addressed by the theory of comparative advantage. The theory of comparative advantage is able to describe only the conditions of supply and the benefits once demand is given. In section 2.3.4 an extension to classical trade theory that incorporates exchange rate determination is developed. But before this step is taken it may be worthwhile relaxing the assumption that trade takes place only by barter and introducing money into the analysis.

2.3.3 Money and comparative advantage

The example of country I and country II exchanging goods A and B produced by a single input labour is our starting point (Table 2.1). Now let each country have its own currency. Let us suppose that monetary values are denominated in pounds in country I and in dollars in country II and that the exchange rate is £1 = $2. With a wage rate of $6 per unit of time expended by labour in country II, the cost of producing one unit of A will be $1.00, while the cost of producing good B will be $1.50 (i.e. $6 for six units of A and $6 for four units of B). For country I, assuming labour is paid £1 per unit of time expended, the cost of producing one unit of good A is £1.00 (£1 for 1A) and the cost of producing one unit of B is £0.50 (£1 for 2B). In terms of country II's currency ($2 = £1) this is $2.00 for good A and $1.00 for good B.

Table 2.3 gives the costs of production in terms of dollars per unit of output produced by one unit of labour. Here we can see that the cost of producing good A in country II is lower than in country I, while for good B the opposite is the case. Thus, A would be bought in country II and sold in country I, whereas the opposite would happen to good B. Although country I is less efficient than country II in the production of good B, this is more than compensated for by the lower wage rate that labour receives in country I. As shown in Table 2.1, country I is only half as efficient as country II in the production of good B. Its workers, however, receive only one-third of the wage rate paid in country II ($6.00 in country II compared to £1 times the exchange rate = $2.00 in country I). The result of this lower wage rate is to make the cost of producing good B in country I lower than that in country II. As long as the wage rate is between one-sixth and a half (the difference in the output per unit of labour) of that in country II, country I will export good B and country II good A.

Table 2.3 Comparative advantage with money: dollar cost per unit of labour

	Goods	
	A	B
Country I	2.00	1.00
Country II	1.00	1.50

The trade flow would be altered if the exchange rate between the pound and the dollar changed. For example, if £1 = $1, the price of good A in country I would equal $1.00 and exports of A from country II to country I would cease. At this exchange rate, however, the price of good B in terms of the dollar would fall in country I relative to that in country II, and so exports of B from country II would increase. With trade stopped in good A but increased in good B, the result would be a trade balance in favour of country II.[4]

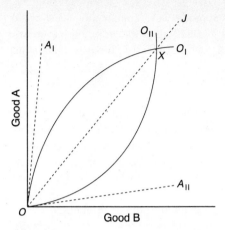

Figure 2.1

2.3.4 *The law of reciprocal demand*

In the 1840s, to determine the ratio at which goods will be exchanged internationally, John Stuart Mill[5] put forward the concept of reciprocal demand. He suggested that trade in two goods between two countries would be carried out at a rate of exchange that would keep the balance of trade between the countries in equilibrium. The development of a framework for analysis that determined precisely the rate of exchange at which this equilibrium would be reached had to await the work of Alfred Marshall (1923). Marshall's approach abstracted from money by concentrating on the real quantities exchanged between the two trading nations. One country's demand for the other country's good was depicted diagrammatically by an offer curve. This curve showed, at each level of imports, the demand of one country for imports in terms of the quantity of export goods it would be willing to exchange in return – i.e. how much of its own domestically produced goods it would offer to exchange for foreign goods.

The offer curves for country I, O_I, and country II, O_{II}, are shown in Figure 2.1. The quantity of goods A and B traded are shown on the vertical and horizontal axis, respectively. Also shown are the autarkic exchange rates (the internal terms of trade), A_I and A_{II}. They are tangential to the respective country's offer curves at point 0, indicating no trade. Between these two rays mutually beneficial trade can take place. The offer curves are shaped in such a way to show that, as trade takes place, each country will be willing to offer fewer exports for each incremental increase in imports. At point X, where the two curves intersect, the exchange rate or terms of trade (or, more precisely, the barter terms of trade) are determined. At this point the amount of each good reciprocally demanded equals the amount reciprocally supplied and the terms of trade (or rate at which A will be exchanged for B) is shown by the ray OJ.

The determination of the terms of trade was a major advance for the classical theory of trade. The models presented up to this point, however, are constrained to the two-good, two-country case. This restriction is relaxed in the following sections.

2.3.5 Two nations and n goods

It can be shown that the principles underlying the standard two-country, two-good ('two-by-two') model can also be applied to situations where two countries produce more than two goods. The first two rows in Table 2.4 give the costs of producing five goods in country I and country II expressed in dollars at an exchange rate where £1 in country I equals $2 in country II.

Table 2.4 Two countries and many goods: dollar cost per unit of labour

| | Goods | | | | |
	A	B	C	D	E
Country I	12	8	6	4	2
Country II	2	4	6	8	10
Country I* (£1 = $3)	18	12	9	6	3

At this exchange rate, the costs of producing goods A and B are lower in country II than in country I, while the opposite is the case for goods D and E. In contrast, good C has the same cost of production in both countries. In this example, country I will export goods D and E and import goods A and B. Country II will export A and B and import D and E. Neither country will trade good C.

The costs of production for goods A to E in dollar terms in country I when the exchange rate is changed to £1 = $3 are given in the bottom row of Table 2.1. With this exchange rate, not only are the costs of production lower for A and B in country II but they are less for good C as well. As a result, good C will be exported from country II to country I. If unbalanced trade resulted and was sustained, the exchange rate would adjust to bring about equilibrium.

By examining and ranking the costs of production in each country one can develop a hierarchy or chain of comparative advantage. Of all the goods produced, good A requires fewer inputs in country II relative to country I. Thus, country II has a comparative advantage in A relative to country I. This advantage declines and eventually becomes a disadvantage as one proceeds along the list of goods. The opposite is true for country I.

2.3.6 n nations and two goods

The classical model can also be extended to take into account more than two countries trading two goods and, although a little more complex, the general principles of exchange still hold. Assume that there are five countries, I–V, and that each country has an internal price ratio between goods A and B (price of A, P_A, divided by the price of B, P_B), as shown in Table 2.5.

Table 2.5 Many countries and two goods: national ranking in terms of price ratios

	Country				
	I	II	III	IV	V
P_A/P_B	5	4	3	2	1

If the countries are open to trade, the equilibrium ratio of P_A to P_B will settle between 1 and 5. If the equilibrium P_A/P_B ratio were 3, countries IV and V would export A while I and II would export B. Country III would not enter trade as the pre-trade price ratio of A to B equals the equilibrium trade ratio. Should the equilibrium ratio move from 3, country III will enter trade – exporting A or B depending on whether the ratio moves above or below 3. It should be noted, however, that one cannot infer anything about the bilateral trade links (i.e. exactly which country exports what to whom) but only what they will export.

It is possible to generalise the classical model further to include many countries and many goods. Again, countries will export the goods in which they have a comparative advantage and so will tend to specialise in the production of those goods. Countries will only produce the same range of goods under autarky and when trade takes place if the price ratios when trade is allowed equal the autarky price ratios. Thus, multidimensional trade does tend to resemble the patterns predicted by the simple two-by-two model. Strictly interpreted, classical trade theory suggested that specialisation would be complete with no country producing more than one good. Haberler (1936) reinterpreted classical theory in terms of opportunity cost, thus casting aside Ricardo's labour theory of value (the single-resource assumption). The major theoretical implication of Haberler's contribution was that incomplete specialisation becomes a legitimate outcome when countries trade. This development in classical theory is discussed in the next section.

2.4 Haberler's restatement of classical trade theory

A significant criticism of the Ricardian formulation of classical trade theory was its reliance on the labour theory of value. Very simply, this maintained that the value of a good was determined by the amount of labour that went into its production. The important implication of this proposition was that other factors of production were either of no significance or so evenly spread across the labour force that they combined with it in some fixed proportion. Alternatively, the other factors of production were perceived as simply some form of stored up labour. This last view allowed the incorporation of capital goods into the single measure of input because labour had been used in their production. The labour theory of value has, as a fundamental assumption, the proposition that labour is homogeneous – or at least can be broken down into standard units such as unskilled labour.

Obviously, labour is not the only factor of production; for example, land and capital are both used in the production of goods and they are not so insignificant that they can be ignored. The considerable variability in the proportions of inputs actually used in production makes it implausible to value goods solely in terms of their labour input. It would be unrealistic to suggest that a particular good had a higher value than another because its labour content was larger.

Leaving aside these objections, if goods were to be valued by the amount of their labour input, their prices would be determined by the labour time expended in their production. Trade patterns would thus reflect differences in the labour time needed to produce goods and countries would export the good that required a low labour time input. To undertake this evaluation, it must be assumed that labour is homogeneous and that each labourer is equally productive. If this assumption does not hold, variations in labour productivity would render labour time an elastic – and hence inconsistent – measure of value. This would be the case even if the contributions of other factors of production were assumed to be non-existent. Since labour productivity varies, value may not be proportional to labour time expended and trade patterns would not, therefore, be explained by the Ricardian formulation of classical trade theory.

Non-homogeneity of labour could affect trade patterns in another way (Cairns, 1874). The assumption made by the early classical economists was that labour is mobile not only between industries but between occupations. In an economy dominated by non-competing groups – where labour is specialised and, hence, not perfectly interchangeable – the effect on the value of a good of a shift in demand could be significant. For example, if the demand for one good rose, the demand for its labour inputs would increase as the sector expanded. Demand for labour would decline in a contracting sector. If, under Ricardo's system, full employment is assumed, labour would flow out of one occupation and into another. The price of labour would remain the same owing to this process of labour arbitrage and, as a result, labour time expended would still reflect value. However, where non-competing labour groups exist the increase in demand would lead to a rise in the price of that good's specialised labour and, thus, in the cost of the good. Although labour time remained the same, the cost of the good would have risen.

It is against this background of theoretical difficulties with the labour theory of value that Haberler (1936) recast classical trade theory in terms of opportunity cost. By adopting this new approach he was able to incorporate factors of production other than labour into classical trade theory. More importantly, attention was no longer focused on the quantity of resources employed in the production of a commodity. The issue of how much of each factor or how many factors were employed in the production of a good left the

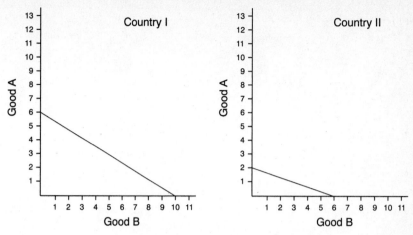

Figure 2.2

centre of the stage and was replaced by how much of another good could be produced by the same factors.

Instead of implying that a specific amount of labour time (e.g. a day or a week) will produce a given amount of good A or good B, one can suggest that all factors of production will produce specified amounts of A or B or some combination in between. Figure 2.2 shows countries I and II both producing goods A and B on the vertical and horizontal axes, respectively, of each diagram. The diagram on the left shows that under autarky country I can, using all its resources, produce six units of A or ten units of B or some combination in between. Without trade, country II can produce two units of A and six units of B or, again, some combination in between. The use of the opportunity cost approach, hence, does not say what is produced but what can be produced if each country's factors of production are fully utilised. It is assumed that in both countries resources are fully employed, meaning that they produce on the production possibility frontier. Furthermore, the straight-line, or constant-cost, production possibility curves show the prices at which goods are exchanged within an economy. In our example, in country I goods A and B are exchanged at a 6:10 ratio and at 2:6 in country II. Thus, the price ratios and the opportunity cost ratios are the same in each country. Along the entire length of the production possibility frontier, whenever resources are shifted out of the production of good A into good B they can always produce goods in the ratio of 6:10 for country I and 2:6 in country II. With the opportunity cost ratio equal to the domestic price ratio, a higher price for, say, good A in country I will result in resources flowing out of the production of good B into good A until the supply of A is increased and the original price ratio is restored. If trade is opened between the two countries, country II will export good B because its domestic opportunity cost of producing an extra unit of good A domestically (6B for 2A) is greater than country I's opportunity cost of producing the same extra unit of good A (5B for 3A) and

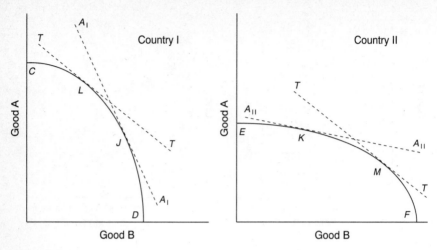

Figure 2.3

trading it. Country I has a comparative advantage in the production of A, while country II has a comparative advantage in the production of B.

The simple assumption of constant opportunity costs whereby the transfer of factors of production from one activity to another does not affect their productivity (i.e. that production possibility frontiers are straight lines) was seen to be unrealistic. It is more realistic to model factors of production as being not equally adaptable in the production of all goods. Thus, some inputs are more efficient in the production of one type of good and some in the production of another good. Hence, instead of constant costs one has increasing costs – which result in the more common concave production possibility curves depicted in Figure 2.3.

The production possibility frontiers for two countries are shown in Figure 2.3 as the curves *CD* and *EF* for country I and country II, respectively. From these it can be seen that country I is more efficient at producing good A than country II, the opposite being the case for good B. Under autarky, it is assumed that domestic price ratios (A_I–A_I for country I and A_{II}–A_{II} for country II) give rise to equilibrium production and consumption points *J* for country I and *K* for country II. When the economies are opened up to trade the internal price ratios are replaced by the international price ratio *T–T*. As a result, new production points *L* and *M* are established. Country I increases its output of A but reduces its production of B and so moves from *J* to *L*. Country II does the opposite, reducing its production of A while increasing that of B – i.e. moving from *K* to *M*. As a result of trade, each country will increase the output of the good in which it has a comparative advantage and reduce that in which it has a comparative disadvantage.

What effect will these changes have on consumption and, hence, on trade? To answer these questions the concept of community indifference curves must

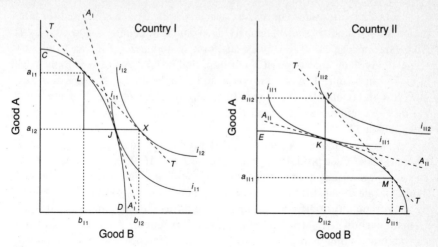

Figure 2.4

be introduced. Community indifference curves are constructed, in theory, by aggregating the indifference curves of all the individual consumers that make up a country's population (Leontief, 1933). An individual's indifference curve shows his or her willingness to trade off possible combinations of consumption goods. Each curve illustrates the individual's trade-offs at a fixed level of satisfaction – the combination of goods between which he/she is indifferent. For example, an individual may be equally satisfied to have two pieces of pizza and six beers or three pieces of pizza and four beers. Of course, each person will value pizza and beer in his or her own way. Combinations that give greater satisfaction put the individual on a higher curve.

Rational individuals are assumed to want to consume combinations of products that give them the highest level of satisfaction. As with the individual, it is assumed that a nation attempts to achieve the greatest satisfaction, which means that it tries to conduct its consumption on the highest attainable community indifference curve. Under autarky, what constrains the nation in attaining higher community indifference curves is the productive capacity – as shown by the production possibility frontier. This can be illustrated as in Figure 2.4, which reproduces the case developed in Figure 2.3. Start with country I. The highest attainable community indifference curve is i_{I1}, when no trade takes place. For example, community indifference curve i_{I2}, which is further from the origin and, hence, depicts a higher level of satisfaction, is not attainable because all the combinations of A and B depicted on it exceed the production abilities of the economy, as represented by production possibility curve C–D. With no trade, production and consumption take place at J and the domestic price ratio for goods A and B (A_I–A_I) is now determined at the point where i_{I1}–i_{I1} is tangential (has the same slope) to C–D. For country II, the autarkic production and consumption point K are derived in a similar fashion.

If trade is allowed, each country specialises. The price ratio used for international exchanges is simultaneously determined in country I and country II. Consumption can now take place at point X and point Y in each country, respectively. Note that at point X consumption of both A and B is higher than at point J in country I. A similar observation can be made when one compares Y with K in country II. The slopes of $i_{I2}-i_{I2}$ at X and $i_{II2}-i_{II2}$ at Y are equal, giving the common price ratio, $T-T$. How is this increase in consumption accomplished?

Under autarchy, consumption and production took place at J and K, whereas under trade production takes place at L and M. With trade, each country can consume at any point along the international price line $T-T$, where its marginal rate of substitution of good A for good B in consumption as depicted by its community indifference curve is equal to the marginal rate of transformation shown by its production possibility curve. As long as the new consumption combination is on a higher indifference curve (i_{I2} and i_{II2}, respectively) than the one associated with its autarkic equilibrium, the country will gain from trade. In our diagram the new equilibrium points show that each country will consume more of the good in which it has a comparative disadvantage and that for these it will exchange the good in which it has a comparative advantage. In terms of our diagram, country I will produce more of A but will exchange $a_{I1}-a_{I2}$ of this extra output to import $b_{I1}-b_{I2}$ of B from country II. Country II will exchange $b_{II1}-b_{II2}$ of B so that it can import $a_{II1}-a_{II2}$ for consumption.

Incorporating the concept of opportunity cost into classical trade theory made very little difference to its main conclusions. Although complete specialisation did not occur, each country still concentrated its production on the good in which it had a comparative advantage. The classical conclusions concerning the gains from trade were still upheld. The adoption of opportunity costs and increasing, as opposed to constant-cost, production possibility curves gave the theory some added realism.

Despite its reformulation, classical trade theory did not explain the reasons for comparative advantage. By and large, it was suggested that differences in the quality of the resources available to each country and/or climatic factors lead to the differences in production functions that exist between countries.

2.5   The neoclassical, Heckscher–Ohlin or factor proportions theory of trade

While Haberler (1936) was incorporating opportunity cost as a replacement for the labour theory of value, Ohlin (1933) was simultaneously developing a separate and more general theory. His theory was both a refinement and further development of ideas embodied in a 1919 article by Heckscher.[6] The resulting Heckscher–Ohlin model did not only try to explain trade patterns but it also attempted to explain the underlying basis of comparative advantage.

Put simply, the Heckscher–Ohlin theory proposed that production functions for a given good are the same in all countries but that they differ between goods. This means that good A could be capital-intensive in its production while good B, using relatively more labour, would be labour-intensive. With factors of production distributed unequally between countries, some nations would be capital-abundant while others would be labour-abundant. This difference in relative capital endowments, along with the difference in factor intensities in the production of goods, means that capital-abundant countries have comparative advantages in the production and export of capital-intensive goods whereas labour-abundant countries have a comparative advantage in labour-intensive goods. In other words, capital-abundant countries will export capital-intensive goods while labour-abundant countries will export labour-intensive goods. Thus, the relative abundance of factor endowments would determine the trade pattern of countries.

To show this more formally, it is first necessary to be more precise about what we mean by abundance. Again, a simplification is made by assuming that there are only two factors of production, normally capital and labour. There are two ways of defining abundance. The first relates to factor prices, while the second equates abundance with physical quantities of resources. These definitions are not equivalent, and it is only when factor abundance is defined in terms of relative prices that the Heckscher–Ohlin conclusions follow unequivocally.

According to the definition based on prices, country I would be capital-intensive if its price ratio of capital to labour were less than that in country II – for example, where $P_I K / P_I L < P_{II} K / P_{II} L$, where P is price, K is capital, L is labour, and the subscripts I and II refer to the countries. Hence, if capital is relatively cheap in country I, country I is capital-abundant, while if labour is relatively cheap in country II, country II is labour-abundant. With these definitions we can now illustrate Heckscher–Ohlin's proposition.

Figure 2.5 shows two isoquants (which show the different combination of inputs required to produce a fixed quantity of output), AA and BB; the former pertains to a capital-intensive good and the latter to a labour-intensive good. Relative factor prices in country I, where capital is relatively cheap, are shown by the line P_1–P_1. Assuming that each isoquant represents one unit of output of each good, A will be produced by OK_1 of capital and OL_1 of labour. Since capital and labour can be substituted for one another in the ratio shown by the price line P_1–P_1, it follows that OL_1 of labour is equal to $K_1 G$ of capital and OK_1 of capital is equal to $L_1 H$ of labour. From this, the cost of producing A can be considered in terms of labour alone (or capital alone). In the same way, the cost of producing one unit of B can be expressed as being either OG in terms of capital or OH in terms of labour.

In country II capital is relatively more expensive than in country I and, hence, it is labour-abundant, meaning that the slope of its price line will be less steep than in country I. The price line for country II is depicted as P_2–P_2 in Figure 2.5 and is tangential to isoquant AA at point E, which shows that it costs

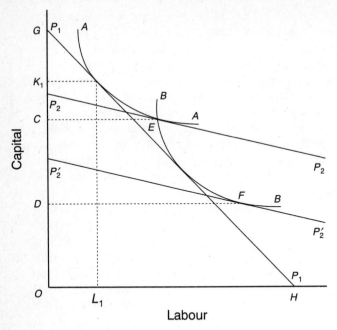

Figure 2.5

OC in terms of capital to produce one unit of A. By moving P_2–P_2 down parallel to itself (to keep the price ratio constant) until it becomes tangential to isoquant *BB* (i.e. P'_2–P'_2), one can determine the cost of producing B in terms of capital. With tangency at *F*, one can see that it costs *OD* to produce one unit of the labour-intensive good B compared to a cost of *OC* to produce one unit of the capital-intensive good A. Thus, it is relatively cheaper to produce good B than good A in country II. Comparing the production costs across countries, one can see that it is cheaper to produce good A in country I and good B in country II. Thus, country I has a comparative advantage in and will export good A, while country II has a comparative advantage in and will export B. By defining capital and labour abundance in terms of relative factor prices, one is able to derive Heckscher–Ohlin's conclusions.

What will be the result if factor abundance is defined in terms of physical abundance? This definition implies that country I is abundant in capital if K_I/L_I > K_{II}/L_{II}, where *K* and *L* are, respectively, the total amounts of capital and labour and I and II refer to the countries. To answer this question we will make use of Figure 2.6, which shows that of the two goods produced, A is the capital-intensive good while B is the labour-intensive good. The production possibility frontier of country I (the capital-abundant country) is shown by curve P_1–P_1 and P_2–P_2 is that of country II. Let us assume further that both these countries produce goods A and B in the same proportions (e.g. 60 per cent of good A and 40 per cent of good B). Thus, country I would produce at point *X* and country II

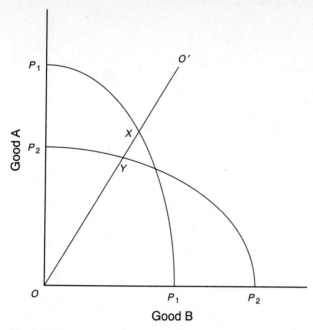

Figure 2.6

at *Y* along a line from the origin. Remember that the price ratio of A and B is determined by the slope of the production possibility frontier at the point where production takes place. The slope of country I's production possibility curve at *X* is steeper than country II's at *Y*, which implies that good A is cheaper in country I than in country II, while the opposite is the case for good B. At *X*, less of B must be given up to gain an additional unit of A than is the case at point *Y*. Hence, the opportunity cost of producing more of good A is lower in country I than it is in country II, and the former has a bias towards the production of capital-intensive goods. It follows that country II has a bias in favour of producing labour-intensive good B.

Despite these biases in favour of producing goods which use the abundant factor of each country, it does not necessarily follow that country I actually exports good A and country II exports good B. It could be the case that demand conditions prevailing in each country would lead to country I exporting good B and country II exporting good A. We can illustrate this using Figure 2.7. This is the same as Figure 2.6 except that we have included two indifference curves I_1 and I_2, which reflect the preferences of consumers in countries I and II, respectively. In country I demand is biased in favour of the capital-intensive good, while the opposite is the case in country II. Under autarky this leads to good A being more expensive in country I than in country II – as seen by the slope of the production possibility curves at the point of tangency with the indifference curve I_1. In other words, more of good B must be given up to gain

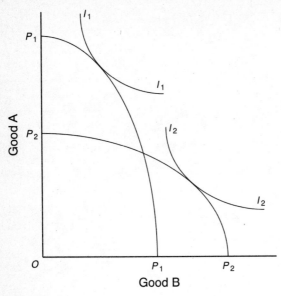

Figure 2.7

an additional unit of A in country I than in country II. By examining demand
conditions in country II, we can say that good B is relatively more expensive
there than in country I. When trade is opened up between the two countries it
follows that country I will export good B while country II will export good A.
When one compares these results with those presented in the previous section,
it is clear that it is only when abundance is defined in terms of relative prices
that countries will export the good that uses the abundant factor intensively. This
clarification of the definition of abundance will be important when empirical
tests of the neoclassical model are discussed in Chapter 3.

2.6 Importance and implications of the assumptions underlying the Heckscher–Ohlin model

For the Heckscher–Ohlin model to yield its predictions, a number of underlying
conditions have to be met and a host of assumptions made. Some of these were
made for illustrative simplicity and pedagogic clarity, while others – especially
those encompassing conditions of production and market structure – are more
fundamental. The more important of these conditions and assumptions will now
be examined in detail. It should be borne in mind that some of the comments
justifying the importance of the assumptions are of considerable importance
for the empirical studies that are discussed in Chapter 3. They are included here
to make the exposition in Chapter 3 easier and to provide some prior insights
into the criticisms arising from empirical studies that have been directed at
neoclassical trade theory.

2.6.1 Two countries, two commodities and two factors of production

The two-by-two-by-two assumptions are made for illustrative purposes only – even three-dimensional graphs can be difficult to grasp – and it has been shown that these can be generalised to the nth dimension and the conclusions still apply. As in the Ricardian case, demand factors have to be introduced to complete ('close') the model (Jones, 1974).

2.6.2 No trade barriers or transport costs

A free-trade, no transport cost situation would lead each country to specialise to the point where commodity prices are equalised. The existence of tariffs and transport costs limits the level of specialisation to the point at which commodity prices differ by an amount equal to the value of the tariffs and transport costs. The existence of trade barriers in the form of import quotas means that trade and specialisation are physically restricted. Assuming trade barriers and transportation costs away, however, does not affect the model's results in any significant way. The real world is, of course, littered with trade barriers and is subject to transportation and other costs associated with organising international transactions (Kerr and Perdikis, 1995). If these are sufficiently high, they may affect the empirical results.

2.6.3 Similar production functions in each country

It is assumed in the Heckscher–Ohlin trade model that both countries use the same technology. This means that producers would use exactly the same technology in the production of a similar good. More formally, the isoquant for a given good is the same in each country. However, as factor prices differ between countries, an economy will use more of its abundant factor in the production of one good than will be the case in other countries. In other words, although the technologies available to all countries are the same, there is no reason why one country should not use more capital and less labour while another uses more labour and less capital in the production of a particular good.

By relaxing the assumption of similar technologies it is possible to alter the predictive results of the model. Take the situation shown in Figure 2.8(a), where country I uses *OK* capital and *OL* labour to produce the level of output A, given the factors' relative prices. Compared to country II, shown in Figure 2.8(b), it can be seen that the production of output level A in country I is more capital-intensive as it uses more capital and less labour. This is not due to the difference in factor prices – the slope of P_1–P_1 is the same in both countries – but to the difference in the shape of the isoquants.

If one changes the factor prices in both countries, one can plot the changes in the capital–labour ratio and derive capital intensity schedules for good A in each country, as is shown in Figure 2.9. By lowering the price of labour (i.e. changing the slope of the P_1–P_1 lines in Figure 2.8) one can trace out a curve that represents the points of tangency between the moving factor price lines P_1–P_1 and the isoquant A. As country I produces A with a higher capital–labour

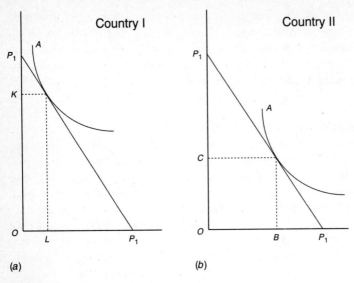

Figure 2.8

ratio, its capital-intensity schedule will be above that for country II and will
continue to be so at all factor prices. Similar intensity curves can be constructed
for good B.

By making some assumptions about good B, one can see the effect on
Heckscher–Ohlin's conclusions if the same production technology is no longer
assumed to be used in both countries. First, assume that good A is always the
capital-intensive good in either country and that the technology used to produce
good B in both countries is the same (i.e. the isoquants are the same in both).
The factor intensity curve for good B will be above those for good A in both
countries. Further, the factor intensity curves for good B in each country will
coincide. This is illustrated in Figure 2.9. The figure also shows that at any price
ratio country I, being capital-abundant, will prefer to produce A, which is
capital-intensive, whereas country II, which is labour-abundant, will by default
prefer to produce good B, which is labour-intensive. These results are consistent
with Heckscher–Ohlin's predictions, but they can be overturned if it is assumed
that good B is produced labour-intensively in country I, the capital-intensive
country, and capital-intensively in labour-abundant country II. One would then
have a situation where the factor intensity schedule for good B in country I
would lie between those for good A produced in country I and country II. In this
situation country I would still prefer to produce good A because it uses more of
its abundant factor. Country II would, however, also prefer to produce good A to
good B because it uses less of its scarce factor, capital. These results imply that
country II would export good A along with country I, a result which would
contradict the model's predictions as well as being logically inconsistent in a
world with only two countries.

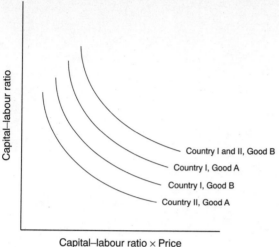

Figure 2.9

Whether trade took place would depend on how close country II's factor intensity schedule for good B was to country II's factory intensity schedule for A. The closer the two schedules, the less the likelihood of specialisation but the larger the effect on comparative costs. Where country II's factor intensity schedule for good B is close to country II's factor intensity schedule for good A, the less likely it is that country II will specialise since there will be little difference in the use of its factors. However, the closer the curves, the wider the gap will be in comparative costs between country I and country II in the production of goods A and B, respectively. In this situation country I would be willing to export A in return for B, which is intensive in its relatively expensive factor, and trade will take place. The further away country II's factor intensity curve for B is from its factor intensity curve for A, the more it will want to specialise in A. The situation would then arise that there would be no comparative cost differences between the production of good A in country I and good B in country II, and trade would not take place.

These results can be generalised to include the situation where the technologies used in production differ for both goods in both countries. Country I would now produce good B labour-intensively while country II would produce B capital-intensively. In this case the factor intensity schedules would be those shown in Figure 2.10. Country II has a comparative advantage in producing good A over B and in producing A over country I, while the opposite is the case for country I. The trade pattern that would arise would be the opposite to Heckscher–Ohlin's predictions, with the capital-abundant country exporting the labour-intensive good and the labour-abundant country exporting the capital-intensive good. Whether trade took place would depend on the differences in comparative costs between the two countries.

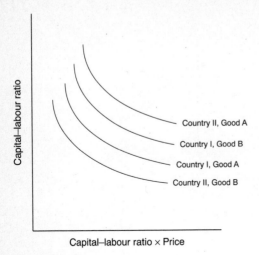

Capital–labour ratio × Price

Figure 2.10

Hence, the assumption that similar production techniques are available to both countries is fundamental to the use of the Heckscher–Ohlin model to derive predictions regarding trade patterns. Whether similar production technologies are used in different countries at any point in time is, of course, an empirical question.

2.6.4 No factor intensity reversals

A further assumption on which the Heckscher–Ohlin theory depends is that not only can the goods be classified as either capital-intensive or labour-intensive but that the classification will not be altered by a change in factor prices. More formally, the assumption of no factor price reversal of product classification means that the isoquants will not cross one another more than once. In Figure 2.11(*a*) isoquants A and B cross once. At factor price ratio P_1–P_1 one can say that good A is relatively more capital-intensive than good B. If the price ratio is changed to P_2–P_2, the same conclusion will hold. In fact, the conclusion will be true no matter what the price ratio. The opposite situation is shown in Figure 2.11(*b*), where the isoquants cross more than once. Good A is capital-intensive relative to B at the P_1–P_1 price ratio but is labour-intensive relative to B at the P_2–P_2 price ratio.

The effect of factor intensity reversal can also be illustrated by referring to the factor intensity curves in Figure 2.12, where R is the point at which factor intensity reversal takes place at factor price ratio PR. If points C_I and C_{II} represent the factor price ratios in countries I and II, respectively, country I (capital-abundant) would prefer to produce good A – but so would country II, which is labour-abundant. Thus, when trade is opened up country I would wish to export good A in accordance with the Heckscher–Ohlin theory, but country II would also wish to export A. Hence, if factor intensity reversals are allowed, Heckscher–Ohlin's predictions will not be fulfilled.

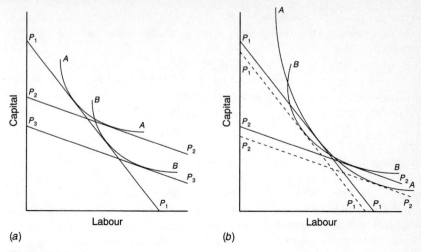

Figure 2.11

2.6.5 Constant returns to scale

Another important assumption of the Heckscher–Ohlin model is that constant returns to scale in production are manifest in each country. In other words, if one doubled the amount of capital and labour in the production of good A, its output would also double. There are, as a result, no cost savings from long-run increases in production. If economies of scale are present, trade can take place in a variety of situations. For example, if demand increases for capital-intensive goods that are subject to economies of scale, a labour-abundant country could well find itself exporting capital-intensive goods. Furthermore, trade could also arise in a situation where, while factor endowments between countries are identical,

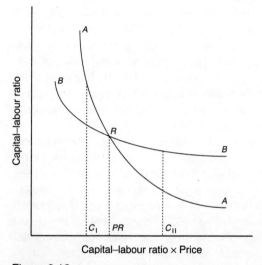

Figure 2.12

economies of scale exist in only one country. This situation could arise if sufficient demand did not exist in one country to justify plants of sufficient size to exploit economies of scale.

Another important implication of the existence of economies of scale is that price ratios can no longer be used as a simple measure by which costs of production can be compared. This is because the same price ratio could apply to production technologies with differing efficiency levels.

2.6.6 Perfect competition

The possibility of economies of scale in production sets the stage for a discussion of the role of the assumption of perfect competition in the Heckscher–Ohlin model. With perfect competition no single producer, consumer or trader of the commodity will be powerful enough to dictate price or output. Competitive forces ensure that the factors of production earn their marginal product and no more. Prices, therefore, reflect marginal costs, and any deviation will lead to entry or exit from the industry until equilibrium is restored. For the Heckscher–Ohlin model it means that as long as the costs of producing the two goods differ between the two countries, so will their prices. It is, after all, the difference in relative prices that induces trade to take place. Deviations from perfect competition and, hence, prices that no longer reflect marginal costs may lead to a different set of relative prices. As a result, a different trade pattern can result from those based on factor intensities predicted by the Heckscher–Ohlin model.

2.7 Conclusions

The Heckscher–Ohlin model is very elegant in its formulation and precise in its predictions. It is a powerful theory that is, moreover, more general than its classical counterpart. It became, and remains, one of the most popular models used by international trade economists. Not only could it explain trade but it could also explain the source of comparative advantage. Its general equilibrium nature enabled it to be used not only in analysing the imposition of trade barriers, such as tariffs, but also to investigate the effects of economic growth, technological progress, changing costs and resource availability. Exploring these extensions of the Heckscher–Ohlin model required considerable intellectual effort and tended to divert discussion away from other factors that may influence trade. Ohlin (1933) himself was very much aware that factor proportions were only one explanation of trade flows. Other influences that he stressed were location and transport costs, economies of scale, technology, innovation, skills, product differentiation, quality and income distribution. He did not ignore the effects of qualitative differences in products, nor the ability of countries' political, legal and administrative institutions to influence trade. He suggested that the latter were particularly important in explaining trade between developed and developing countries. Thus, in this self-criticism he anticipated ideas developed later by the *alternative* theoreticians which are presented in Chapter 4.

To Ohlin, location combined with transport costs were important factors in explaining trade patterns. Once an industry's location had been determined, the ease and cheapness of transportation could determine the profitability of exporting. Hence, effective internal transport systems enabled a country to exploit its resources to the full and enabled it to overcome the disadvantage of long haulage distances.

He also noted the importance of economies of scale by taking a hypothetical good that could be produced equally well in two countries but for which the markets were individually too small to reap economies of scale. Once the decision had been taken to set up a plant large enough to exploit economies of scale in one country, the pattern of trade would be established.

Innovation, improved technology and investment skills were used by Ohlin to explain the industrial specialisation and trade patterns of the US. He believed that these activities lowered the cost of products and, thus, enabled a country to establish and maintain a comparative advantage in production.

Ohlin also suggested that product differentiation and differences in quality could explain intra-industry trade. Consumers did not necessarily have identical tastes and producers could exploit these differences across frontiers.

He felt that demand factors could contribute substantially to the volume of trade between countries – citing the example of Britain and the Netherlands, which had a high level of bilateral trade despite similar factor endowments. In contrast, Britain and Iceland had low bilateral trade volumes and dissimilar factor endowments. The strength of trade in the first case could only be explained in terms of similar income levels, while in the latter case the dearth of trade could be accounted for by the disparity in income.

One should not, however, place too much emphasis on these aspects of Ohlin's (1933) work. He was, fundamentally, propounding a theory of international trade based on factor endowments. To him the dissimilarity of factor endowments between countries was the main determinant of trade. All the other factors influenced trade and occasionally provided an odd exception to the rule, but they did not explain the bulk of international trade.

To what extent actual trade patterns could be explained by factor endowments was an empirical question that was put to the test as soon as the appropriate quantitative tools to carry out such work became available. The empirical testing of Heckscher–Ohlin's theory and the controversy it produced form the basis of the discussion in Chapter 3.

Notes

1 Adam Smith published his famous *Wealth of Nations* in 1776. Interested readers are referred to Smith (1976) for an accessible modern version.
2 David Ricardo published his major work, entitled *Principles of Political Economy and Taxation*, in 1817. Interested readers are referred to Sraffa (1951–73).

3 See Torrens (1820) for a clear statement of comparative advantage. He had set out the problem in an earlier (1815) version of this book and thus predates Ricardo's 1817 formulation.
4 Of course, over the long run this situation could not be sustained. If one assumes a flexible exchange rate system, a trade surplus in country II would push the value of its currency upward in terms of dollars until trade was brought into equilibrium.
5 See *Of the Law of Interchange Between Nations* (1844) and *Principles of Political Economy with Some of their Applications* (1848), both to be found in Robson (1963–85).
6 Heckscher's (1919) original article was published in Swedish in *Ekonomisk Tidskriff*, pp. 497–512. An accessible translation can be found in the volume published by the American Economic Association (1949), where it appears as Chapter 13: 'The effect of foreign trade on the distribution of income'.

References

American Economic Association (1949), *Readings in the Theory of International Trade*, Philadelphia: Blackeston.

Cairns, J. E. (1874), *Some Leading Principles of Political Economy Newly Expounded*, London: Macmillan.

Haberler, G. (1936), *The Theory of International Trade with its Application to Commercial Policy*, London: William Hodge and Co.

Jones, R. W. (1974), 'Trade with non-traded goods: the anatomy of interconnected markets', *Economica*, 41, pp. 121–38.

Kerr, W. A., and Perdikis, N. (1995), *The Economics of International Business*, London: Chapman and Hall.

Leontief, W. (1933), 'The use of indifference curves in international trade', *Quarterly Journal of Economics*, 47, pp. 493–503.

Marshall, A. (1923), *Money, Credit and Commerce*, London: Macmillan.

Ohlin, B. G. (1933), *Interregional and International Trade*, Harvard Economic Studies no. 39, Cambridge, Mass.: Harvard University Press.

Robson, J. M. (ed.) (1963–85), *Collected Works of John Stuart Mill*, Toronto: University of Toronto Press.

Smith, A. (1976), *An Inquiry into the Nature and Causes of the Wealth of Nations*, in R. H. Campbell, A. S. Skinner and W. B. Todd (eds), *Works and Correspondence of Adam Smith*, vol. II, Oxford: Clarendon Press.

Sraffa, P. (ed.) (1951–73), *The Works and Correspondence of David Ricardo*, Cambridge: Cambridge University Press.

Torrens, R. (1820), *An Essay on the External Corn Trade*, London: Longman, Rees, Orme, Brown and Greene.

CHAPTER 3

Empirical testing of the classical and neoclassical trade theories

3.1 Introduction

The increasing emphasis on empirical testing of economic theories, particularly since the widespread availability of computers starting in the 1960s, has had a major impact on the study of international economics. The earliest, and extremely influential, empirical examinations of both the Ricardian and neoclassical theories of trade, however, predate the computer revolution in economics. MacDougall (1951, 1952) was able to test Ricardian theory using information on productivity in British and American industries. Utilising input–output analysis, which quantifies all the factor inputs required to produce a unit of output, Leontief (1953) undertook a test of the Heckscher–Ohlin model.

A flurry of activity followed these early empirical investigations and their sophistication and number increased with the availability of computers. Both the classical and Heckscher–Ohlin model were subjected to considerable scrutiny. The results of these tests failed to confirm the predictions of either the classical or neoclassical models and set in motion an unparalleled degree of academic inquiry, which continues to this day. In this chapter greater emphasis is placed on testing the Heckscher–Ohlin model, largely because of the importance of the neoclassical model in economic theory and, particularly, for the study of international trade. The empirical evaluations of the Ricardian model are presented in section 3.4.

3.2 Tests of the Heckscher–Ohlin theorem

Leontief's (1953) approach was to examine the actual factor composition of US imports. Given the generally accepted proposition that, at the time, the US was a (if not the most) capital-abundant country in the world, one would expect from the theoretical prediction of the Heckscher–Ohlin model that the US would have been an exporter of capital-intensive goods and an importer of labour-intensive goods. As input–output tables were not available for the trade partners of the US, Leontief adopted the novel approach of examining the factor content of import substitutes. These are goods which could be produced domestically but are imported. Leontief posed the question: if $1 million of imports had to be produced by the US domestically, what would have been their factor content? This basic method of analysis has been used in all subsequent tests involving input–output analysis. This is the case both for subsequent tests conducted for the US and for tests undertaken for other countries.

Leontief's (1953) results, using data from 1947, were startling in that the US appeared to be a capital-importing and a labour-exporting country. This conclusion, which clearly confounded the widely accepted theoretical predictions of the neoclassical model, was quickly challenged. Swerling (1954) argued that 1947 was not a typical year since both the US and the world economy were still recovering from World War II. In response, Leontief carried out a further study (1956) using data for 1954. Once again the US was found to be an importer of capital-intensive goods, and there then followed a whole host of studies that attempted to explain this apparent paradox – a paradox which was to become associated with Leontief. In two studies of US trade flows using input–output tables for 1958 and 1963, respectively, Baldwin (1971, 1979) confirmed the paradox. Some studies of other countries also produced paradoxical results – but in general the results were mixed. A sample of these studies is reported in Table 3.1. For example, Japan, a labour-abundant country in the 1950s, exported capital-intensive goods to the US (Tatemoto and Ichimura, 1959). India was also found to export capital-intensive goods to the US (Bharadwaj, 1962). Labour-short Canada, however, appeared to export capital-intensive goods to the US and, hence, provided evidence to support the predictions of neoclassical theory (Wahl, 1961).

Table 3.1 Capital–labour ratios for exports and imports – selected countries

	Exports to US	Imports from US
Japan		
Capital (yen)	1,026,387	2,741,786
Labour (man-years)	18.9	141.2
Capital–labour ratio	54,352	19,415
Canada		
Capital (dollars)	1,838,000	1,627,000
Labour (wages and salaries)	421,000	435,000
Capital–labour ratio	4.4	3.7
India		
Capital (rupees)	10,481,883	9,552,619
Labour number	12,185	14,436
Capital–labour ratio	860.2	661.7

Sources: Tatemoto and Ichimura (1959); Wahl (1961); Bharadwaj (1962).

Faced with this conflicting, and often counterintuitive, empirical evidence, a number of attempts were made to explain the paradox. On the whole they concentrated on the theoretical treatment of labour, the inclusion of other factors of production, such as resources, and the technical conditions attendant on production and demand factors. These efforts enjoyed varying degrees of success.

3.2.1 Labour superiority and productivity

To explain his paradoxical results, Leontief (1953) put forward the suggestion that labour in the US was more productive than that of its trading partners. This explanation required US labour to be three times more productive than the labour of countries that exported to the US. The higher level of productivity had to be achieved with the same amount of capital per head. In other words, the superior productivity of US labour could not be explained by the large amounts of capital available for each worker. Superior managerial or organisational ability were the reasons hypothesised for the relatively greater efficiency of labour. Leontief's explanation, however, was not found to be compelling. If superior organisation increased labour productivity, it should also have raised capital productivity. As a result the capital–labour ratio would stay the same and, hence, the paradox remained unresolved. When production functions in different countries were estimated, the results showed that although efficiency differences did exist between countries, they tended to be neutral between capital and labour (Arrow *et al.*, 1961). The absence of any empirical support cast severe doubt on the validity of the superior organisation argument.

A related explanation, however, has found more general acceptance as a means of resolving the paradox – labour skills. Both Leontief (1956) and Kravis (1956) found that US export industries employed more highly skilled labour than import-competing industries. If one redefines capital as consisting of physical capital plus human capital, US exports become capital-intensive relative to imports and the paradox is reversed. Empirical studies have shown skilled labour to be an important factor in determining trade patterns. Kenen's (1965) early quantitative work, in particular, was seen as being successful in providing evidence that reversed the paradox. He estimated that physical plus human capital amounted to $30,610 for exports and $29,830 for imports.

Given the small differences in Kenen's (1965) estimates – meaning that the paradox was only just resolved – it is worth examining the method of estimation that was used in order to ascertain the level of confidence which can be placed on the results. The approach taken by Kenen to calculate the level of human capital was to take the difference between the wages earned by skilled and unskilled workers and attribute this difference to a return on education and training. If the wage difference was, for example, $100 and the rate of return on education was 10 per cent, then the level of human capital invested in education would be $1,000.

This method of estimation has a number of drawbacks. First, it assumes that all differences in wage rates are a function of education and training. Hence, it ignores market imperfections, such as unions, which can affect relative wages. Second, Becker (1964) and Hannah (1967) have also shown that returns on lower levels of education are higher than those for more advanced levels. By including the amount of human capital in labour, Kenen (1965) underestimated the total amount of human capital involved in producing both exportables and importables. The effect was to reverse the paradox when import-competing industries were more labour-intensive than exporting industries. Third, long-run equilibrium conditions were assumed to exist in capital markets so that rates of return were equilibrium rates. Fourth, and more importantly, it was assumed that in the long run capital moved freely between physical and labour factors of production. In developed countries it might be the case that capital could find its best return and, hence, could be considered fungible in the long run. In less-developed countries, however, market imperfections make it difficult for physical capital to be treated in this way. Investing in physical capital may be constrained in developing countries and, hence, investment capital cannot flow to where it will receive its highest return. Fifth, by considering only formal training and education as human capital, the on-the-job training component of human capital was completely ignored. This would underestimate the total amount of capital involved in industries which had a high labour input – industries that comprised the export sector of the US.

In his study of the US, Baldwin (1971) found that even when physical and human capital were combined the Leontief paradox still persisted. When the labour force was broken down by skill groups and goods were divided into exports and import-competing categories, US exports used more skilled labour while import-competing industries used more unskilled labour. The Heckscher–Ohlin predictions were, thus, upheld as the US exported goods that used its abundant factor, skilled labour, intensively and imported goods incorporating its scarce factor, unskilled labour.

A later study carried out by Stern and Maskus (1981) used a single measure of human capital based on rates of pay. They argued that the higher the rates of pay received, the higher are the workers' skills. The study tracked the US economy over time. Despite confirming the paradox for 1958 using a capital–labour ratio of 1.07, they discovered that imports were less skill-intensive than exports, embodying only 80 per cent of the skill-intensity found in the latter. This figure fell to 60 per cent when resource-intensive industries were excluded. By 1972 the paradox had disappeared, with imports more labour-intensive than exports (i.e. the capital to labour ratio increased but with the net export of human capital sharply reduced). The result was that imports and exports had fairly similar intensities that could only be explained if the US had become relatively less well endowed with skilled labour relative to its trading partners. This may well have been the case as other more advanced countries increased the education levels of their workers.

Clearly, including human capital in an analysis could explain the Leontief paradox. Accounting for human capital was also consistent with Ohlin's (1933) seminal work, in which labour was broken down into a number of skills. The results, however, were not conclusive and depended, to a considerable extent, on the measure of human capital used. Although periodic examinations of this avenue of empirical research are conducted – often on new countries – it is no longer a central theme for empirical research on international trade.

Wood (1994) attempted to rekindle the debate, but taking a new tack. He suggested that the difficulty encountered in testing the Heckscher–Ohlin hypothesis lay not in the labour variable but with capital. As capital is internationally mobile, it cannot explain patterns of trade. Wood suggested that trade patterns could be explained only by immobile factors such as skilled and unskilled labour. His results indicated that trade in manufactures between developed and developing countries follow patterns suggested by the predictions of the Heckscher–Ohlin model.

3.2.2 Natural resources and multiple factors

Economic models are abstractions. In the period before most economists received even a modest degree of mathematical training, graphical analysis predominated. Although, as suggested above, the results of the neoclassical model can be generalised mathematically to *n* goods, countries and factors, it became commonplace to assume away the effects of factors of production other than capital and labour. In part, this focus on capital and labour arose out of the great Marxian/anti-Marxian debate surrounding the long-run trend in the 'share' received by labour. In the debate capital was considered the only other claimant to a share. As the validation of Marx's predictions of a declining share for labour spilled over into cold war politics, the debate provided a focus for a great deal of effort by economists. There is, however, no theoretical reason why neoclassical predictions regarding trade flows should focus exclusively on whether exports and imports are capital-intensive or labour-intensive. By confining his empirical analysis to capital and labour alone and leaving out natural resources (which economists have often called 'land'), Leontief (1953) may well have excluded an important factor of production. It may be the case that the initial abundant endowment of natural resources in the US had been run down after years of intensive industrialisation. As a result, the US would have imported resource-intensive products and paid for these by exporting goods that were intensive in both capital and labour.

Leontief (1953) excluded non-competing imports from his analysis. These included natural resource-intensive imports such as coffee and minerals as well as other resource-based products not produced in the US. Where there was some domestic production, however, he did include resource-intensive products. It could be argued that their inclusion was invalid because import substitution could not take place at a reasonable cost given the shortage of natural resources in the US. Adopting this reasoning in his later work, Leontief (1956) found that the paradox disappeared. The capital–labour ratio per year in exports and imports became $10,110 and $9,270, respectively, whereas the corresponding figures in his earlier work had been $14,000 and $18,000. The change in the capital–labour ratio for both exports and imports showed that resource-based industries were more capital-intensive on average than other sectors. Resource-intensive domestic production that competed with imports was very capital-intensive – as was evident from the very large change in the capital–labour ratio of $18,000 to $9,200. This conclusion had intuitive appeal because, if 'cheap' natural resources had already been depleted in the US, the remaining natural resources would be likely to be capital-intensive to extract. Hence, it appeared that the paradox was resolved.

Baldwin's (1971) study, however, failed to confirm Leontief's (1956) result. The capital–labour ratios for imports did fall from 1.27 to 1.04 after the adjustments were made but did not fall below 1.00. Only when total capital was calculated with the human capital component measured by the total cost of education did the capital–labour ratio fall to 0.93. In a later study, however, Baldwin (1979) found that the paradox was removed when natural resource products were excluded. These conflicting studies did little to clear the waters.

Leaving the composition of exports and imports in the original Leontief (1953) study unchanged, Vanek (1963) attempted another approach to incorporating the effect of natural resources. This involved calculating the combination of natural resource inputs per million dollars of imports and exports. Vanek argued that the land (natural resources) input was proportional to the amount of this resource used directly and indirectly (as incorporated in intermediate goods) per million dollars of exports and imports. Utilising Leontief's (1953) input–output data, Vanek found $680,000 worth of natural resource inputs per million dollars of import substitutes and only $340,000 worth per million dollars of exports. Thus, US imports were more natural resource-intensive than exports.

However, Vanek (1963) went one stage further by showing that there was a high degree of complementarity between natural resources and capital but that little, if any, existed between natural resources and labour. The US imported resource-intensive products with which capital was unavoidably linked. Hence, imports appeared to be capital-intensive. The Leontief paradox could be explained by this complementarity.

A number of studies other than Leontief's (1956) have invoked the natural resource factor as an explanation for the Leontief paradox. Naya's (1967) study of Japanese trade found that capital–labour ratios per man-year rose in exports from ¥395,000 to ¥512,000 and for imports from ¥236,000 to ¥520,000 when natural resources were excluded. The paradox for Japan was, thus, removed. One can also explain the factor intensities of the trade of Canada and India using similar reasoning. The high capital intensity of Canada's mineral exports to the US could account for Wahl's (1961) finding. India's capital-intensive exports can be explained by the fact that in the year Bharadwaj carried out his study (1962), India imported an abnormally high level of US agricultural commodities.

Agricultural products are produced by labour-intensive methods in India and, as a result, analysis using Leontief's methodology would tend to bias the results.

A strict theoretical interpretation of the Heckscher–Ohlin model, however, would mean that the failure to include natural resources could not be an explanation for Leontief's paradox. Heckscher–Ohlin assumes that factor price equalisation is realised. As a result, the factor proportions used to produce any one commodity are the same in all countries and each country consumes all commodities in equal proportions. These conditions can only be achieved if the capital-abundant country is exporting capital-intensive goods.

For example, if country I is capital-abundant relative to country II in terms of either labour or natural resources, then $K_I/L_I > K_{II}/L_{II}$ and $K_I/NR_I > K_{II}/NR_{II}$, where K is capital, L is labour and NR is natural resources. Given that the model's equilibrium conditions require that the consumption ratios of these factors are equal, it follows that country I must export capital-intensive goods. In a capital-abundant country like the US, which is poor in natural resources, it would imply that exports would be more capital-intensive than natural resource imports. For labour- and natural resource-abundant countries, the result would be highly labour-intensive exports (Baldwin, 1971). Factor price equalisation, however, is unlikely. As with the labour quality explanations of the paradox, the emphasis of empirical research has moved on. Without factor price equalisation, explanations invoking other factors are ad hoc and difficult to defend.

3.2.3 Factor intensity reversals

Ellsworth (1954) suggested that the paradox could easily be explained if one accepted the proposition that, when faced with substituting labour-intensive imports, a capital-abundant country would simply produce the goods with capital-intensive techniques. The only way one could test whether the US's or any other countries' imports were capital-intensive was to examine the capital–labour ratios of those goods in the countries in which they were produced. If the capital–labour ratio of the US imports, weighted by the volume of trade from each country, were greater than the capital–labour ratio of US exports, then a true paradox would arise. Ellsworth argued that through not having the input–output tables for the countries from which the US drew its imports, Leontief (1953) had been forced to use his indirect method of estimation. According to Ellsworth, assuming that the importing country would use capital-intensive techniques to produce substitutes had led Leontief into the belief that original producers used capital-intensive techniques.

Despite the initial plausibility of this argument, a little reflection will show that it is not a proper interpretation of the Heckscher–Ohlin theorem. Heckscher–Ohlin's theoretical results show that capital-intensive goods are produced and exported by capital-abundant countries and that labour-intensive goods are produced and exported by labour-abundant countries. In this way, factor endowments are linked to trade patterns. Conversely, Ellsworth's (1954) interpretation leaves the type of commodity exported by each country undetermined and, hence, it cannot be considered a theory of comparative advantage.

For Ellsworth's (1954) interpretation to be valid would require either that production functions vary between countries or that factor intensities reverse. Factor intensity reversal means that at one set of factor prices a good is produced capital-intensively but that at another it is produced labour-intensively. Under Heckscher–Ohlin assumptions, however, although capital could be substituted for labour if the price of the latter rose, the product would remain a labour-intensive product. That is, at all factor prices more labour than capital would be used in its production.

If production functions were similar between countries, it is unlikely that factor reversals would take place. By extending some previous work on production functions, Minhas (1963) proceeded to test this hypothesis by carrying out a cross-section analysis on twenty-four industries in nineteen countries. He found that within a believable range of factor price ratios, factor intensity reversals occurred in textiles, non-ferrous metals, basic chemicals, pulp and paper, grain-mill products and dairy products. In addition to this direct test, Minhas confirmed his results by an indirect method. Starting with the hypothesis that production functions are identical between countries even when their factor prices differ greatly, if one ranks two such countries' industries by capital intensity, a high positive correlation coefficient would confirm identical production functions. Taking twenty industries in the US and Japan and classifying their products on the basis of both direct and indirect inputs, he found rank correlation coefficients of 0.33 for the former measure and 0.73 for the latter. These weak results led Minhas to conclude that factor reversal was a plausible explanation for the paradox and certainly not impossible.

There have, however, been criticisms of Minhas's work. Leontief (1964), using Minhas's own data but refining the calculations, could find only seventeen out of two hundred and ten possible reversals. Even in these cases the production functions approximated each other so closely that they could be considered the same.

Minhas's (1963) study was further criticised by Ball (1966), who objected to the inclusion of agricultural products and natural resource-based industries. He argued that in these industries it is inappropriate to assume identical production functions between countries and, therefore, that they should be excluded from the analysis. Reworking Minhas's figures, Ball found that the correlation coefficient on direct factor inputs rose to 0.83, which led him to conclude that factor reversals were unlikely. These conflicting empirical results thus place some doubt on the validity of factor intensity reversal as an explanation of the Leontief paradox.

3.2.4 Demand patterns

A number of economists, including Valvanis-Vail (1954), Robinson (1956) and Jones (1956), have suggested that the paradox may well be explained by the bias of US demand patterns towards capital-intensive goods. Identical tastes could still exist between countries (the Heckscher–Ohlin assumption), but if per capita incomes differed, different demand patterns could arise at the same price ratios. The capital-abundant country could have a demand bias in favour of capital-intensive goods. The argument is strengthened if one assumes that the capital-intensive goods have income elasticities greater than unity and that the capital-abundant country has a higher per capita income. Conversely, the labour-abundant country is assumed to have a lower per capita income and its labour-abundant goods to have low income elasticities of demand. As a result of these assumptions, the capital-abundant country would have a bias in favour of capital-intensive goods that could outweigh the effect of the existing abundance in capital as a factor input. In this way, the abundant factor would be turned into a scarce factor and the scarce factor into an abundant factor. If the same were true for the labour-abundant country, the capital-abundant country would export labour-intensive goods while the labour-abundant country would export capital-intensive goods. In terms of Leontief's (1953) study, the US would export labour-intensive goods and import capital-intensive goods because its demand patterns were biased in favour of capital-intensive goods.

Despite the intuitive appeal of the demand pattern approach, there is little empirical evidence to support the hypothesis. Houthakker's (1957) study suggested that demand patterns between nations are similar. Of course, this result could still be consistent with bias because per capita incomes vary. Later studies by Brown (1957) and Travis (1964) suggested that if US demand patterns are biased at all, they may in fact be biased towards labour-intensive goods. The reason put forward to explain this bias was that capital-intensive production in the US tends to be found among the basic goods, such as agricultural commodities. Labour-intensive production is concentrated in manufactures. The underlying theoretical basis for this argument is Engel's law, which states that the proportion of food in total expenditure declines as household income increases. Hence, a high-income country like the US would demand relatively more manufactured goods than a country with a lower per capita income. As manufactured goods are more labour-intensive, the demand pattern in the US would be biased in favour of labour-intensive products. The implication of this observation is that demand patterns cannot be used as an explanation of the Leontief paradox.

3.2.5 *International and domestic distortions*
Tariffs and other trade measures could contribute to the existence of the paradox, especially when one considers that labour-intensive products are often the most highly protected. If imports of labour-intensive products were restricted while capital-intensive goods entered freely, the paradox would result. In the two-country, two-factor, two-good case tariffs can only be used to restrict imports. They cannot, however, be used to induce a capital-abundant country to export labour-intensive goods and vice versa.

If one can accept the proposition that a country's aggregate trade flow may conform to Heckscher–Ohlin theory but that individual bilateral trade flows need not, then tariffs could play a role in explaining the Leontief paradox. For example, under free trade a capital-abundant country, A, could export capital-intensive goods to a labour-abundant country, B, in return for labour-intensive imports. If country A was also trading in the same way with another labour-abundant country, C, and its net trade with C was only just capital-intensive, tariffs could have the effect of bringing about a Leontief paradox.

The conditions required for global trade to conform with Heckscher–Ohlin's expectation but to diverge from it on a bilateral basis have been shown to be very restrictive (Caves and Jones, 1977). Moreover, it is unlikely that US trade is structured in a way that would lead to such an outcome.

Diab (1956) held that one should exclude imports produced by US multinationals from the US import figures. The basis for his argument was that US multinationals use technologically sophisticated US capital combined with the know-how of skilled managers and technicians in their offshore production. Hence, the goods produced by these firms should be regarded as an integral part of US domestic commerce and not as imports. As these goods tend to be capital-intensive natural resource products, their exclusion from the analysis could well reverse the Leontief paradox.

For this proposition to be accepted, however, one would have to explain why, when US capital is employed abroad, it is not invested in more labour-intensive industries which, in turn, would export to the US. Baldwin (1971) suggested that US investments may well be made in resource-based industries in developing countries because firms in developing countries are not familiar with the capital-intensive natural resource goods that make up a significant proportion of the inputs used in the sophisticated products demanded in advanced countries. As a result, investments in production facilities for capital-intensive goods in developing countries are made by investors from advanced countries. These investors, however, would be less familiar with opportunities existing outside their own narrow product groups in the less-developed countries. When opportunities outside their specific areas of expertise are identified in developing countries, the lack of a domestic market commensurate with optimal plant size and of sufficient indigenous skilled labour is enough to deter foreign investors. There is some evidence to suggest that foreign-owned resource-based industries do invest in other activities in the countries in which they operate but that these investments are more often in familiar, adjacent sectors where forward and backward linkages to their major activity can be strengthened. In other words, foreign mining firms in developing countries might invest in firms making clothing for miners or sawmills to provide shoring timbers.

It is thus possible to see how less-developed countries' exports could become concentrated in capital-intensive, natural resource industries, which would lead to the Leontief paradox being observed. This argument is, however, similar to Vanek's (1963) suggestion that natural resources be included, along with capital and labour, as an input to production. Hence, it may well have a role in explaining away the Leontief paradox. One has to bear in mind that as markets grow economies of scale may be achieved and educational levels may rise to levels sufficiently high to eliminate the constraints associated with a poorly trained labour force. Developing countries would eventually acquire the ability to export capital-intensive manufactures and Leontief's paradox would be confirmed.

3.2.6 *Conceptual misformulations of factor intensity*

Leamer (1980) argued that when a country exports both capital-intensive and labour-intensive goods Leontief's approach of comparing the capital–labour ratio in exports and imports is inappropriate. He suggested an alternative conceptual formulation in which the capital–labour ratio in net exports is compared to that in consumption and production. By adopting this approach he found that the paradox was removed for 1947.

Leamer's starting point was to take country I's trade as being the difference between its output and its domestic consumption. Thus $T_i = Q_i - C_i$, where T_i, Q_i and C_i are vectors of the country's net exports, outputs and consumption. The factors embodied in country I's trade would be AT_i, where A is the matrix of factor requirements. Thus

$$AT_i = A(Q_i - C_i) \tag{3.1}$$

$$= AQ_i - AC_i \tag{3.2}$$

where AQ_i is the country's vector of endowment. If homothetic tastes are assumed along with equilibrium in factor markets – requiring factor demand to equal factor supply – consumption in country I will be proportional to world consumption and world output. Thus, AC_i can be rewritten as $AQ_w a_i$, where Q_w is world output and a_i is a positive scalar.

Equation (3.1) can therefore be rewritten as

$$AT_i = AQ_i - AQ_w a_i \tag{3.3}$$

The right-hand side of equation (3.3) can also be rewritten in terms of a country's total factor endowments. If E_i is a country's total factor endowment, it must equal AQ_i since trade reveals factor endowments and $E_w a_i$ will equal $AQ_w a_i$ for the same reasons. Hence

$$AT_i = E_i - E_w a_i \tag{3.4}$$

It follows that the capital, K, embodied in net exports is

$$K_t = K_i - a_i K_w \tag{3.5}$$

and labour, L, embodied in net exports is

$$L_t = L_i - a_i L_w \qquad (3.6)$$

where t, i and w refer to trade, the country in question and the world.

If a physical definition of abundance is assumed, country I is capital-abundant if its domestic share of world capital exceeds its share of the world labour force. That is:

$$\frac{K_i}{K_w} = \frac{L_i}{L_w}$$

Capital is then revealed by trade to be abundant relative to labour if

$$\frac{K_i}{\left(K_i - K_t\right)} > \frac{L_i}{\left(L_i - L_t\right)} \qquad (3.7)$$

This can be proved if equations (3.4) and (3.5) are rewritten in terms of K_w and L_w. Taking equation (3.4), one can write

$$K_t = K_i - a_i K_w$$

or

$$-a_i K_w = K_t - K_i$$

or

$$a_i K_w = K_i - K_t$$

or

$$K_w = \frac{K_i - K_t}{a_i}$$

The relationship for L_w can be derived in a similar fashion, and $L_w = (L_i - L_t)/a_i$.

The inequality can be rewritten as

$$\left(\frac{K_i}{K_i - K_t}\right) \Big/ a_i > \left(\frac{L_i}{L_i - L_t}\right) \Big/ a_i \qquad (3.8)$$

which simplifies to

$$\frac{K_i}{\left(K_i - K_t\right)} > \frac{L_i}{\left(L_i - L_t\right)} \qquad (3.9)$$

Equation (3.9) can be rewritten in a number of other ways. If K_c and L_c are the amount of capital and labour embodied in commodities used in the country, then $K_i - K_t = K_c$ and $L_i - L_t = L_c$. By substituting into equation (3.9), one has

$$\frac{K_i}{K_c} > \frac{L_i}{L_c} = \frac{K_i}{L_i} > \frac{K_c}{L_c} \qquad (3.10)$$

Thus a country is capital-abundant if its capital–labour ratio in production is greater than that in consumption.

Equation (3.9) can also be rewritten as

$$K_i(L_i - L_t) > L_i(K_i - K_t)$$

or

$$K_i L_i - K_i L_t > L_i K_i - L_i K_t = -K_i L_t > -L_i K_t \qquad (3.11)$$

and if L_t is positive

$$\frac{K_t}{L_t} > \frac{K_i}{L_i}$$

or

$$\frac{K_t}{K_i} > \frac{L_t}{L_i}$$

Hence a country is capital-abundant if its trade is more capital-intensive than its production or if its share of capital exported exceeds its share of labour exported.

Manipulation of equation (3.11) leads to yet another condition. If we define $K_i = K_c + K_t$ and $L_i = L_c + L_t$, then $-K_i = -(K_c + K_t)$ and $-L_i = -(L_c + L_t)$ and equation (3.11) becomes

$$-(K_c + K_t)L_t > -(L_c + L_t)K_t$$

$$= -(K_c L_t + K_t L_t) > -(L_c K_t + L_t K_t)$$

$$= -K_c L_t - K_t L_t > -L_c K_t - L_t K_t$$

$$= -K_c L_t > -L_c K_t \qquad (3.12)$$

or

$$\frac{K_t}{L_t} > \frac{K_c}{L_c}$$

This says that an exporter of both capital and labour services is capital-abundant if the capital intensity in net exports is greater than the capital–labour ratio in consumption. Conversely, an importer of both services is capital-abundant if the capital intensity of net exports is less than the capital intensity of consumption – i.e. $K_t/L_t < K_c/L_c$.

As we can see from Table 3.2, which reports capital intensities as defined by Leamer (1980), the US was a net exporter of both capital and labour services

Table 3.2 Capital intensity of consumption, production and trade

	Production	Net exports	Consumption[a]
Capital ($10[6)]	328,519	23,450	305,069
Labour (10[6] man-years)	47.273	1.990	45.280
Capital–labour ratio ($/man-year)	6,949	11,783	6,737

a Uses the identity Consumption = Production – Net exports.
Source: Leamer (1980).

Table 3.3 Factor content (direct plus indirect) of total US production, net exports and consumption, 1958 and 1972

	Production[a]	Net exports	Consumption[b]
1958			
Labour (10[6] man-years)	108.72	1.38	107.34
Gross physical capital ($10[6])	1,003,217	11,901	991,316
Human capital ($10[6])	2,338,489	36,305	2,302,184
Gross physical capital/labour ($)	9,228	8,624	9,235
Human capital/labour ($)	21,509	26,308	21,448
Human capital/gross physical capital	2.331	3.051	2.322
1972			
Labour (10[6] man-years)	228.52	−0.43	228.95
Gross physical capital ($10[6])	3,163,347	−2,258	3,165,605
Human capital ($10[6])	11,184,588	−16,178	11,200,766
Gross physical capital/labour ($)	13,843	5,251	13,827
Human capital/labour ($)	48,944	37,623	48,922
Human capital/gross physical capital	3.536	7.165	3.538

a Based on value of shipments, which reflect double-counting of intermediate inputs.
b Calculated as the difference between production and net exports.
Source: Stern and Maskus (1981).

and net exports were more capital-intensive not only in production but also in consumption. Hence, Leamer concluded that the US was a capital-abundant country.

However, Table 3.3 reports the results of subsequent work by Stern and Maskus (1981), who showed that for 1958 the capital–labour ratio of net exports was lower than the capital–labour ratio for consumption goods. For 1972 they found the reverse – that the US was a net importer of capital and labour services – and the paradox was absent. These contradictory results, combined with the very strong assumption of identical preferences between countries, the reliance on a factor price equalisation framework and the adoption of the less than satisfactory physical definition of capital abundance, appear to negate the significance of Leamer's explanation of the paradox.

James and Elmslie (1996) conducted a test of the Heckscher–Ohlin–Vanek model which was restricted to the G7 countries (the US, Britain, Canada, Japan, France, Germany and Italy). Their rationale was that previous tests had ignored the basic assumptions of the neoclassical trade model: factor price equalisation and similar production technology. These conditions, they contended, are approximated among the G7. Their results provided evidence to support Heckscher–Ohlin–Vanek.

3.2.7 Misspecification of Heckscher–Ohlin tests

Using a methodology similar to that of Leamer's (1980) study, Maskus (1985) set out to compare measures of factor intensities, trade patterns and factor endowments. He proposed that the reason for the Leontief paradox was that no one had carried out a complete test of the Heckscher–Ohlin theorem. Tests had generally examined factor intensity and trade patterns across industries and had assumed that the structure of factor endowment was revealed by the factor content of trade. Deviations in the predicted endowments when compared to the actual structure of endowments would, he suggested, be a better test of the theorem. The test developed by Maskus required an independent measures of: a country's trade; its factor endowments; and the factor endowments of the rest of the world. In addition, factor intensities in production would have to be calculated. Thus, the capital–labour ratio in US net exports would be compared to measures of US and world factor endowments.

Maskus followed Leamer (1980) in two ways. First, he adopted Leamer's physical definition of abundance – i.e., a country is abundant in a particular factor if its share of the world supply of this factor exceeds its share of the world supply of another factor. Second, he adopted Leamer's criterion of ranking factors according to their relative abundance. That is: any factor 'net exported' is more abundant than any factor 'net imported'; if two factors such as capital and labour are both exported on a net basis, the share of domestic capital exported must exceed the share of labour exported if the country is capital-abundant; and if both factors are imported on net, the share of capital imported must be less than the share of labour imported to give capital abundance.

Table 3.4 US factor content, 1958 and 1972

Factor	F 1958	F 1972	$F_x - F_m$ 1958	$F_x - F_m$ 1972	$(F_x - F_m)/F$ 1958	$(F_x - F_m)/F$ 1972	Rank 1958	Rank 1972
Engineers and scientists (10^6 man-years)	1.168	1.249	0.047	0.015	0.0402	0.0120	1	1
Other labour (10^6 man-years)	12,990	12,243	0.351	0.024	0.0270	0.0020	2	2
Human capital ($10^6)	1,323,410	1,783,938	28,388	−11,526	0.021	−0.0065	3	3
Gross physical capital ($10^6)	750,178	1,340,929	9,942	−9,593	0.0133	−0.0072	5	4
Production labour (10^6 man-years)	42.339	46.705	6.784	−0.374	0.0185	−0.0080	4	5

F, Total factor content of US production.
F_x, Total factor content of US exports.
F_m, Total factor content of US imports.
Source: Maskus (1985).

By calculating a factor's total content in net exports relative to its abundance in total production, rankings among factors can be established.

Maskus's results for factor intensity are shown in Table 3.4 for the years 1958 and 1972. Labour and capital are disaggregated into: engineers and scientists; production labour; other labour; gross physical capital; and human capital. The results show that the US is most abundant in skilled labour (as revealed by engineers and scientists) for both years. Other labour, human capital, physical capital and production (unskilled) labour follow in the ranking. A scarcity of capital relative to labour is revealed for 1958 and, contrary to previous results, in 1972 as well.

Maskus (1985) then compared US factor intensities to those derived from actual factor endowments in the US and the world. Factor abundance using this latter method would be shown if US expenditure per unit of that factor was less than world expenditure per unit. Given identical homothetic preferences, this would mean that net exports would be related to large endowments. As can be seen from Table 3.5, they were not.

If factor intensity, as revealed by trade, is a true predictor of actual factor endowments, then the factor intensity and factor endowments should coincide. However, as we shall see, the results reported in Table 3.5 do not indicate support for this hypothesis. This is the case whether the calculations are made over a wide range of countries or for only six OECD countries. Three tests were carried out that provided a weak test of Heckscher–Ohlin, a strong test and a ranking test. These are described in turn.

The weak test of factor abundance suggests that a factor is abundant if a country's consumption expenditure per unit of a factor is less than the world's expenditure per unit. Given similar demand patterns, this definition implies that a country is well endowed with the factor that is being examined relative to the world. The strong test requires that a country's net exports of the factor in question, taken as a proportion of total exports, should be accompanied by a larger world expenditure per unit. The rank test requires that the ranking of the factors be equivalent across factors.

Given positive net exports of all three factors in 1958 (Table 3.5), US expenditure should be less than world expenditure to satisfy the weak test. For the thirty-four country case, in 1958 – when the US was a net exporter of skilled and unskilled labour – it spent more than the world per unit. Thus, the Heckscher–Ohlin theorem appears not to hold even though there is some support from the figures on capital – i.e., US = 0.6003, world = 0.6237. For 1972, when the US was a net importer, the expected relationship did hold for all three factors. As a failure of the weak test implies a failure of the strong test, the strong test can only be considered with reference to 1972. Here, Maskus (1985) found that the world expenditure to endowment ratio diverged from the predicted ratio. The percentage deviation is shown in the final column of Table 3.5. The deviation was of a sufficient magnitude to suggest that the data did not support Heckscher–Ohlin.

Table 3.5 Tests of the Heckscher–Ohlin–Vanek theorem for the US

Factor	$(F_x - F_m)/F$	Rank	C/F	Weak HOV prediction	C_w/F_w	HOV holds	US share	Rank	Strong HOV prediction	Per cent deviation[a]
34-country world										
1958										
Professional technical and kindred workers	0.0165	2	$60,157	∨	$37,697	No	0.3189	2	$61,166	38.4
Other labour	0.0181	1	$7,287	∨	$1,752	No	0.1223	3	$7,421	76.4
Gross physical capital	0.0133	3	0.6003	∨	0.6237	Yes	0.4222[b]	1	0.6084	2.5
1972										
Professional technical and kindred workers	−0.0011	1	$95,616	∧	$64,322	Yes	0.2693	2	$95,511	32.6
Other labour	−0.0075	3	$16,229	∧	$4,857	Yes	0.1198	3	$16,108	69.8
Gross physical capital	−0.0072	2	0.7270	∧	0.6283	Yes	0.3460	1	0.7218	13.0
OECD – 6 countries										
1958										
Professional technical and kindred workers	0.0165	2	$60,157	∨	$45,730	No	0.4983	2	$61,166	25.2
Other labour	0.0181	1	$7,287	∨	$3,977	No	0.3795	3	$7,421	46.4
Gross physical capital	0.0133	3	0.6003	∨	0.4941	No	0.5395	1	0.6084	18.8
1972										
Professional technical and kindred workers	−0.0011	1	$95,616	∧	$84,169	Yes	0.4743	2	$95,511	11.9
Other labour	−0.0075	3	$16,229	∧	$11,158	Yes	0.3704	3	$16,108	30.7
Gross physical capital	−0.0072	2	0.7270	∧	0.07314	No	0.5420	1	0.7218	1.3

C, Aggregate US consumption; C_w, Aggregate consumption; $C_{w'}$ Total world (either 34-country or OECD) factor content; HOV, Heckscher–Ohlin–Vanek theorem. F, Total factor content of US production; F_x, Total factor content of US exports; F_m, Total factor content of US imports; $F_{w'}$ Total world (either 34-country or OECD) factor content; HOV, Heckscher–Ohlin–Vanek theorem.
a Absolute deviation as percentage of predicted ratio.
b Computed from 1963 data.
Source: Maskus (1985).

The more restrictive test using only the US and five major OECD countries fared no better, failing to satisfy the weak test in four of the six cases and the strong test in all six. Some doubt, however, attaches to the conclusions concerning physical capital since the estimates are so small. The rank tests in both the thirty-four country and the OECD case fail to confirm the prediction of the Heckscher–Ohlin theorem.

3.2.8 Alternative statistical tests of Heckscher–Ohlin

Harkness and Kyle (1975) provided an alternative test for the Heckscher–Ohlin theorem using a logit model (a description of logit procedures can be found in Maddala (1992)). Prior empirical studies had attempted to explain the volume of trade or the share of an industry's net exports in terms of the factor intensities used. Harkness and Kyle felt that the use of factor intensity was inappropriate on theoretical grounds. Both Jones (1956) and Bhagwati (1972) had shown that in economies with more goods than factors only the direction of trade could be predicted, not the volume. As a result, the size of an industry's trade balance could be ignored and, instead, empirical tests should concentrate on whether an industry was a net exporter or net importer. By designating an industry's net trade balance in terms of a binary dependent variable – that is, 0 if it is a net importer and 1 if it is a net exporter –logit analysis can be employed to estimate the possibility of an industry taking on the value 0 in terms of a vector of industry characteristics. The independent variables (the vector of industry characteristics) in the logit regression are the factors of production that are important in determining the industry's comparative advantage.

Harkness and Kyle's (1975) results are given in Table 3.6 and can be interpreted in much the same way as standard regression analysis. Two logit tests were run on eighty-eight industries, which were subdivided into natural resource and non-natural resource industries. In their first equation the independent variables were: the capital–labour ratio (K/L); and the proportion of the industry's labour force made up of the following four groups: scientists and engineers (SE); middle skills (MS); unskilled and other skills (US); and resource intensity (DUM). In their second equation the skill groups were alternatively aggregated into white-collar labour skills (SEP) and blue-collar skills (OPS).

Harkness and Kyle interpreted their results as showing that the source of the US's comparative advantage in non-resource-intensive industries lay in its abundance of capital and skilled labour. This was the case for both aggregation methods. The significance of the negative DUM variable (1 if resource industry, 0 otherwise) suggested to them that the US was natural resource poor and that resource industries were at a disadvantage compared to their foreign competitors. Moreover, the factors that were relevant in explaining comparative advantage for non-resource industries were not statistically significant in the case of these industries. This difference suggested that there must be very strong structural factors differentiating resource industries even though the hypothesis was that in a capital-rich country like the US capital and skill intensities should have some

Table 3.6 Logit estimates of factors affecting US comparative advantage

Equation	KL	SE	MS	SEP	OPS	US	DUM	Constant	LRT
(1) Non-NR	8.574 (2.43)[b]	0.788 (1.97)[a]	0.722 (2.07)[a]			-0.095 (0.24)		2.522 (1.12)	36.56[b]
NR	-0.792 (0.96)	-1.386 (0.80)	0.034 (0.78)			-0.187 (1.14)	-75.097 (2.17)[a]		
(2) Non-NR	7.762 (2.08)[a]			0.785 (2.17)[a]	0.682 (1.89)	-0.045 (0.11)		3.78 (1.33)	37.61[b]
NR	-0.618 (0.71)			-0.645 (0.79)	0.053 (0.92)	-0.051 (0.21)	-73.70 (2.06)[a]		

DUM, Dummy variable (1 if resource industry, 0 otherwise); KL, Capital per worker; LRT, Likelihood ratio test chi-square with nine degrees of freedom; MS, Percentage of non-technical professionals in an industry's labour force (managers, clerks, foremen and operatives); NR, Natural resource industries; OPS, Percentage of 'blue-collar' skills (craftsmen, foremen and operatives); SE, Percentage of scientists and engineers; SEP, Percentage of 'white-collar' skills (scientists, engineers, professionals, managers and clericals); US, Percentage of unskilled (non-farm labourers and service workers).

a Significant at the 95% confidence level on a one-tailed test.
b Significant at the 99% confidence level on a one-tailed test.
Source: Harkness and Kyle (1975).

effect on export probabilities. Harkness and Kyle's results, therefore, upheld the Heckscher–Ohlin theorem that the US non-resource-based export industries were capital-intensive. Skilled labour, however, also contributes to comparative advantage. This latter result supports both the idea that labour should be disaggregated into skilled and non-skilled segments and that US export industries obtain their comparative advantage from research and development. Scientists and engineers were considered proxies for research and development activities.

Testing net exports in a binary form was not, however, the end of the debate as Harkness and Kyle's (1975) results were not fully accepted. Branson and Monoyios (1977), using US data for 1963 and 1967, retested a binary variable using probit analysis (a description of probit procedures can also be found in Maddala (1992)). A positive coefficient suggests that the variable contributes to comparative advantage. The results of their tests of two models are presented in Table 3.7. In model 1 capital, K, has a negative coefficient and is insignificant. The same is also true for labour, L. In 1963 and 1967 human capital, H, has a positive coefficient, suggesting that it played a part in conferring comparative advantage on the US. It was, however, only significant in 1963. Model 2, which tested the capital–labour ratio, K/L, and the human capital to labour ratio, H/L, showed a negative and insignificant coefficient for K/L but positive and significant coefficients for H/L. This is consistent with the results for model 1. Branson and Monoyios's results thus throw doubt on Harkness and Kyle's (1975) conclusions.

Table 3.7 Probit estimates of factors affecting US comparative advantage

	Dependent variable	Independent variables			
Model 1					
		K	H	L	$-2\log_e \lambda$
	Net exports (1963)	−0.0005 (1.66)	0.0005 (2.88)[b]	−0.0079 (1.98)	20.54[b]
	Net exports (1967)	−0.0004 (0.43)	0.00018 (1.94)	−0.0055 (1.58)	10.27[a]
Model 2					
		K/L	H/L	$-2\log_e \lambda$	
	Net exports (1963)	−0.038 (1.88)	0.058 (3.51)[b]	13.86[b]	
	Net exports (1967)	−0.017 (1.97)	0.044 (3.17)[b]	11.46[b]	

K, Capital; *H*, Human capital; *L*, Labour; λ, Ratio of the maximum value of the constrained likelihood function to the maximum value of the unconstrained likelihood function.
a Significant at the 5% level.
b Significant at the 1% level.
Source: Branson and Monoyios (1977).

Baldwin (1979) also took issue with Harkness and Kyle's results. His main criticism was based on theoretical grounds. He argued that, in a multi-country setting, a country may not import only those commodities which are intensive in its scarce factor – a point that was also strongly made by Caves and Jones (1977). Baldwin therefore believed that tests using a binary dependent variable were inappropriate.

Stern and Maskus (1981) also undertook a probit analysis but used a different approach. Availing themselves of a data series covering the years 1958 to 1976, they were able to increase their sample and break away from the cross-section analysis used in the previous studies. As can be seen from Table 3.8, net exports were found to be negatively related to the K/L ratio. Although when natural resource (Ricardo) industries were left out of their sample the capital/labour coefficients turned positive, they were not statistically significant. Stern and Maskus also used scaled regression involving industry cross-sections at the three-digit Standard Industrial Classification (SIC) level with net exports as the dependent variable and physical capital, labour inputs and human capital

Table 3.8 Probit analysis of US net exports of manufactures

| | Independent variables | | |
Year	K/L	H/L	$-2\log\lambda$
All manufactures			
1958	−0.022 (1.99)	0.050 (3.49)[b]	13.411[b]
1967	−0.017 (2.22)[a]	0.046 (4.44)[b]	21.800[b]
1976	−0.015 (2.25)[a]	0.018 (3.51)[a]	13.430[b]
Excluding Ricardo industries			
1958	0.017 (0.95)	0.059 (3.96)[b]	26.53[b]
1967	0.012 (0.81)	0.051 (4.78)[b]	33.48[b]
1976	0.003 (0.29)	0.023 (4.35)[b]	28.55[b]

The numbers in parentheses are the profit coefficients divided by their standard errors. Significance levels are based on a table of *t*-values and hence are only approximate here. The final column gives a log transformation of the likelihood ratio statistic $-2\log\lambda$. This is distributed as chi-squared in large samples and the reported significance levels reflect this fact. It is analogous to a regression *F*-statistic in that it tests for the existence of an overall relationship.
a Significant at the 5% level.
b Significant at the 1% level.
Source: Stern and Maskus (1981).

as independent variables. In this case as well the coefficients on K/L were negative while that for human capital was positive and statistically significant. As their probit analysis produced contradictory results, Stern and Maskus concluded that Harkness and Kyle's results could not be upheld even if the theoretical objection to the use of binary dependent variables was ignored. Furthermore, their regression analysis – and their preferred model – supported the Leontief paradox.

3.3 Summary of tests of the Heckscher–Ohlin theory

In view of the extent to which the Heckscher–Ohlin hypothesis has been tested, the complex nature of the tests and the subsidiary issues they raised, a short summary of central issues may clarify the arguments and refocus the discussion.

The attempts at verification using input–output analysis produced, in the main, paradoxical results. Countries with an abundance of a particular factor imported goods which incorporated that factor intensively in their production and exported goods that used those countries' less abundant factor intensively in their production. Research efforts then focused on finding ways to reconcile theory with the empirical evidence. These efforts followed a number of paths, ranging from: a more detailed treatment of labour inputs and the inclusion of additional factors in production functions; an examination of differences in demand patterns; the existence of trade distortions; the reformulation of factor intensity; the respecification of the empirical tests; and, finally, alternative statistical testing using logit and probit techniques. The implications that these empirical results had for the Heckscher–Ohlin theory will be evaluated at the end of this chapter. First, however, tests of the Ricardian – or classical – theory are examined.

3.4 Empirical tests of Ricardian trade theory

Ricardian trade theory suggests that one country will have a comparative advantage over another if its labour costs are lower. The crucial assumption of this theory is that all of a good's costs can be assigned to a common labour unit – i.e. it is a *labour theory of value*. The theory states that the only way a high wage-cost country can compete effectively with a low wage-cost country is if its labour productivity is high enough to equalise or outweigh the advantage of the low wage-cost country. For example, if country I's labour costs were only half of those of country II, the latter could only compete if its labour productivity was twice as high as country I's.

MacDougall (1951, 1952) initiated and carried out the first test of the relative labour productivity hypothesis using labour productivity data from the US and UK for 1939. Subsequent studies using more recent data were carried out by Stern (1962), MacDougall *et al.* (1962) and Balassa (1963), although the last used a different approach for part of his analysis (see section 3.4.2).

The thrust of this empirical work was to examine whether the US, with wage rates twice those of the UK, was nevertheless able to compete and achieve a share in world exports in a comparable range of products. As suggested above, the only way the US could be expected to compete internationally was through superior labour productivity. Hence, the basic approach was to examine the relationship between export shares and wage rates adjusted for labour productivity. Two related issues were also examined: whether labour productivity or unit costs, taken alone, could predict export market shares.

3.4.1 Testing for a relationship between wage rates and market share

To test the first hypothesis – that wage rates adjusted for productivity determine export market share – MacDougall (1951, 1952) and Stern (1962) used two approaches. The first, direct, approach examined each industry independently to see if it conformed to the hypothesis regarding labour cost and export share and then tabulated the number of industries that conformed to the hypothesis. The second approach employed statistical estimation procedures.

Taking the direct approach, MacDougall (1951, 1952) and Stern (1962) used both average and individual industry wages and then adjusted for productivity levels. MacDougall found that in 1939, when average US wages were twice those of the UK, the former only had a higher export share than the latter when its labour productivity was twice that of the UK. This was the case in twenty of the twenty-five industries examined. In a repeat study for 1950, when the average US wage was 3.4 times higher than that of the UK, Stern (1962) obtained a similar result for twenty industries out of a sample of twenty-four. In a larger sample of thirty-nine industries only five did not conform to the expected pattern. Data limitations prevented MacDougall from applying industry-specific wage levels to more than thirteen industries. Despite this smaller sample, however, the results were slightly improved over those for average wage rates. Stern, using the same sample of industries as MacDougall but for 1950, found a slight weakening of the results although the same general pattern was maintained.

Both MacDougall and Stern regressed the log ratio of US exports/UK exports against the log ratio of US and UK labour productivity. MacDougall found that his regression line, when fitted to data for 1937, passed through the point where US and UK exports would be equal – to the left of the US/UK labour productivity ratio of $2:1$. For the same sample of industries for 1950 Stern found a similar trend, although his results were not quite as marked as MacDougall's. In Stern's thirty-nine industry sample the regression line passed through the $2:1$ US/UK labour productivity ratio. In Stern's period of study US wages were, it will be recalled, 3.4 times the British level. What both MacDougall's and Stern's results for the 1950 period imply is that the UK had greater advantage over the US than wage rates alone would imply. The results were interpreted as an indication that the benefits of Britain's imperial preference trade regime and perceived quality advantages were declining over time.

3.4.2 Testing for a relationship between export share and labour productivity

MacDougall (1951, 1952) tested a second hypothesis – whether there was a relationship between export share and labour productivity – by regressing the ratio of US/UK export share against the ratio of US/UK labour productivity. The results showed that as US labour productivity increased relative to UK labour productivity, the larger was the proportion of US exports relative to UK exports. MacDougall's results are given in Table 3.9. Balassa (1963) also tested this hypothesis. His approach was slightly different in that he preferred to work with export values rather than quantities on the grounds that labour productivity and output quantities were positively correlated. His choice of 1951 was based on his belief that 1950 was an abnormal year. His results for both direct estimation and in logs (Table 3.9) appear to confirm the hypothesis that there is a positive relationship between export share and labour productivity.

3.4.3 Testing for a relationship between labour cost ratios and export shares

The relationship between labour cost and export shares was tested by both Stern (1962) and Balassa (1963). Their results are also presented in Table 3.9. Stern tested the relationship between the log of export shares and the log of the unit cost ratio, and his regression showed some support for the hypothesis that they were negatively correlated, although not strongly so. Balassa used the wage ratio as an explanatory variable in conjunction with the labour productivity ratio. The wage ratio was not significant (at the 5 per cent confidence level) in either the log or non-log regressions, and the minor improvement it gave to the multiple correlation coefficient suggests that it adds little explanatory power.

3.5 Summary of tests of Ricardian trade theory

Taking the three studies together, it appears that the Ricardian analysis was vindicated. Bhagwati (1964), however, took issue with this conclusion on theoretical grounds. His objections were threefold. First, he argued that Ricardian theory addresses itself to a situation where two countries are trading with one another and not where they are competing for sales in a third market. Thus, attempting to test for comparative advantage using third markets was an inappropriate approach. As the Ricardian model can be expanded to take into account many-country, many-commodity trade, Bhagwati's criticism on this point may not be particularly important.

His second objection centred on the problem of interpreting results drawn from a general analysis for a specific case. For example, a reduction of input costs for a specific industry may well lead to a reduction in the price of the good produced and to an increase in its share in third markets by a specific proportion. However, it would be wrong to assume that a reduction of input costs of the same magnitude would increase the share of all of a nation's exports by that same proportion. The amount of increase would clearly depend on the elasticity

Table 3.9 Tests of Ricardian trade theory

Study	Data year	Dependent variable		Intercept	Independent variables					Correlation coefficient	Multiple correlation coefficient
		X	LogX		Y	LogY	LogZ	W	LogW		
MacDougall	1950		Quantity	−2.19		+1.89				0.61	
Stern	1950		Quantity	+0.01	—		−1.40			−0.43	
Balassa	1951	Value		−181.2	+0.691 (0.167)			+0.140 (0.102)			0.81
Balassa	1951		Value	−5.164		+1.457 (0.328)			+1.250 (0.566)		0.88

W, US/UK wage ratio; X, US/UK export ratio; Y, US/UK labour productivity ratio; Z, US/UK unit cost ratio.
Source: Bhagwati (1964).

of demand for each individual good. MacDougall's (1951, 1952) methodology, which was based on cross-section analysis, assumed that a fall in input costs would translate into an equiproportional increase in market share for all goods. Clearly, this caution was aimed at those who might misuse the results by attempting to make forecasts rather than being a criticism of the test itself.

Bhagwati's third theoretical objection is perhaps more serious. According to his argument, the direction of causation should run from comparative costs to relative prices to export shares. MacDougall's (1951, 1952) results were based on the relationship between the latter two variables. There should, however, also be a statistical relationship between comparative costs and relative prices, but Bhagwati could not find one. Bhagwati's empirical tests involved two measures or proxies for comparative cost: labour productivity and unit labour costs. His results are presented in section (*a*) of Table 3.10. The linear regressions of export price on labour productivity ratios have only poor explanatory power and the independent variables are not significant. When unit labour costs are

Table 3.10 Comparative costs and relative prices

Date	Regression equation		Coefficients
(a) Labour productivity ratios and export price ratios			
1937	$Y = 1.72$ (0.2291)	$-0.211X$ (0.0450)	$r^2 = 0.525$ $r = -0.724$
1937	$\log Y = 0.252$ (0.1925)	$-0.525 \log X$ (0.432)	$r^2 = 0.0686$ $r = -0.262$
1950	$Y = 1.58$ (0.32605)	$-0.169X$ (0.1204)	$r^2 = 0.129$ $r = -0.359$
1950	$\log Y = 0.264$ (0.3769)	$-0.611 \log X$ (0.5155)	$r^2 = 0.0912$ $r = -0.302$
1950	$Y = 1.7044$ (0.3291)	$-0.1470X$ (0.1095)	$r^2 = 0.0728$ $r = -0.2698$
1950	$\log Y = 0.2056$ (0.0816)	$-0.2773 \log X$ (0.1831)	$r^2 = 0.0906$ $r = -0.301$

Y, Export price ratio; *X*, labour productivity ratio.

(b) Unit labour cost ratios and export price ratios

Date	Regression equation		Coefficients
1950	$Y = 0.7227$ (0.33194)	$+0.4141X$ (0.23021)	$r^2 = 0.1233$ $r = 0.3512$
1950	$\log Y = 0.03785$ (0.0335)	$+0.42113 \log X$ (0.1997)	$r^2 = 0.162$ $r = 0.40248$

Y, Export price ratio; *X*, unit labour cost ratio.

Standard errors in parenthesis.
Source: Tables III and IV of Bhagwati (1964).

regressed against price ratios, as can be seen in section (*b*) of Table 3.10, the results are also not encouraging. The lack of significance in these two sets of results led Bhagwati to conclude that because a causal link cannot be established, the Ricardian approach should be rejected.

Bhagwati's (1964) conclusion does not necessarily hold if the competitive assumption of the model are relaxed. Except in the very long run, profits will vary among industries owing to the presence of an element of monopoly. Prices will be independent of labour costs. Costs would still be important because the lower the costs, given a set of prices, the higher would be the profits from export earnings. Hence, the incentive to export would be greater. By rejecting Bhagwati's assumption that labour costs and labour productivity reflect comparative costs, the results of the empirical tests of the Ricardian hypothesis can be viewed in a more favourable light.

Interest in tests of Ricardian theory, however, has waned, with no major empirical work undertaken over the subsequent thirty years (Leamer and Levinsohn, 1995).

3.6   Implications of the empirical tests of classical and neoclassical trade theories

The impact that the empirical evidence had on both the Ricardian and Heckscher–Ohlin theories was twofold. First, the evidence affected the relative standing of the two models. Second, it influenced the development of Heckscher–Ohlin theory and led to the formulation of alternative approaches.

Earlier generations of trade theorists, on seeing the empirical evidence supporting the Ricardian view and contrasting it with the weaker support for the Heckscher–Ohlin theory, concluded that the former was superior as an explanation for international trade. Their conclusions, however, can be challenged on both a theoretical and an empirical level.

Theoretically, the Ricardian explanation of trade can be regarded as inferior in that it does not explain what factors give rise to a country's comparative advantage – which is taken as a given – whereas Heckscher–Ohlin links this explicitly to factor endowments. How can one rely on a theory that cannot explain how comparative advantage is established?

To base the assessment of the two theories purely on empirical criteria one would have to be satisfied that the results obtained could not be explained by alternative models. Deardorff (1984), utilising earlier work by Ford (1967) and Falvey (1981), suggested that the results obtained from the empirical work that supports the Ricardian hypothesis can also be used to support the Heckscher–Ohlin hypothesis. In a two-country, two-commodity, two-factor world with factor price equalisation Ricardian theory would not hold because the assumption of factor price equalisation leads to the equality of labour productivity between countries. In a world where factor prices do not equalise, and at best only tend to equality, the implication is that labour productivity differs between countries. If a capital-abundant country has a comparative advantage in producing and selling capital-intensive goods, its labour productivity would be closely related to its capital intensity. In other words, labour productivity would be highest in those industries producing more capital-intensive goods. Hence, a capital-abundant country's exports would be related to high labour productivity. A labour-abundant country would have a comparative advantage in labour-intensive industries and, when its economy was opened up to trade, it would experience an increase in demand for labour-intensive goods. Although initially labour productivity would be lower than in capital-abundant countries, the differences would be smallest in the labour-intensive industries where capital and labour are not close substitutes.

Leontief's (1953) original tests and many of those which followed gave paradoxical results. It was clear from the approaches taken to reconcile the empirical evidence with the theory – either by including other variables or by allowing for human capital – that the simple, or strict, Heckscher–Ohlin model did not provide a satisfactory explanation of trade. This led to dual research paths where one group set about constructing a new theory while others attempted to rehabilitate Heckscher–Ohlin. The latter refined the tests and restated the theory. Even so, paradoxes still occurred – although not in all tests and not for all time periods. Many economists, however, still tended to support Heckscher–Ohlin, or its modifications, as a general theory of trade. This suggests that alternative theories of trade that were developed in the wake of the inability to find a definitive resolution of the Leontief paradox also suffered from difficulties with empirical validation. It is to this question that we turn in Chapters 4 and 5.

References

Arrow, K. J., Chenery, H. B., Minhas, B. S., and Solow, R. M. (1961), 'Capital–labour substitution and economic efficiency', *The Review of Economics and Statistics*, 43(3), pp. 225–50.
Balassa, B. (1963), 'An empirical demonstration of classical comparative cost theory', *The Review of Economics and Statistics*, 45(3), pp. 231–8.
Baldwin, R. E. (1971), 'Determinants of the commodity structure of U.S. trade', *American Economic Review*, 61(2), pp. 126–46.
Baldwin, R. E. (1979), 'Determinants of trade and foreign investment: further evidence', *The Review of Economics and Statistics*, 61(1), pp. 40–8.
Ball, D. S. (1966), 'Factor-intensity in international comparison of factor costs and factor use', *Journal of Political Economy*, 74(1), pp. 77–80.
Becker, G. (1964), *Human Capital*, New York: National Bureau of Economic Research.
Bhagwati, J. N. (1964), 'The pure theory of international trade: a survey', *Economic Journal*, 74, pp. 1–84.
Bhagwati, J. N. (1972), 'The Heckscher–Ohlin theorem in the multi-commodity case', *Journal of Political Economy*, 80(5), pp. 1052–5.

Bharadwaj, R. (1962), 'Factor proportion and the structure of Indo-US trade', *Indian Economic Journal*, 10(2), pp. 105–16.

Branson, W. H., and Monoyios, N. (1977), 'Factor inputs in US trade', *Journal of International Economics*, 7, pp. 111–31.

Brown, A. J. (1957), 'Professor Leontief and the pattern of world trade', *Yorkshire Bulletin of Economic and Social Research*, 9(1), pp. 63–75.

Caves, R., and Jones, R. (1977), *World Trade and Payments*, Boston: Little Brown and Co.

Deardorff, A. V. (1984), 'Testing trade theories and predicting trade flows', in R. W. Jones and P. B. Kenen (eds), *Handbook of International Economics*, vol. I, Amsterdam: North-Holland, pp. 467–517.

Diab, M. A. (1956), *The United States Capital Position and the Structure of Its Foreign Trade*, Amsterdam: North-Holland.

Ellsworth, P. T. (1954), 'The structure of American foreign trade: a new view examined', *The Review of Economics and Statistics*, 36(3), pp. 279–85.

Falvey, R. E. (1981), 'Comparative advantage in a multi-factor world', *International Economic Review*, 22(2), pp. 401–13.

Ford, J. L. (1967), 'On the equivalence of the classical and the factor-proportions models in explaining international trade patterns', *The Manchester School of Economic and Social Studies*, 35(2), pp. 185–98.

Hannah, G. (1967), 'An economic analysis of earnings and schooling', *Journal of Human Resources*, 2(3), pp. 310–46.

Harkness, J., and Kyle, J. F. (1975), 'Factors influencing United States comparative advantage', *Journal of International Economics*, 5, pp. 153–65.

Houthakker, H. S. (1957), 'An international comparison of household expenditure patterns, commemorating a century of Engel's law', *Econometrica*, 25(4), pp. 532–51.

James, A. M., and Elmslie, B. T. (1996), 'Testing Heckscher–Ohlin–Vanek in the G7', *Weltwirtschaftliches Archiv*, 13(1), pp. 139–57.

Jones, R. W. (1956), 'Factor proportions and the Heckscher–Ohlin theorem', *Review of Economic Studies*, 25, pp. 1–10.

Kenen, P. B. (1965), 'Nature, capital and trade', *Journal of Political Economy*, 73(5), pp. 437–60.

Kravis, I. B. (1956), 'Wages and foreign trade', *The Review of Economics and Statistics*, 38(1), pp. 14–30.

Leamer, E. E. (1980), 'The Leontief paradox reconsidered', *Journal of Political Economy*, 88(3), pp. 495–503.

Leamer, E. E., and Levinsohn, J. (1995), 'International trade theory and evidence', in G. Grossman and K. Rogoff (eds), *Handbook of International Economics*, vol. III, Amsterdam: Elsevier Science, pp. 1339–94.

Leontief, W. (1953), 'Domestic production and foreign trade: the American capital position re-examined', *Proceedings of the American Philosophical Society*, 97, pp. 332–49.

Leontief, W. (1956), 'Factor proportions and the structure of American trade: further theoretical and empirical analysis', *The Review of Economics and Statistics*, 38(4), pp. 386–407.

Leontief, W. (1964), 'International factor cost and factor use', *American Economic Review*, 54(4), pp. 335–45.

MacDougall, G. D. A. (1951), 'British and American exports: a study suggested by the theory of comparative costs, part I', *Economic Journal*, 61, pp. 697–724.

MacDougall, G. D. A. (1952), 'British and American exports: a study suggested by the theory of comparative costs, part II', *Economic Journal*, 62, pp. 487–521.

MacDougall, G. D. A., Dowley, M., Fox, P., and Pugh, S. (1962), 'British and American productivity, prices and exports: an addendum', *Oxford Economic Papers*, 14, pp. 427–34.

Maddala, G. S. (1992), *Introduction to Econometrics, 2nd edn*, New York: Macmillan.

Maskus, K. E. (1985), 'A test of the Heckscher–Ohlin–Vanek theorem: the Leontief commonplace', *Journal of International Economics*, 19, pp. 201–12.

Minhas, B. S. (1963), *An International Comparison of Factor Costs and Factor Use*, Amsterdam: North-Holland.

Naya, S. (1967), 'Natural resources, factor mix, and factor reversals in international trade', *American Economic Review*, 57, pp. 561–70.

Ohlin, B. G. (1933), *Interregional and International Trade*, Harvard Economic Studies no. 39, Cambridge, Mass.: Harvard University Press.

Robinson, R. (1956), 'Factor proportions and comparative advantage: part I', *Quarterly Journal of Economics*, 70(2), pp. 169–92.

Stern, R. M. (1962), 'British and American productivity and comparative costs in international trade', *Oxford Economic Papers*, 14, pp. 275–96.

Stern, R. M., and Maskus, K. E. (1981), 'Determinants of the structure of US foreign trade, 1958–1976', *Journal of International Economics*, 11, pp. 207–24.

Swerling, B. C. (1954), 'Capital shortage and labour surplus in the United States', *The Review of Economics and Statistics*, 36(3), pp. 286–9.

Tatemoto, M., and Ichimura, S. (1959), 'Factor proportions and foreign trade: the case of Japan', *The Review of Economics and Statistics*, 41(4), pp. 442–6.

Travis, W. P. (1964), *The Theory of Trade and Protection*, Cambridge, Mass.: Harvard University Press.

Valvanis-Vail, S. (1954), 'Leontief's scarce factor paradox', *Journal of Political Economy*, 62(6), pp. 523–8.

Vanek, J. (1963), *The Natural Resource Content of United States Foreign Trade, 1870–1955*', Cambridge, Mass.: MIT Press.

Wahl, D. F. (1961), 'Capital and labour requirements for Canada's foreign trade', *Canadian Journal of Economics and Political Science*, 27(3), pp. 349–58.

Wood, A. (1994), 'Give Heckscher and Ohlin a chance!', *Weltwirtschaftliches Archiv*, 130(1), pp. 20–49.

CHAPTER 4

Alternative theories of international trade

4.1 Introduction

The absence of even weak support for Heckscher–Ohlin predictions in the early empirical investigations of neoclassical theory led a number of economists to abandon it as an explanation of trade and provided the incentive for them to seek new explanations. For them, the development of alternative theories was perceived as a solution that was preferable to patching up a theory that was considered faulty in its foundations (Wijnhold, 1955). The subsequent theoretical developments were, therefore, largely based on departures from the neoclassical assumptions of perfect competition, factor immobility, identical production functions, constant returns to scale, similar tastes and homogeneous goods.

This chapter will outline these new theoretical developments and focus on what have come to be recognised as the main rivals to the Heckscher–Ohlin model. That is, alternatives that have been important in the development of a line of reasoning or for having achieved a wide degree of acceptance in the economics profession. These include: the vent for surplus model; the availability thesis; the technology/product-cycle theory; formulations allowing for economies of scale; and the modelling of imperfect competition. Each of these approaches has a section devoted to it where its development is chronicled and its strengths and weaknesses are analysed. Empirical evidence relating to these alternative theories will be dealt with in Chapter 5.

4.2 The vent for surplus model

To explain the opening up and evolution of trade between developing and developed countries, Myint (1958) made use of an idea that had its origins in Adam Smith's *Wealth of Nations* (1776). Williams (1929) had taken a similar approach in an earlier paper, but Myint developed this alternative to Heckscher–Ohlin more fully. Neoclassical trade theory presupposes that economies are

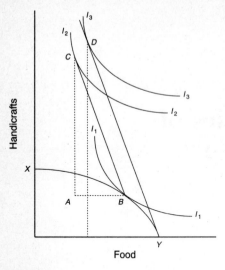

Figure 4.1

operating on their production possibility frontiers both before and after an economy is opened to trade. Once countries began to trade there is a reallocation of resources as export goods industries increase their output while import-competing goods industries contract. In short, there is a movement along the production possibility frontier. Myint proposed an alternative whereby once a country was opened up to trade, exports would increase but there would be no decline in the output of other sectors. Hence, a situation was postulated in which idle resources exist prior to trade. These surplus resources are only brought into production use once trade commences. As a result, the contraction of the non-export sector is avoided. Of course, Myint's pre-trade situation implies that the country is not operating on the production possibility frontier but somewhere inside it. Hence, trade acts as a provider of new effective demand for the output of surplus resources – i.e. as a *vent for surplus*.

Figure 4.1 can be used to illustrate Myint's argument. The economy produces two goods, handicrafts and food products, with a production possibility frontier XY. Instead of producing on XY, the country produces inside this frontier at point A. In this model it is assumed that the only constraint on the output of both goods is labour – i.e. there is no capital or land constraint. Before proceeding, it is important to explain why the economy operates at point A rather than on the production possibility frontier. One line of reasoning suggests that the output of the food sector can be limited by the saturation of wants. In other words, so much food is produced in the absence of the opportunity to trade that its marginal utility is zero. Similarly, enough handicrafts are produced to satisfy local demands, so when faced with the choice between working (and producing more handicrafts) or consuming more leisure, producers of handicrafts choose leisure.

In Figure 4.1 the economy produces at point *A*. When consumers are given the opportunity, through international trade, to acquire the goods being offered by developed countries the opportunity cost of leisure rises and food production rises to pay for imports. The economy moves from *A* to point *B* on the production possibility frontier. When trade is opened up the new terms of trade allow an economy to consume at *C*, which is a point tangential to a higher community indifference schedule – I_2–I_2 compared to I_1–I_1 (see Chapter 2 for an explanation of community indifference curves). Thus, by increasing its production of food by *AB*, the country can exchange this extra production for new manufactures (which add to non-food consumption) equal to *AC*. In the long run handicrafts are not expected to be competitive with manufactured products produced in the developed countries and handicraft production eventually falls to zero. Food production, in contrast, expands to point *Y* and additional amounts are traded for manufactured products. The terms of trade line would be shifted out parallel to *CB* and would pass through point *Y* – enabling the economy to consume at point *D*. Once all the land had been brought into food production it would be impossible for the country to expand its food exports in order to purchase additional manufactured products unless land productivity could be increased.

If the productivity of land cannot be increased, the growing population would literally eat into the food surplus and reduce the country's ability to buy industrial goods. The result would be a decline in the exports of food products and a reduction in imports. In addition to providing an alternative to Heckscher–Ohlin, the vent for surplus approach would appear to account for the often observed rise and fall of developing countries' traditional exports.

The population that the agricultural sector could not absorb could possibly find its way into an expanding import-substituting industrial sector. Lack of sufficient investment capital may, however, prevent this sector from becoming established – and even more so from expanding sufficiently fast to employ surplus labour.

Lewis (1954) has suggested an additional reason why agricultural labour may fail to move to the industrial sector. His explanation is based on the behaviour expected from peasant proprietors. If those working in the export sector obtain an income based on the joint sharing of the product of a family plot of land, they will only move to the industrial sector if they can be compensated for their loss of earnings in the agricultural sector plus the costs of moving. This incentive wage rate may, however, be beyond the ability of a newly establishing industrial sector to pay.

If the industrial sector of developing countries fails to arise, or if incentive wage rates cannot be paid, the result of population increases would be a contracting export sector accompanied by rising unemployment and underemployment. This outcome contrasts with that indicated by the Heckscher–Ohlin model, which would predict a rise in the proportion of output contributed by the labour-intensive commodity as the ratio of labour to land increased.

Although the vent for surplus model is useful for understanding the *opening up* phase in the development of some countries, it does not follow that it explains the persisting situation of rising unemployment and falling exports that often characterises the economic performance of developing countries. The model suggests that the growth of the domestic manufacturing sector is constrained by trade. If the goal of the government is to foster growth in manufacturing, restrictions on trade are the obvious policy prescription. Hence, empirical tests of the vent for surplus model may be important for determining the trade policy regime a nation may wish to follow.

4.3   The availability thesis

In the mid-1950s trade between industrialised countries and countries characterised as producers of primary products constituted an estimated 50 per cent of world trade. To explain this observed trade pattern, Kravis (1956) developed what has been termed the *availability thesis*. He suggested the straightforward proposition that the primary reason that goods are bought abroad is simply because they are not available at home. Unavailability can take on both an absolute meaning – when goods simply do not exist in a country – or a relative meaning – where increased production of a product can only take place at rapidly rising cost because supply is highly inelastic. Examples of the former might be oil or diamonds, while the latter could be bananas or grapefruit in cold climates.

Kravis' (1956) theory can be illustrated by starting with a highly simplified model of the world and then making the model correspond more closely to the real world by dropping some of the more restrictive assumptions. The explanation of Kravis that follows draws heavily on Findlay (1970). Initially, let us assume that there are *n* countries and *m* commodities and that each commodity requires a specific input which is exclusive to it. Each country is endowed with only one of these factor inputs. Assume, also, that all countries demand all commodities, the exact magnitudes depending on relative prices. The supply of an individual commodity will then be limited by the quantity or endowment of the special input that is *available* in the supplying country. The relative price of the commodity is determined by aggregating the demand of the individual countries. As long as a country is willing to exchange some of its unique commodity for those produced by other countries, a pattern of trade will be established whereby each country will export one commodity in exchange for one or more commodities. The volume of trade that results will be determined by the terms of trade – i.e. how much of a foreign good can be acquired in exchange for a domestically produced good.

In the simplified world economy described above the theory of comparative advantage would not come into play because trade patterns are determined by the *availability* of the unique commodity. Would trade be determined in the same way in a more complex world where some countries produced more than one good? To answer this question let us now assume a world in which there are four countries – A, B, C, D – and two goods – food and manufactures. Both goods require land and capital for their production, but manufactures also require an extra input – say, technological knowledge. All countries possess capital, but only A, B and C are endowed with land, while B, C and D possess technological knowledge. Country A is thus confined to producing only land-intensive products and country D is limited to manufactures. Countries B and C can produce both goods as they are endowed with both land and technical knowledge.

For countries A and D to acquire goods they do not produce they have to export food and manufactures, respectively. The exports of countries B and C will be determined by relative prices. At one set of relative prices they would be importers of food and exporters of manufactures, while the opposite could be true at another set of relative prices. For example, assume a constant marginal rate of transformation in both countries: e.g., in country B five units of food exchange for one unit of manufactures, and in C the ratio is 3:1. Both countries would export manufactures if the world price ratio were greater than 5:1 and export food products if it were less than 3:1. If the world ratio lies in between – say, at 4:1 – country B would export food and country C would export manufactures. Thus, *availability* describes the trade pattern only of countries A and D. Although B and C possess land and capital, it is relative prices that determine the exports and imports of food and manufactures between themselves and between countries A and D. Thus, the Ricardian or classical theory of trade explains the trade of countries B and C, the availability model explaining only the trade patterns of countries A and D.

In a similar fashion, *availability* can be integrated with the Heckscher–Ohlin model. Let us assume that country B and country C have equal endowments of labour, capital and technical knowledge, but let B have more land than C. Both countries could produce the same level of manufactures, but B is able to produce more food because of its larger land endowment. This can be illustrated using production possibility curves. In Figure 4.2 country B (curve *JB*) would lie outside that of country C (curve *JC*). Given the terms of trade – as shown by the slope of the parallel lines *KK* and *K'K'* – and demand patterns – represented by the slope of the line from the origin *OM* – we can determine the level of the exports of both B and C. Country B consumes a combination of manufactures and food represented by point *X*, but it produces domestically the combination consisting of fewer manufactures and more food at point *Y*. The difference is made up by exporting food and importing manufactures to satisfy domestic demand. The opposite is the case for country C, which exports manufactures and imports food – it consumes at *Z* but produces at *W*. The reason that this trade pattern arises is that land in B, owing to its plentiful endowment, is cheaper than capital. Hence, factor proportions have a determining role in trade.

The availability thesis can, however, produce results opposite to those predicted by the Heckscher–Ohlin model. For example, let us assume a two-

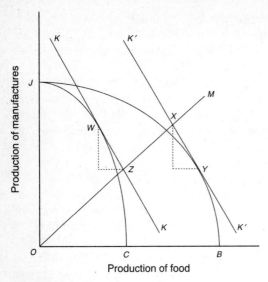

Figure 4.2

country world in which both country B and country C are endowed with capital
and labour but where B has a higher capital to labour ratio. Let us also assume
that two goods – manufactures and food – are produced but that the former
requires a higher capital/labour ratio than the latter. The production of manufactures, however, also requires, for example, iron ore, which is specific to country
C, and food products require land, which is specific to country B. The availability thesis would correctly predict that country B would export food products
whereas manufactures would be exported by country C. The Heckscher–Ohlin
theory does not give us this result because its central focus is on only two factors
– for example, capital and land. Thus, Heckscher–Ohlin predicts that country B
would export manufactures and country C food products. For the Heckscher–
Ohlin model to give the same results as the availability thesis one would have to
take these specific factors into account. This means that the model is no longer
generally applicable but rather applies only to a special case. Hence, when a
three-factor model is used it is not always clear whether a capital-abundant
country or a labour-abundant country will export a good that requires both
capital and land more intensively than labour.

     The absolute and relative concepts of *availability* and their importance in
determining which goods are traded have already been discussed. A question
remains as to whether availability is a necessary and/or sufficient condition for
the determination of trade patterns. In the case of a highly differentiated product
(e.g. Scotch whisky) it is not surprising that demand is higher for whisky
imported from Scotland than domestically produced scotch. One cannot say,
however, that without this characteristic domestic scotch would not be exported
as, given a country's endowments, it could still be produced and exported.

Is availability a sufficient condition to justify trade? Again, the answer must be no since it may be in a country's interest, given its factor endowments, to produce a commodity which sells in greater volume even if the country has no special reputation for its production.

When relative availability is based solely on technological differences (rather than physical factor endowments), any trade advantage is likely to be short-lived. Since technology is transferable, other countries will soon acquire the know-how to produce the goods in question and the initial advantage will be eliminated.

4.4 Economies of scale

A major underlying assumption of neoclassical trade theory is that of constant returns to scale. International specialisation, however, can be explained if unit cost falls as output increases. For example, if economies of scale lead to the need for only one plant to supply the world market, the country where the plant is located will export the product while other countries will import. In other words, economies of scale can be important in determining trade patterns. Certainly, allowing for the existence of economies of scale has a great deal of common sense appeal. Large-scale enterprises permit workers to concentrate on the functions they do best as well as providing opportunities for entrepreneurs to introduce more specialised and productive machinery.

Economies of scale can be of two types – internal and external to the firm. Although theories based on internal economies of scale that are compatible with perfect competition do exist, internal economies of scale usually lead to monopoly. In trade theory, however, it is usually assumed that scale economies are external and, therefore, are equally available to all firms in the economy. Hence, a country can specialise in a line of production but still maintain a competitive domestic market structure for that commodity.

Figure 4.3 shows a convex production possibility schedule, *BB*, which would be applicable for a country that experienced economies of scale in production. Before the specialisation that can arise from opening the country to trade, the country can produce any combination of goods X and Y located on this curve. Let us assume that under autarky the internal price ratios are such that they are tangential to *BB* at *D*. Thus, the country's social indifference curve depicting its preferences and tastes is also tangential to *BB* at point *D*. At *D* the country is producing and consuming X_1 and Y_1. This equilibrium position is, however, unstable in that once trade is allowed it makes sense for this country to specialise completely in the production of one good (either X or Y) and to exchange some of this for the other good. In this example, the country specialises completely in X – at X_2 on the production possibility curve – and exchanges some of this, $(X_3 - X_2)$, for Y_2 at the international terms of trade shown by *TT*. By specialising and exchanging the country is able to consume more of both goods and obtain a higher level of satisfaction – moving from I_1-I_1 to I_2-I_2.

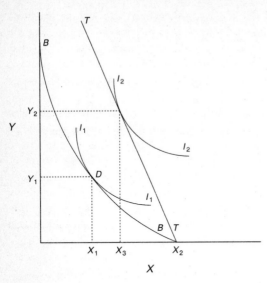

Figure 4.3

Why does the country specialise completely? The reason is that once the process of specialisation has begun there is no turning back. The falling cost per unit allows the country to undercut its rivals in the commodity to an ever-increasing extent. Hence, once specialisation begins, it is unlikely to stop until it is complete.

The question of which goods a country will specialise in remains and can only answered by understanding the factors that affect demand for individual products. The Heckscher–Ohlin theory (with, of course, the assumption of constant returns to scale) would predict that each country specialises in the good that uses its abundant factor intensively. When economies of scale are permitted the opposite may hold. Demand patterns could be such that when trade is opened up from a position of autarky, a country specialises on the basis of the economies of scale available and, therefore, establishes a comparative advantage in a good that does not use its abundant factor intensively. As a result, it is possible for a country to export the *wrong* goods from a Heckscher–Ohlin perspective.

One implication of the economies of scale argument is that small countries could now produce goods on a scale commensurate with a world market – they can build world-scale plants. In this way they can break away from any small-scale (and, thus, higher cost) production imposed on them by the limited size of their domestic market. By producing for the international market they not only gain advantages in the production of standardised goods where economies of scale play an important part but also in that of differentiated products. Production costs for differentiated products are also likely to decline as output rises so that the larger the output, the lower the cost. For example, prior to European integration, US firms had lower average costs than European firms for the same product. It has been suggested that the reason for this was that European firms were largely limited by the size of their home markets, so each plant produced a larger range of products, product styles and package sizes than its US counterpart. By having access to large international markets it is possible for small countries to acquire comparative advantages in the production of differentiated goods.

Drèze (1960), however, came to a different conclusion. He postulated that goods are differentiated not so much by national tastes but rather by national regulatory standards. An example would be electrical goods, which are subject to safety regulations. If there is no international harmonisation of safety standards, small countries face regulations in other countries that act as effective (although often unintentional) non-tariff barriers. These barriers, coupled with the smallness of the home markets, diminish their export potential. The observable export pattern of small countries would, therefore, be dominated by non-differentiated products of an intermediate type such as metal products, minerals, paper, pulp and wood products where specialised regulations are not required. Belgium's trade patterns appeared to support Drèze's hypothesis.

Despite the unrealistic conclusion that an economy would specialise completely in the production of one good, the economies of scale theory does have considerable intuitive appeal. As we will see in Chapter 5, it also enjoys some degree of empirical support. When economies of scale are recast in a dynamic rather than a static framework their implications for trade theory become more far-ranging. These dynamic considerations are explored in the next section.

4.5 Technological theories of trade and dynamic economies of scale

Although technological factors were referred to by Kravis (1956), their importance was more formally analysed by Posner (1961) and Hufbauer (1966), who proposed them as important determinants of trade between industrialised countries. Balogh (1963) extended this work to encompass trade between developed and underdeveloped countries. He also explored the welfare aspects of trade explained by technological factors. Building on this work, Vernon (1966) advanced a theory that not only emphasised the role of inter-country technological differences in determining trade but also suggested how this pattern might change over time.

4.5.1 Posner's theory of trade
In 'International trade and technical change' Posner (1961) had two objectives. First, he proposed an additional trade theory – one that was not put forward as a replacement for the traditional or orthodox Heckscher–Ohlin model. Second, he wished to show that technology had a central role in the determination of trade patterns.

According to Posner (1961), commodities and processes are developed through time and do not occur simultaneously in all countries. They are developed and introduced on to markets because they confer a quasi-monopoly profit on the firm that first introduces them. This supernormal profit can be reaped until the new product or process is imitated by competitors, not only at home but in other countries. During the period prior to international imitation a reason to initiate trade between countries exists. Posner stressed that inasmuch as new processes (or new products that require new processes) are developed, countries' production functions will differ. This violated an important assumption of the Heckscher–Ohlin approach. As technical change and product developments were related to economic growth, trade was related to economic growth rather than to factor endowments.

In his formal model, Posner (1961) assumed that all industries exist in all countries, as do the factors of production. Further, he assumed that they are distributed in equal proportions. However, differences in technological knowledge, or *know-how*, would lead to different processes being adopted or different products being produced between given industries in different countries. Posner also assumed zero tariffs and transport costs, identical tastes, fixed exchange rates, stable growth and full employment.

The forces at work that provide the inducement for trade were reasoned to be as follows. The introduction of a new product or process would confer on a firm an advantage over its rivals. In the process of introduction, the new product or process might also adversely affect a whole set of complementary goods. Rival domestic firms would react to this threat by developing and marketing their own products but, given the complex nature of technological goods, only after a lag. This *domestic lag* would be made up of two components – a *reaction lag*, consisting of the time taken for the new product to arrive on the market and, subsequently, for rivals to respond, and a *learning period*, which would correspond to the time it takes rivals to assimilate the new product or process. The length of the domestic lag would depend very much on the nature of the industry. The domestic firm(s) would also attempt to supply the new product abroad to exploit any foreign markets for the new product. Again, there would be a lag until rival foreign firms reacted and were able to compete by supplying their domestic market.

As the response by foreign firms would not be instantaneous, during the period of this foreign reaction lag a *one-way* trade flow would develop, with technological goods being exported to the foreign country from the home country. As the length of the foreign reaction lag is finite, the one-way flow would also be finite. A trade flow in technological goods from the innovating country to the imitating country would be maintained as long as there were new innovations in additional industries and at different times. A two-way flow in technological goods could also arise as long as the two trading countries were equally dynamic innovators. In the situation where one country innovated more than another – unequal (trade) partners – a trade deficit might well be created, resulting in the less dynamic country exporting more traditional goods to pay for more technologically sophisticated products. In this way, technological factors might encourage the expansion of trade in traditional goods.

Balogh (1963) examined the relationship between unequal partners more closely and came to the conclusion that once a country lost its *dynamism* (the rate at which innovations are introduced) it would lag perpetually behind the technological leader. The reason for this was that a prolonged one-way flow of goods would lead to balance of payments problems, which would be dealt with by contractionary policies. The country's growth rate would be reduced, which would further slow the rate of innovation. Thus, the weaker partner would be destined to lag continuously behind its rival. This situation may have characterised the post-World War II position of the British economy with respect to its main trading rivals. Britain's low rate of economic growth prevented the take-up and development of innovations. As a result, Britain began to lag behind its rivals. They, in their turn, embarked on a virtuous self-fulfilling circle of trade surpluses, rising incomes and economic growth, more new innovations and commensurately expanding exports.

A country may not be able to maintain its position as a technological leader (Gremmen and Vallabergh, 1986). A leading country might well have an initial advantage in the introduction of a product or process but could lose its advantage if its rivals improved and developed it further, while the once leading country would be stuck with the original, and now inferior, product or process. Furthermore, a leader may not necessarily keep its advantage as other countries, by devoting enough resources to research and development, catch up and overtake it. An example of this is the expanding level of innovation in Europe and, in particular, Japan relative to the US.

Posner (1961) recognised that the internal logic of his theory might be open to criticism, for example, over the assumption of equal factor proportions between countries but dissimilar methods of production. Moreover, he foresaw that similar conclusions could arise from theories that explained trade patterns by adding factors of production to Heckscher–Ohlin or economies of scale. Posner tried to pre-empt these criticisms. It does seem difficult to accept that countries endowed with the same factors and in the same proportions will not adopt the same technology to produce a particular good. To forestall this criticism, Posner suggested that although factor endowments, including technical knowledge, might not differ in aggregate between two countries, the difference in technical knowledge may be quite marked at the disaggregated level. As technical knowledge can be acquired, albeit with a lag, the advantage that an industry in one country has over the same industry in another country is temporary and limited to the learning period. Posner was, therefore, suggesting that – given a time lag – country B can produce country A's output exactly if it adopts country A's manufacturing techniques and labour policies. In other words, *potential* similarity can become *actual* after a lag, but in the interim differences can exist.

By innovating a country would, however, accumulate capital. Hence, the ratio of factor endowments between it and a potential trading partner would change. As a result, the observed trade pattern could not be divorced from a factor endowments theory. By insisting that the industry level is the appropriate focus for analysis, Posner (1961) was suggesting that it is unlikely that investments in one sector would be so great as to unbalance the equality of factor endowments between two countries at the aggregate level. In this way, equality of factor endowments could be maintained as an assumption of his model. Over time, factor endowments might well differ as one country built up its capital stock through advances in innovations. However, the trade could not be said to arise from this difference. Technical progress and innovation are the real source of the existing trade pattern.

Explanations of the trade patterns based on the existence of multiple factors of production or economies of scale were also rejected by Posner (1961). He accepted that one could generate differences in factor endowments between countries by breaking down the factors of production, particularly labour, into highly specific groups. Although trade could be explained by these differences, the resulting, more orthodox, theory would become less general and more descriptive. Furthermore, sub-factors were assumed to be non-interchangeable in that labour or capital are highly specific to one line of production and cannot easily be used in another. Posner suggested, however, that both workers and machine tools can be switched from one line of production to another. Further, over a period of time both capital and labour, and their subcategories, could also be switched between industries.

Even if the multi-factor proposition could be accepted as a working hypothesis, Posner (1961) suggested that it should be rejected for three reasons. First, if the comparative advantage were derived from using a specific form of machinery or labour, then a domestic producer in an importing country could simply buy the appropriate equipment or hire the necessary labour. Posner further suggested that as labour skills are a function of time spent on the job, they could be obtained through a period of protection from imports. Hence, an explanation of trade based on multiple factors of production would only explain an unstable situation – one that could be upset by a chance disturbance such as the acquisition of special machinery or skills.

Second, a multiple factor of production theory could not explain why a country had acquired a comparative advantage in the first place. In contrast, Posner's (1961) theory was able to provide an explanation by linking technical change to economic growth.

Third, it is difficult to account for the different distribution of sub-factors of production between countries. It is more likely that the growth of a particular industry gives rise to any differences rather than vice versa. Posner's (1961) theory was able to explain how differences in the distribution of sub-factors could arise as well as explaining the impact of technical change on trade.

Posner (1961) was also highly sceptical of trade theories based on static economies of scale. Although intuitively plausible as an explanation of trade patterns because firms and countries experiencing these economies would obtain cost advantages over rivals, he found the argument unconvincing. First, theories based on economies of scale could not explain why they appeared in one country rather than another. To Posner it seemed as if a country's advantage arose out of some historical accident. Accidents, however, were not an acceptable hypothesis and rather, the occurrence required an explanation. Second, many commodities that are traded are not mass produced (e.g., machine tools) and, hence, could not confer the benefits of economies of scale.

Posner's (1961) view was that, although economies of scale are important, the idea should be recast in terms of *dynamic* economies of scale. These, he suggested, are related to the innovations and technical improvements carried out by a firm, coupled with the benefits the firm gained through its experience in producing a particular good. He felt that these advantages were positively correlated with the volume of production. For example, if a German firm produced a good ten years before it was taken up by a British firm, the experience gained over this ten-year period (attributable to the sheer volume of output produced) would give the original firm a considerable advantage over its British rival. German firms, due to their familiarity with the product, would be more likely to discover better methods of production and make improvements. These dynamic economies of scale were based on firm-specific 'learning by doing' – which, hence, were also country-specific, whereas static economies of scale were available to all. Countries experiencing dynamic economies of scale would be able to maintain competitive advantages in lines of production. The emergence of dynamic economies of scale was no historical accident but, rather, was closely linked to a willingness of entrepreneurs to invest. The willingness to invest was, in turn, linked to demand factors related to the rate of economic growth and the cost of inputs.

In summary, Posner (1961) provided an explanation of trade patterns based on innovations that occurred through time. Technical progress and innovation take place in the more dynamic countries and, as long as they are distributed randomly between countries and industries, they can lead to stable two-way trade. Advanced countries that have lost their innovating potential and less-developed countries that lack it find themselves doomed to producing traditional goods and exchanging these for newer and more advanced products. The dynamic economies of scale reaped by the innovating countries compound their lead, thus widening the gap between themselves and their less dynamic rivals. This trade pattern could only be upset if less dynamic countries were able to regain or acquire the wherewithal to become innovative.

4.5.2 Hufbauer and technological trade

Working essentially within but improving on Posner's (1961) framework, Hufbauer (1966) was able to put forward a more comprehensive theory. His hypothesis differed from Posner's in two respects. First, he proposed a slightly different interpretation of dynamic economies of scale and, second, the assumption of equal factor endowments was relaxed.

Hufbauer differed from Posner on the issue of dynamic economies of scale in that he perceived them to be more a function of time than of production volume. He incorporated Kaldor's (1962) hypothesis, which emphasised that *learning* took time as well as activity. Hufbauer suggested that the productivity of the '*n*th machine will depend not only on the cumulative total machines which have been previously built, but on the time interval over which the total was constructed' (p. 27). Thus, if a small country introduced a new product or process before a larger country, it would still have an advantage over the larger country despite the smaller volume of its output. The underlying reason for this advantage was that the smaller country's workforce would be far more familiar with its product or process than the workforce in the larger country. Thus, dynamic economies of scale were a function of an *imitation lag*. The small country could prolong its advantage over the other country because its experience in producing would enable it to cut costs ahead of a rival who entered the market at a later time. In the long run, however, technological improvements would cease and the later entrants would be able to catch up. If this equilibrium was actually reached, the smaller country's exports to the larger country would end.

Hufbauer (1966) foresaw two criticisms of his hypothesis, one dealing with initial production dates and the other with the neglect of firms in the imitating country other than the initial imitator. He appreciated that differences in initial production dates for old products would have little bearing on present-day technological differences. For example, if one country had a lead of five years over another in the production of a good, this would mean very little if the good had existed for seventy or eighty years. Over this time span the technology involved would have been perfected in both countries and they would be competing on equal terms. Hufbauer suggested that one way of incorporating this loss of advantage over time into his analysis would be to apply a system of weightings. As the product's age grew a country's initial advantage would diminish. A difficulty remains, however, because it is not possible to know whether a ten-year lag incurred in the production of goods introduced, say, forty years ago, should have a higher or lower weight than a ten-year lag on a good first introduced twenty years ago. Hufbauer suggested that one way around this difficulty would be to add the imitation lags of all products together with each lag weighted by the output of that product so that 'the resulting aggregate imitation lag will in fact minimise the role of older products' (p. 28). He felt that this approach was justified because newer products outsell older products.

The second potential criticism – that relating to the focus placed on the first foreign firm to imitate – was also important because imitation lags were calculated from the production date of this pioneering foreign firm. Using the pioneering foreign firm might be inappropriate since imitation may well be determined more by the wider adoption of a new process or production of a new good by other foreign firms in the industry than by an isolated pioneering firm. Hufbauer (1966) suggested that this empirical difficulty could be taken into account by obtaining the initial dates of production or adoption by each firm and weighting them appropriately. He felt, however, that using this approach was both difficult (in that one had to derive a method of weighting) and unnecessary. He suggested that one could justify simply letting the innovating firm's experience, as represented by its date of innovation in production, act as a proxy for the industry as a whole. This simplification was acceptable for a number of reasons. First, the leading firm tended to set the pace for subsequent domestic imitation and, therefore, determined the overall efficiency of the industry. Second, since it was easier for skilled workers to move between firms in their own country than it was for them to move between countries, it was likely that technology would be more homogeneous within a country than between countries. Hence, rival firms in the same country were unlikely to lag very much behind the leader, and one could measure the foreign lag from the date the innovator first introduced the product or process.

Hufbauer (1966) also relaxed the assumption of equal factor endowment proportions (and equal factor prices) between the innovating country and the imitating country. In the real world, he maintained, there were differences in factor endowments and prices and, therefore, the model had to be modified.

What effect did relaxing these assumptions have? To Hufbauer the key to this question lay in the source of the difference in the factor price ratio. Differences in factor price ratios did not arise from 'variation in the division of the economic pie (as the factor proportions theory would assert), but from substantial changes in the size of the pie itself' (Hufbauer, 1966, p. 29). In other words, one country could have a higher wage–profit ratio than another country. The resulting price difference need not arise because profits in one country were greater than in another but because wages were much lower. If wages were related to productivity and productivity, in turn, was related to the application of science and technology to industrial problems, low-wage countries would not be technological leaders. One would therefore expect high-wage countries to be the exporters of technologically advanced products. Low-wage countries would, however, have an advantage in the production of goods that required substantial inputs of labour. Older products that required relatively fewer technological inputs relative to labour were, therefore, more likely to be produced and exported by low-wage countries.

An international trading pattern would be established in which high-wage countries exported technologically advanced goods while low-wage countries exported goods whose prices were sensitive to wage levels. Hufbauer (1966) further suggested, however, that the high-wage country's lead in technologically advanced goods was finite. Over time, manufacturers in the low-wage country would react defensively to high-technology products by producing imitations. Their advantage would, however, arise from the prevailing low level of wages. As a product became older and wage costs became more important, low-wage countries would acquire a comparative advantage. Imports would first be replaced by home production and, eventually, the goods would be exported to the innovating country. Trade is based on a *technology gap* and requires that substantial new advances take place in that particular good or that new goods and innovations arise in other lines of production. The latter is more realistic. Hufbauer showed clearly that trade based on a technological gap and trade based on low wages complement each other over time. Furthermore, a country's lead in technologically advanced goods would be reduced if its wage rates were substantially higher than its potential rival. The lag would also be reduced if the imitator country had a supply of entrepreneurs able to react quickly to the introduction of new goods.

Hufbauer allowed that there were two exceptions to his account of trade based on a technology gap. Advanced countries that were similarly endowed with factors could experience a two-way flow of trade based on technology gaps in different industries. The importing country might not export low-wage exports to pay for imports incorporating a technology gap but could sell new or improved products of its own.

Hufbauer's (1966) second exception comes into play when multilateral trade rather than bilateral trade is possible. In the multilateral trade case, a country could send exports incorporating a technological advantage to one trading partner and low-wage exports to another. Imitation lags would not be the only determinant of this pattern of trade, which would also depend on a 'pecking order of trade' (Hufbauer, 1966, p. 32). An advanced innovating country would export technologically advanced goods to pay for low-wage imports. A low-wage country with a very long imitation lag would, therefore, rely on selling low-wage goods to pay for technologically advanced goods. The longer the imitation lag, the more likely a country would be to rely on low-wage exports. Hufbauer examined a world economy consisting of an advanced innovating country, a less advanced country but one lagging only a little behind, and a third country that lagged considerably behind the second country. The advanced country would export technological goods to the less advanced country and receive low-wage imports in return. The less advanced country would export technology-gap goods to the much less advanced country, accepting its low-wage goods in return.

By incorporating a more sophisticated theory of dynamic economies of scale and dropping the assumption of inter-country equality in factor endowments, Hufbauer (1966) was able to improve on Posner's (1961) theory. Why entrepreneurs based their initial production in the high-wage home country and did not take immediate advantage of the lower wages existing abroad was left unexplained. In his attempt to answer this question, Vernon (1966) made a major contribution to the development of technology-based trade theories.

4.6 The theory of the product cycle

4.6.1 Vernon's approach

To answer the question why entrepreneurs with innovations based on technological advances do not locate in low-wage countries, Vernon (1966) invoked
the degree of ease or difficulty entrepreneurs have in obtaining information
about markets. Their awareness of, and response to, market opportunities are a
function of communications, which, in turn, are related to geographical distance.
The importance of market information in a firm's decision-making process had,
Vernon maintained, been shown in a number of empirical studies. A firm located
near a market was, therefore, more likely to be aware of the market's characteristics and any changes that might be taking place than a firm located in a
different market, such as another country.

Vernon accepted that new products would be generated primarily in
countries with high average incomes and high labour costs. High income would
give rise to a plethora of new wants that could only be satisfied by the development and introduction of new goods. High labour costs would act as a stimulus
to the development of new, capital-intensive processes. The expectation of
supernormal profits (accruing to those firms which supplied the market early)
would induce entrepreneurs to strive to convert an abstract idea of what was
required into a marketable product.

Vernon believed that these market and industrial characteristics described
the US and provided the explanation for why a host of new products and
processes were first introduced there and why American firms spent more than
their foreign rivals on product development. Other countries could innovate and
produce new goods but, given the characteristics of its economy, these activities
were more likely to take place in the US. In our development of Vernon's model
we will not refer to the US explicitly but to a 'leading' country.

Although firms may benefit from geographical proximity to a market, it
does not follow that production should take place at the same location. Strict
cost criteria might dictate that a firm had its marketing research and development
teams near the point of sale but that production should take place elsewhere to
reap cost advantages. If the firm was a multinational, it would make sense for it
to produce at one of its overseas locations where labour costs were lowest.
Existing work on regional economics led Vernon (1966) to believe that other
factors, such as external economies, played a more important role than conventional production costs in determining the location of production in the early
phase of a product's development. As the product progressed from being a
new product to becoming a maturing and, finally, a standardised product, the
importance of external economies declined while those associated with direct
production costs increased.

Vernon considered that a variety of characteristics of a country contribute
to the external economies that support the production of innovative goods. The
unstandardised nature of a new product carries with it a number of locational

implications. First, entrepreneurs would not wish to be tied to a particular combination of inputs until the good's characteristics had become fully established and/or the appropriate production process more clearly defined. Although input costs would be important, their importance would be secondary to the need for flexibility. For example, a well-educated labour force and the availability of engineering services increase flexibility. Hence, traditional cost factors would not be uppermost in entrepreneurs' minds when they make their location decisions.

Second, in the early phases of production a high degree of product differentiation or market power would confer a low price-elasticity of demand on each firm's good. In such a situation cost differences would count for less in an entrepreneur's calculations than they would in more mature and, hence, more competitive periods of production.

Third, and perhaps most important, is the need for entrepreneurs to be in close touch with customers, suppliers and rival firms in the early phase of a product's introduction so that they can respond quickly to any changes in market behaviour. After all, no one at this introductory stage would know the size of the market, nor could they be certain of the way rival firms might try and pre-empt them. Further, firms could not know the exact nature of the inputs required in production, nor the specifications of the product which would be most likely to satisfy consumer wants.

For all of the above reasons, production of a new good in its early phase is more likely to take place near the point of sale, where communication between the market and entrepreneurs is greatest. Of course, Vernon (1966) was writing about a period prior to the revolution in electronic information technology, which has greatly reduced the transaction costs associated with international communications (Kerr and Perdikis, 1995).

In the maturing, or intermediate, phase of a product's development a certain amount of standardisation takes place. Standardisation has implications for location. Product differentiation would increase because sub-varieties could be tailored more closely to the tastes of individual consumers. Vernon (1966) cited, as an example, radios – which developed into clock radios, car radios, portable radios and so on. Although experimentation with new products might proliferate as firms tried to stave off price competition, surviving products would develop more standardised characteristics. This standardisation would also apply to the production process. A more standardised product sold in a less uncertain market means that entrepreneurs would not have to give such a high weighting to flexibility in their calculations. They could, therefore, pay more attention to supplying their markets in the cheapest possible way. Hence, the location of production would, in the first instance, move away from the point of sale to areas in the advanced country where production costs are lower. As overseas markets grow, entrepreneurs may also decide to set up overseas plants to satisfy foreign markets and to take advantage of even lower input costs. The extent and speed with which this foreign investment takes place depends on factors such as transportation costs, tariff barriers, wage costs, the availability of suitable labour, foreign patent laws and the size of the foreign market. The latter leads to the potential for economies of scale. Vernon suggested that perhaps the most important stimulus for setting up overseas is the fear that entrepreneurs have of rivals gaining a competitive advantage by locating abroad first. Furthermore, he pointed out, when one firm invests abroad rivals are quick to follow in the hope that such a move will neutralise the competitor's perceived advantages.

In this maturing phase production abroad will stem from local as well as foreign investment. In relatively advanced foreign countries domestic firms would see the opportunity and react to foreign investment by setting up their own plants. Domestic investment might be openly encouraged by governments seeking to foster local employment and growth. An import-substitution policy could provide one form of encouragement.

In the final, mature phase of a product's life cycle, Vernon (1966) suggested that although there would still be product differentiation, both the product and the method by which it is produced will have become standardised. Standardisation implies that a large number of firms can buy the technology to produce a good and that they can sell it in a well-defined market. The increased number of suppliers and, therefore, the degree of competition reduces the product's price-elasticity and increases the importance of direct costs relative to externalities. In the mature phase production locations will move once again. This time the move is away from advanced to the developing countries, which offer a plentiful supply of unskilled labour that is able to carry out routine tasks and is paid lower wages.

The consequence of the three-phase *product cycle* – and the associated locational shifts – in trade patterns can be summarised as follows. In the early, unstandardised, phase the innovating country produces and exports the good to other advanced countries with similar income levels. In the maturing phase, as foreign plants are set up in other advanced countries, the latter become not only producers but also exporters. Exports could even be directed back to the original innovating country as well as to other, third countries. In the standardisation phase, with competition at its height, firms would supply the original innovating country as well as other advanced nations from locations in developing countries.

Not only was Vernon (1966) able to explain why the production of new products would take place in the advanced countries, but he was also able to show how trading patterns would change over time as a product developed, matured and became standardised. He provided, moreover, an explanation of the Leontief paradox (see Chapter 2). The US, being an advanced industrialised country with one of the highest per capita incomes in the world, should be in the forefront of product innovation and process development. In its early phase a product would require a high degree of labour input. As a country's comparative advantage lay in the production and sale of new products, it would be an exporter of labour-intensive goods. Japan was an importer of new products at the time of Vernon's writing. Hence, it is not surprising that its exports were capital-intensive relative to its imports.

Impressionistic evidence lent some credence to Vernon's (1966) views, and there was stronger support for his hypothesis when trade patterns were examined. Apart from a few of examples, such as electronics components facilities in Taiwan and computer accessory plants in Argentina, Vernon could not, however, find evidence of foreign investments made specifically to export advanced standardised goods back to the innovating and other advanced countries. Most foreign investment by manufacturing firms in developing countries was undertaken to circumvent threatened import restrictions. Trade patterns did follow his predictions, with developing countries exhibiting a build-up of industries exporting highly standardised goods – such as textiles and steel – that require unsophisticated manufacturing processes.

4.6.2 Hirsch's skilled labour approach
Hirsch (1967) also proposed a three-phase product cycle consisting of new, growth, and mature phases. But whereas Vernon (1966) stressed information factors as the main determinant of the location of new products in their first phase of production, Hirsch emphasised the availability of skilled labour – labour qualified in the sciences, engineering and technology.

Like Vernon, Hirsch accepted that, in the early phase, the production process for new goods is not settled with respect to inputs – largely because product specifications are not yet well defined. Hence, assembly-line production is rare and production runs are small. In the early stage, flexibility in production is paramount because changes in the product and/or production process need to be accommodated quickly. The early or new phase is not, therefore, characterised by highly capital-intensive means of production but by highly flexible and, hence, labour-intensive methods. Thus, the newness and experimental nature of both the good and the production process require a high degree of flexibility in the labour force. The labour force, therefore, must have substantial scientific and technical skills. Firms also depend on outside specialists and consultants in the early phase, adding to the need for skilled labour. A firm's ability to produce and market a new product successfully is determined by the availability of a pool of advanced scientific and technical knowledge, or know-how, on which it can draw. Given that skilled labour makes up a higher proportion of the total labour force in advanced countries than in other countries, Hirsch concluded that the production of new products would be concentrated in advanced countries.

The availability of these advanced skills endow developed countries with a comparative advantage over developing countries. In common with Vernon (1966), Hirsch (1967) suggested that as both the product and the production process became mature and standardised, inputs with advanced skills became less important and more direct costs became the primary concern of firms. Thus, a particular good's production would be transferred from the leading (developed) country to other developed countries and, finally, to developing countries.

One could not, however, conclude that at any one point in time production would be skewed in favour of mature goods in developing countries, new products in a leading country and growth goods in other developed countries. It is possible that some mature products require a high level of inputs that are scarce in developing countries. For example, a product, although mature, could be capital-intensive and capital might be scarce in developing countries. A developed country with abundant capital would then have a comparative advantage over developing countries in the production of a good that required a large proportion of capital in its input mix. Although developed countries would tend to produce goods at the newer end of the product-age spectrum, production would be more normally distributed over the whole range of product ages.

4.7 Further developments in product-cycle theories

4.7.1 Inter-industry and intra-industry cycles

The product cycle, as constituted by both Vernon (1966) and Hirsch (1967), involved the transfer of a good's production location at each of the three stages. The exact nature of the good was never clearly stated. Were they referring to a *new* good that had never existed before and required the setting up of a new industry, or to one that was new but could be accommodated within traditional industrial structures? The traditional view had emphasised the former.

As a country develops and its incomes and wages rise – along with the accumulation of capital, technology and skills – the demand for technology and capital-intensive goods rises, as does the ability to produce them. Concurrently, it becomes relatively more expensive for the country to produce standardised, labour-intensive, goods. This loss of comparative advantage in such goods leads to the transfer of their production to countries abundant in unskilled labour. Hence, if one examined the manufacturing sector in any developed country, one would expect to see some industries growing while others would be in decline. A country's pattern of exports, imports and industrial production would be the result of the sum of all individual product cycles, each product having its own timing and relative importance according to a country's income level and factor availability.

It is possible, however, to envision a slightly different pattern, one which does not require the transfer of whole industries to other countries. The nature of the product itself may change in response to competitive factors. The new product is still produced in the developed country and industrial decline and relocation of the industry are not observed. Rapp (1975) suggested that textiles provide an example of product evolution where the nature of the basic article changes from, say, wool to cotton to synthetics. He classified this type of product cycle as an intra-industry cycle – in contrast to inter-industry cycles, where whole industries are expected to be on the move.

4.7.2 The form of technology transfer

McGee (1977) explored the industry life-cycle model further. He proposed the *appropriability* theory to account for the high incidence of new product development and technology transfer between and within multinational firms. Vernon (1966) had suggested that there were three ways in which new products and processes could be transferred from the innovating country to the rest of the world. These were by: exporting the goods; a firm setting up a subsidiary plant in a host country; and leasing the rights to a product or process to a domestic firm in the host country. The nature of licensing agreements, however, means that the innovating firm loses control over the production process. This loss of control over information is, according to McGee, why firms may prefer intra-firm transfers between countries. When property rights are not well developed or are poorly enforced a further incentive is provided for vertical integration internationally (Kerr, 1993).

McGee viewed multinational companies as being producers of and traders in information. A product's life cycle is characterised by a process that required the generation of a great deal of information in the early phase and a diminishing need for information in the subsequent developing and mature phases. During the development of new products the market generates five types of information. These are: information regarding the need for and initial conceptualisation of new products; the information required to develop the product; information regarding the form of the production function – i.e., what it should be like given a set of input prices; information relating to the creation of new product markets; and information concerning the extent to which the originator of an idea could expect to acquire the value society places on the idea. The latter was what McGee called *appropriability*.

Drawing on the work of Arrow (1962) and Johnson (1964), McGee pointed out that new information (including a new good or process) can be regarded as both a private and public good. Once produced, the good will give rise to a stream of future benefits not only to the originator but to anyone else who can acquire the means to produce it. In this way, those who have not contributed to the development of the new product can also benefit. In the long term the ability of others to acquire part or all of the benefits that arise from new information will reduce the effort by those who invest their time or other resources in invention, research and development. The flow of new ideas will therefore be reduced unless a mechanism exists (or is created) that allows innovators to capture all the benefits.

Although the generation of new products or information is not wholly confined to large firms, the other four types of information are closely correlated with firm size. Large firms are the only institutions that have the resources required to develop products, production processes and product markets. Above all, they are the only institutions that can carry the cost of maintaining appropriability by defending patent rights and trade secrets through the legal system.

This last point is one of the main reasons why the international transfer of information takes place at an intra-firm level. A firm expands to internalise the externality or public-good aspects of a new product or process. In other words, it tries to keep the secrets or know-how involved in the production of a product for as long as possible.

The other reasons why intra-firm transfers might be more economically desirable than country-to-country transfers of products or processes are largely bound up with the nature and requirements of new goods. For example, new products tend to benefit from production experience (or volume) and, hence, require a larger optimum firm size than goods manufactured using standard pro-duction processes. As a result, multinationals are more likely to set up their own production plants than to license smaller domestic firms to undertake production. New goods will also require sophisticated technical support and service facilities, adding to the required overhead. This overhead cost can be spread over a larger number of output units by adding a subsidiary. Complementarities between the four types of information (development, production, marketing, and appropriability) means that the range of products that can be produced is large. Furthermore, such complementarities also mean that costs are reduced if information is transferred on an intra-firm basis. Lastly, the spread between buyers' and sellers' evaluations of new information is higher for new products than for standardised goods. Transfers of information are, therefore, more likely to take place on an intra-firm basis.

In summary, McGee's (1977) appropriability theory hypothesises that multinational firms are specialists in the production of information. Given the nature of new information and the requirement that large firms are needed to produce it, the easiest way of transferring it abroad is on an intra-firm basis. Hence, new products are more likely to appear in foreign countries via the subsidiary of a multinational than through an international market transfer. This predilection for intra-firm transfers of information rather than firm-to-firm sales of goods between countries alters the pattern of trade. Trade statistics take no account of information transfers.

4.7.3 *Product development as a form of competition*

Finger (1975) suggested that one should take a different view to that traditionally held concerning the nature of a new good. His approach suggested that product development was undertaken by firms in an attempt either to maintain old markets or to gain new markets. Product development was, therefore, a form of competition between rival firms. Each competing firm would strive to offer the public a series of goods which, in the view of the buyers, were different from those currently on offer. The intensity of this competition could be measured by the rate of product turnover – defined as the rate of change of the list of products offered for sale in a particular market.

In Hirsch's (1967) view of the product cycle, a good was new because the technological process used to produce it was also new. The characteristics associated with new technological processes are short production runs, the intensive use of skilled labour, reliance on external economies and the relative unimportance of price competition. In Finger's (1975) view, some products – for example, fashionable clothing – possessed these characteristics but could not be considered new. Other standardised products may use highly sophisticated new technology. An example would be the new float-glass process for producing an old or established good – plate glass. Another is injection-moulded footwear produced by new technology in less-developed countries and exported to the US. Leather footwear made with traditional technology is, however, produced in and exported from European countries to the US.

Finger suggested that Vernon's (1966) view of the product cycle was even more restrictive in that new goods had not only to be produced by a new process but also had to satisfy a new set of wants. A conflict would therefore arise between Hirsch and Vernon over what should be classified as a new good. Under the former's definition, plate glass would be a new product because new technology was used in its production. The latter would disagree because plate glass produced by the float-glass method would not satisfy new wants.

Finger (1975) attempted to develop a theory that incorporated both views of a new good. The product cycle should be perceived not as a passing dis-equilibrium between two equilibrium points but as a 'more or less permanent equilibrium'. Whereas both Hirsch and Vernon saw an equilibrium as being disturbed by the development of technology or the introduction of a new good, Finger suggested that firms attempt to develop products at an optimal rate over time – a rate that does not add more to a firm's costs than to its revenues. Competition between firms through product development can take place irrespective of technology. He cited annual model changes in automobiles and appliances as well as new fashions in the garment industry. Further, product development does not necessarily lead to the satisfaction of new wants. It occurs, Finger suggested, to keep interest in the product alive.

Although technological breakthroughs can take place in industries that are going through a period of product development, the role of technological change in the determination of trade patterns is distinct from that of product development. Insofar as product development is more prevalent than the intro-duction of new goods, in the Vernon (1966) sense of technological break-throughs their importance as a determinant of trade patterns is downgraded.

Finger (1975) emphasised that his concept of product development should not be confused with product differentiation. Once the methods of production had been learnt, production would gravitate to countries which possessed a comparative advantage. What he suggested was that product differentiation was irrelevant when compared to product turnover. A country could maintain its exports in a particular product line even if it was not differentiated as long as it kept improving the characteristics of the product – i.e. new and old models of automobiles are not produced simultaneously. The higher the rate of product development, the more likely a country was to be able to maintain its exports in a particular line of production. Finger suggested that there was confusion in the literature between 'standardised' and 'unstandardised' goods, the former referring to a higher degree of product differentiation than the latter. He proposed that a more appropriate definition would be to ascribe the term standardised to goods that did not have high rates of product development. Standardised goods were, therefore, those whose quality did not change year by year rather than goods which were indistinguishable from others. For example, textile exports from developing countries could be classed as standardised not because they were indistinguishable from those exported by advanced countries but because they were similar to those they previously exported.

Finger (1975) highlighted the importance of style changes in influencing trade patterns. Whether his hypothesis offers a better alternative explanation of trade (to theories based on factor proportions) can only be assessed after we have examined the empirical evidence in Chapter 5.

4.8 Income and tastes as determinants of trade

In Ricardian and neoclassical trade theory, comparative advantage is determined by the difference between countries' relative production costs. These, in turn, are based on the difference in factor prices. The greater the difference in factor prices between countries, the greater is the scope for trade. Since the differences in capital–labour ratios are larger between developed and developing countries than among the developed countries, one would expect to find a higher volume of trade between the former. Trade statistics, however, do not support this hypothesis as the volume of trade between developed countries far outweighs that between developed and developing countries (Linder, 1961). One explanation for this anomaly is that industrialised countries have such large productive capacities that small differences in factor costs are sufficient to generate a large volume of trade. It could also be the case that developed countries' demands for imports cannot be met by developing countries because of capacity constraints and have to be met through trade with other developed countries.

Linder (1961) offered an alternative hypothesis to explain the apparently anomalous pattern of trade by incorporating innovations but, at the same time, putting greater emphasis on similarities between incomes and tastes in different countries. His thesis presupposed that the greater the similarity of per capita income between countries, the more similar their internal demand patterns would be. Although manufacturers in a particular country orientate their production largely towards supplying the home market, they would find it relatively easy to export their products to countries that have similar incomes and, hence, demand patterns. Thus, the greater the similarity in incomes, the larger the volume of trade between countries. Similarities in demand determine trade rather than differences in relative factor costs.

For Linder, home demand was very important as it determined the parameters of potential trade. In his (1961) model entrepreneurs would supply goods in order to meet clearly defined economic needs. In a world beset by uncertainties and imperfect knowledge, they would react to opportunities of which they were aware. The information on opportunities was more likely to become available the nearer the firm was to the market and, thus, physical proximity determined supply. Entrepreneurs would initially concentrate on supplying the domestic market, but once established might then embark on an export-orientated expansion strategy. Over time the export market could grow to dominate a firm's sales, but the certainty of the domestic market was needed in the initial phase of production. Linder's approach is very much in line with that of Frankel (1943), who proposed that a country with a large internal market for, for example, low-quality goods, is more likely to compete successfully in countries with a demand for similar goods than in a market where demand is geared to higher-quality goods.

The home market may well act as a stimulus to innovation and new goods. Innovations often arise as a response to a problem that has arisen in production or consumption. Before adopting the invention simultaneously in all its markets, a firm is likely to evaluate its potential in the home market. Only when the teething troubles are overcome will the new product or process be produced or utilised abroad.

Linder (1961) suggested that the extreme case of an entrepreneur producing and selling goods purely for export was unlikely not only because physical and cultural distance would lead him to produce the wrong goods but also because the costs involved in obtaining the relevant marketing information would outweigh any comparative advantage he might believe himself to have. In this way, Linder was echoing Kravis' (1956) concept of availability.

In Linder's view, production functions were not identical in all countries but were rather the production functions of those goods produced at home that proved to be the most advantageous when it came to exporting. Exceptions to this might exist, but they would be limited to those goods for which it was easy or cheap to obtain information about the foreign market and/or where the product required very little inventive activity or development effort.

In the same way as potential exports were determined by what was already being produced at home for consumers with similar levels of income, so too were potential imports. Internal demand determines potential imports. Hence, all products for which there is a demand at going prices are potential imports. The actual level of trade, however, is determined by the similarity in per capita incomes. The greater the similarity, the greater the volume of trade between countries; the larger the difference, the smaller the volume of trade.

Although the volume of trade is determined, Linder (1961) did not explain what determines the pattern of trade – namely, what goods one country will export to another. Nor is he clear in explaining what factors confer comparative advantage on trading partners, suggesting only that the same forces that give rise to trade within each of the countries create trade between them. Moreover, he attributed the trading of essentially the same goods between countries as being due to the unlimited scope for product differentiation. This was a view that was examined later by Grubel and Lloyd (1975) and gave rise to the subsequent large body of literature on intra-industry trade, which is examined in greater depth in Chapter 6.

Linder did not totally discount the factor proportion hypothesis. He accepted that if a good has a strong home demand and also uses the country's abundant factor intensively, it is more likely to be an export good. The converse would be true for products which are intensive in the country's scarce factor. Linder's assertion, however, that capital abundance is strongly correlated with rich countries because the accumulation of capital is closely bound up with past savings and investment patterns puts his conclusions at variance with the Heckscher–Ohlin model. In Linder's world, countries with similar per capita incomes will have similar capital–labour ratios and will trade intensively with one another. In the Heckscher–Ohlin world, similar capital–labour ratios between countries would mean little trade. Thus, in Linder's view, factor proportions exert some but not a great deal of influence on trade patterns.

Linder's (1961) theory was criticised for its inability to explain the factors that confer comparative advantage. Johnson (1964) went further and called it a 'non-theory'. He questioned critically the tautology of a strong home market being essential to the creation of tradable products. He also took issue with what he considered to be Linder's naive account of the difficulties entrepreneurs encounter in obtaining information about and exporting to countries dissimilar to their own.

Nevertheless, empirical evidence gathered later lent some support to Linder's hypothesis and led to its further development. Arad and Hirsch (1981) reconciled Linder's theory with Heckscher–Ohlin. Markusen (1986) attempted to build a model explaining the direction and volume of trade among developed countries and between developed and undeveloped countries utilising Linder's framework. As Markusen's approach involves a discussion of intra-industry trade, it will be discussed in Chapter 6.

Arad and Hirsch (1981) invoked the concept of international transfer costs to facilitate the incorporation of Linder's (1961) approach into a Heckscher–Ohlin framework. They defined transfer costs as the difference between the costs incurred in selling in a foreign and a domestic market. Although they accepted that transfer costs are made up of several components, including transport, shipping and insurance, those positively correlated with physical distance were formally ignored in order to concentrate on those associated with the marketing of products. In other words, Arad and Hirsch placed their emphasis on the costs involved in market research and in adapting goods initially produced for the domestic market to export markets. Following Linder (1961), they accepted that these marketing transfer costs fall as countries' per capita incomes and, hence, demand patterns converge. A point where no exports would take place would exist where per capita incomes were equal but transfer costs remained positive. If perfectly competitive factor markets and free, instantaneous technology transfers within and between countries were assumed, trade would be ruled out in Linder's model as local firms would always have an advantage. This is because it is cheaper (costs less) to acquire the technology while transferring goods has a non-zero cost. However, by including transfer costs within a Heckscher–Ohlin framework Linder's hypothesis can be reinstated.

Arad and Hirsch reformulated Linder's model by asserting that the tradability of a good is dependent on its relative costs of production where transfer costs are included as part of production costs. Hence, capital-abundant countries would have the edge over labour-abundant countries in the production and export of capital-intensive goods. The opposite would be the case for labour-abundant countries and labour-intensive goods. In this way, capital-rich countries would still export capital-intensive goods to capital-poor countries. However, a country's ability to export its goods to other countries would be limited by the transfer costs involved. As exporting countries with similar per capita incomes and, hence, demand patterns incur lower transfer costs, it is only to be expected that trade between such countries will be of a higher intensity. Furthermore, as capital availability is often correlated with a country's income levels, it is also to be expected that capital-rich countries will trade intensively amongst themselves. Thus, for Arad and Hirsch, the Heckscher–Ohlin model determines countries' potential exports while the Linder (1961) hypothesis determines their actual trading partners.

4.9 Summary

The unease surrounding the Heckscher–Ohlin model engendered by the empirical investigations of Leontief and others led to a search for alternative and more satisfactory theories to explain observable patterns of trade. The formulations that subsequently appeared were largely based on relaxing the assumptions underlying Heckscher–Ohlin. The result was a variety of models based primarily on assumptions that allowed for the existence of economies of scale, differences in technology, differences in demand patterns between countries and the international mobility of capital over the product cycle.

It is interesting to note that these theoretical developments took David Ricardo's and Adam Smith's assumptions of differences in production functions as their starting point. Even Myint's (1958) theory arose from an idea that had been set down in the *Wealth of Nations* but was neglected by subsequent writers. Unlike the classical writers, however, the alternative trade theorists concentrated on evolving technology as a determinant of trade. The debate was moved away from equilibrium economics and towards disequilibrium economics.

Kravis (1956) provided an important impetus to the development of theories based on a technology gap and product cycles. By stressing the importance of technical know-how, he showed that countries which innovated and produced new goods could compete and trade effectively with low-wage countries. In other words, the availability of technology gave them a comparative advantage. Theories based on static economies of scale were also important because they suggested that countries could specialise in unlikely goods. These static approaches, in turn, led researchers to consider dynamic economies of scale. Posner (1961) built on the various threads of this earlier work by explicitly introducing the concept of an *imitation lag*. In the period immediately after inventing new goods or processes a country had an advantage over its rivals and exported. This advantage would, he suggested, persist until the rivals had acquired the necessary technology. How quickly imitation took place depended on a number of structural factors in the rival economies and also on how soon a good invented in one country was demanded in another. Home demand was considered a prerequisite for any domestic investment in plant and machinery.

The question as to why both innovation and production took place in rich advanced countries when lower-cost locations existed elsewhere was not explained by Posner (1961). This issue was left to Vernon (1966) and Hirsch (1967) to address. Their explanations were based on the changes in the factors required by a product as it moved through its life cycle from inception to maturity. In the initial phase there was a great deal of uncertainty surrounding not only a good's method of production but also its marketability. This uncertainty required flexibility on the part of the producer. In Vernon's view, flexibility was achieved by firms locating themselves close to their market in order to respond to changes in customers' needs. Hirsch emphasised flexibility in production and suggested that firms would avoid investing heavily in expensive, capital-intensive technology, which was itself subject to rapid change. Instead, firms would invest in a flexible but highly skilled labour force that would be more adaptable to changing methods of production. This investment would be smallest in developed countries with their high levels of general and technical education. Since *dynamism* in consumer markets and production was associated with innovation, both Vernon and Hirsch concluded that new goods would be produced and exported from rich and large economies. As the product matured, its production processes would become standardised and competitors would appear on the market. Cost factors would then become more important in determining competitiveness, forcing manufacturers to seek lower-cost locations. Capital investment would take place abroad. In other words, comparative advantage would shift away from the innovating country towards those with lower labour costs.

The *product-cycle* theory was subsequently expanded and refined by a number of researchers. Rapp (1975) contributed to the argument by clarifying the nature of the new goods – distinguishing between those which could be accommodated in an existing industry and others that required the establishment of a totally new industry. An explanation for the concentration of product development and technical transfer within multinationals was provided by McGee's (1977) *appropriability* theory. Finger (1975) contributed by arguing that the development of new products reflected a conscious attempt by companies to maintain old markets or gain new markets. He suggested a product-cycle theory that took style changes into account. His contribution should be seen as an attempt to incorporate price factors as determinants of patterns of trade.

Linder (1961) argued that, in manufacturing, demand factors determined trade patterns more than differences in factor endowments. Manufactured products would not be exported until a domestic demand for the product existed. Furthermore, production would be located near the market so that manufacturers could obtain the necessary information to improve their goods. In this way Linder was in advance of, and influential in, the development of the product-cycle model. As the range of potential imports depended on the pattern of domestic demand – or, more precisely, per capita incomes – the intensity of trade would be greater the more similar per capita incomes were between countries.

Whereas the Heckscher–Ohlin framework was offered as an all-embracing model explaining trade in all goods, the alternative models concentrated on manufactured goods. Collectively, they account for aspects of trade not covered by the Heckscher–Ohlin model. In addition, the product-cycle theory offers an explanation of the Leontief paradox. As products in their initial phase of development are labour-intensive, rich countries will export these and import standardised capital-intensive goods. The product-cycle theory does, moreover, provide an explanation for changing trade patterns over time. It does not, however, explain satisfactorily why some countries are more innovative or dynamic than others.

The plethora of alternative trade models clearly provides a large number of testable hypotheses. These hypotheses relate to their own validity in determining patterns of trade; their explanatory power compared to more orthodox Ricardian and Heckscher–Ohlin models of trade and their relative explanatory power among the set of alternative trade models. Whether the alternative theories outlined in this chapter are rivals to or replacements for the Heckscher–Ohlin model or whether they are, along with the latter, parts of a more general model can only be assessed after we have examined the empirical evidence presented in Chapter 5.

References

Arad, R. W., and Hirsch, S. (1981), 'Determination of trade flows and choice of trade partners: reconciling the Heckscher–Ohlin and the Burenstam Linder models of international trade', *Weltwirtschaftliches Archiv*, 117, pp. 276–97.
Arrow, K. J. (1962), 'Economic welfare and the allocation of resources for invention', in *The Rate and Direction of Inventive Activity: Economic and Social Factors*,

A report of the National Bureau of Economic Research, Princeton: Princeton University Press, pp. 609–25.

Balogh, T. (1963), *Unequal Partners*, Oxford: Blackwell.

Drèze, S. J. (1960), 'Quelques réflexions sereines sur l'adaptation de l'industrie Belge au Marché Commun', *Comptes Rendus des Travaux de la Société Royale d'Economie Politique de Belgique*, no. 275, pp. 47–62.

Findlay, R. (1970), *Trade and Specialisation*, Harmondsworth: Penguin Books.

Finger, J. M. (1975), 'A new view of the product cycle theory', *Weltwirtschaftliches Archiv*, 111, pp. 79–99.

Frankel, H. (1943) 'Industrialisation of agricultural countries and the possibilities of a new international division of labour', *Economic Journal*, 53, pp. 189–201.

Gremmen, H. J., and Vallabergh, A. H. J. (1986), 'An input approach to European comparative advantage in advantaged products: a study with special emphasis on the Netherlands', *Weltwirtschaftliches Archiv*, 122, pp. 270–80.

Grubel, H. G., and Lloyd, P. J. (1975), *Intra-Industry Trade: The Theory and Measurement of International Trade in Differentiated Products*, New York: John Wiley and Sons.

Hirsch, S. (1967), *The Location of Industry and International Competitiveness*, Oxford: Oxford University Press.

Hufbauer, G. C. (1966), *Synthetic Materials and the Theory of International Trade*, London: Duckworth.

Johnson, H. G. (1964), 'Book review of Linder', *Economica*, 31(1), pp. 86–90.

Kaldor, N. (1962), 'Comment on the production function symposium', *Review of Economic Studies*, 29, pp. 246–50.

Kerr, W. A. (1993), 'Domestic firms and transnational corporations in liberalizing command economies – a dynamic approach' *Economic Systems*, 17(3), pp. 195–211.

Kerr, W. A., and Perdikis, N. (1995), *The Economics of International Business*, London: Chapman and Hall.

Kravis, I. B. (1956), 'Availability and other influences on the commodity composition of trade', *Journal of Political Economy*, 64(2), pp. 143–55.

Lewis, W. A. (1954), 'Economic development with unlimited supplies of labour', *The Manchester School of Economic and Social Studies*, 22(2), pp. 139–91.

Linder, S. B. (1961), *An Essay on Trade and Transformation*, New York: John Wiley and Sons.

Markusen, J. R. (1986), 'Explaining the volume of trade: an eclectic approach', *American Economic Review*, 76(5), pp. 1002–11.

McGee, S. P. (1977), 'Multinational corporations, the industry technology cycle and development', *Journal of World Trade Law*, 11(4), pp. 297–321.

Myint, H. (1958), 'The classical theory of international trade and the underdeveloped countries', *The Economic Journal*, 68(2) pp. 317–37.

Posner, M. V. (1961), 'International trade and technical change', *Oxford Economic Papers*, 13(3), pp. 323–41.

Rapp, W. V. (1975), 'The many possible extensions of product cycle analysis', *Hitotsubashi Journal of Economics*, 6(1), pp. 22–9.

Smith, A. (1976), *An Inquiry into the Nature and Causes of the Wealth of Nations*, in R. H. Campbell, A. S. Skinner and W. B. Todd (eds), *Works and Correspondence of Adam Smith*, vol. II, Oxford: Clarendon Press.

Vernon, R. (1966) 'International investment and international trade in the product cycle',

Quarterly Journal of Economics, 80(2), pp. 190–207.

Wijnhold, H. W. J. (1955), *International Trade and Payments: An Introduction to the Theory of International Trade, Commercial Policy and Other Economic Relations*, Pretoria: Academic Press.

Williams, J. H. (1929), 'The theory of international trade reconsidered', *Economic Journal*, 39(2), pp. 195–209.

CHAPTER 5

Empirical testing of the alternative theories

5.1 Introduction

The discussion of the empirical testing of alternatives to the neoclassical explanation of trade patterns will concentrate on three theories: the technology gap theory; the product cycle theory; and the similarity of demand patterns theory (see Chapter 4). These theories are the main competing explanations of trade to arise in the wake of the early empirical work that failed to confirm Heckscher–Ohlin's predictions. Empirical testing in economics is seldom straightforward. This is particularly true in the case of the alternative trade theories. Therefore, in addition to reporting the empirical results of the tests of the alternative theories, the chapter highlights the practical difficulties involved in trying to carry out empirical work when information on many of the independent variables has not been routinely collected and, hence, proxies had to be devised. We will first examine the empirical studies of the technology gap theory, then move on to the product cycle model and finally to Linder's (1961) hypothesis concerning demand patterns.

5.2 Tests of the technology gap theóries

Numerous studies have taken a technology gap as their basis and applied it to individual cases and/or refined the theory in scope or detail. The 1960s saw the most sustained period of empirical effort in this area of alternative trade theories. A great many of the studies from that time can be classed as documentary, attempting to assess the size of the technological gap between countries and how it changed over time. Even in the 1960s, most economists were not well versed in econometric theory or sufficiently computer-literate to undertake a rigorous programme of hypothesis testing using even the limited econometric methods available at the time. This had two consequences. Those who proposed the theories seldom tested them, and, when testing did take place, it was after the

Table 5.1 Labour requirements for export production by skill class, 1962

Country	Person-years per billion dollars of exports (000s)	Percentage distribution of labour requirements by skill class							
		1	2	3	4	5	6	7	8
US	48.2	5.02	2.89	2.74	4.85	8.38	14.96	15.73	45.42
Canada	34.9	4.17	2.33	4.43	4.76	5.39	16.45	14.70	49.76
UK	49.8	3.77	2.29	2.36	4.79	7.20	15.01	14.91	49.68
Austria	52.9	2.76	1.76	1.91	4.15	5.71	15.97	12.87	54.87
Belgium	48.6	2.83	1.71	1.98	3.86	4.67	17.35	12.75	54.85
France	49.3	3.15	1.92	2.15	4.58	5.28	15.55	14.14	53.24
Germany	50.4	3.89	2.48	2.33	4.69	8.44	15.84	14.54	47.79
Italy	52.3	2.75	1.75	1.97	4.33	4.32	12.78	13.24	58.86
Netherlands	44.5	3.62	2.39	2.31	4.65	5.04	15.62	14.50	51.87
Sweden	49.9	3.53	2.34	2.23	4.41	8.92	18.87	13.73	45.96
Switzerland	54.9	3.50	2.39	2.18	5.29	7.76	12.66	15.65	50.56
Japan	57.8	2.48	1.66	1.78	3.96	4.56	15.15	12.04	58.38
Hong Kong	74.3	0.69	0.49	1.13	3.75	1.34	8.48	10.39	73.73
India	66.5	0.71	0.58	1.06	3.47	1.33	11.13	9.62	74.09

Skill classes: (1) scientists and engineers; (2) technicians and draftsmen; (3) other professionals; (4) managers; (5) machinists, electricians and tool- and diemakers; (6) other skilled manual workers; (7) clerical and sales workers; (8) unskilled and semiskilled workers.
Source: Keesing (1966).

theories had been much discussed by economists. While most studies took the existence of a technology gap as a given, what could be considered the more ambitious studies attempted actually to test the validity of the technology gap theory.

The methodology used to assess the validity of technological gap theories was fairly consistent across a number of investigators. This standard approach involved a detailed examination of what could be considered radical innovations in products or production processes and related these changes at the industry level to changes in the trade flows of a particular product over time. Hufbauer's (1966) work on the plastics and synthetic fibres industries showed that there were distinct lags between when production began in the innovating country and when it began in the imitator country. For example, the lag between the invention of galalith in Germany and its first commercial production in the UK was fifteen years. For polymethyl methacrylate, on the other hand, the lag was three years. A strong link was also found between being the first country in commercial production and being an exporter. Some early producers/exporters did eventually become importers as either low wages and/or economies of scale abroad reduced the early production advantage over time.

The focus of empirical examinations of the technology gap theory, however, rapidly moved on from the case study approach into more general attempts to test the relationship between trade patterns and either innovations or technical superiority, the latter proxied by research and development activity and/or the use of skilled manpower. These relationships were examined in the work of Keesing (1965, 1966, 1968), Gruber and Vernon (1970), Goodman and Ceyhun (1976) and Soete (1981), as well as in the study by Baldwin (1979) discussed in Chapter 3.

In his 1966 paper Keesing used data from the US and nine other leading industrial countries to test the relationship between technology, as embodied in labour skills, and exports. He applied US skill requirements by industry, based on the 1960 population census, to both the exports and imports of forty-six manufacturing industries in fourteen countries. Hong Kong was not included in the analysis of imports because of its position as a hub for entrepôt activity. He divided labour requirements into eight skill categories:

(1) Scientists and engineers
(2) Technicians and draftsmen
(3) Other professionals
(4) Managers
(5) Machinists, electricians and tool- and diemakers
(6) Other skilled manual workers
(7) Clerical and sales workers
(8) Unskilled and semiskilled workers

The labour requirements, by skill category, of each country's exports and imports are shown in Tables 5.1 and 5.2. A comparison reveals that there were

Table 5.2 Labour requirements for import production by skill class, 1962

Country	Person-years per billion dollars of imports (000s)	Percentage distribution of labour requirements by skill class							
		1	2	3	4	5	6	7	8
US	43.7	2.77	1.71	2.02	4.63	3.88	13.87	13.74	57.38
Canada	50.1	4.09	2.37	2.60	4.70	7.05	14.74	15.32	49.12
UK	43.0	3.21	1.98	2.13	4.94	5.30	14.25	14.25	53.96
Austria	49.5	3.38	2.16	2.27	4.72	7.10	14.37	14.45	51.55
Belgium	46.1	3.71	2.26	2.34	4.58	6.10	14.99	14.48	51.54
France	51.1	3.62	2.19	2.33	5.22	6.56	15.65	15.55	48.88
Germany	48.4	3.02	1.88	2.00	4.48	5.26	14.57	13.54	55.24
Italy	48.6	4.22	2.53	2.53	4.59	7.86	16.20	14.58	47.65
Netherlands	50.4	3.89	2.39	2.29	4.41	6.17	14.93	13.91	52.01
Sweden	46.0	3.56	2.28	2.26	4.52	6.26	14.92	14.11	52.08
Switzerland	47.6	3.48	2.14	2.28	4.66	6.41	15.11	14.47	51.46
Japan	46.0	5.12	3.12	2.71	5.10	9.53	15.87	15.94	47.62
India	40.2	4.31	2.62	2.46	4.62	7.08	17.32	14.87	46.71

Skill classes: (1) scientists and engineers; (2) technicians and draftsmen; (3) other professionals; (4) managers; (5) machinists, electricians and tool- and diemakers; (6) other skilled manual workers; (7) clerical and sales workers; (8) unskilled and semiskilled workers.
Source: Keesing (1966).

Table 5.3 Correlation between percentage of labour force by skill class and export competitiveness (46 industries)

	Type of correlation	
Skill class	Simple	Rank[a]
1. Scientists and engineers	0.49*	0.43*
2. Technicians and draftsmen	0.37*	0.47*
3. Other professionals	0.41*	0.55*
4. Managers	0.16	0.17
5. Machinists, electricians and tool and diemakers	0.22	0.29
6. Other skilled manual workers	0.11	0.29
7. Clerical and sales workers	0.35*	0.54*
8. Unskilled and semiskilled workers	−0.45*	−0.54*

*Statistically significant at the 0.05 level.
a Rank correlations are Spearman coefficients.
Source: Keesing (1966).

sharp contrasts between countries' export and import requirements for skilled labour (classes 1–5). The exports of the US were the most skill-intensive, while those of Hong Kong and India were the least skill-intensive. The reverse was true for the imports of the US, which appear to have been less skill-intensive than those of India. The US had the greatest relative abundance of hard-to-acquire skills, notably scientists and engineers, technicians and draftsmen, and professionals.

Having based his work on the assumption that foreign goods were produced as if they were manufactured in the US, Keesing (1966) did not feel it would be appropriate to test his hypothesis that skill abundance was an indication of export power for all the countries in his sample. For the US, however, he calculated the correlation between the skill requirements of US goods and an index of those goods' export competitiveness. The index was constructed by calculating the proportion of the total imports of all fourteen countries that US exports comprised. The results are presented in Table 5.3. For both the simple and rank correlations, there was a strong positive relationship between skills and export competitiveness.

Keesing's (1966) reservations about applying his conclusions to other countries were to some extent overcome when in a study published in 1968 he found that US skill coefficients were highly correlated with those of other advanced industrialised countries. This was true not only for the correlations based on scientists, engineers and technicians but also for those based on white-collar workers as a percentage of the total labour force. Baldwin (1971) also found a significant relationship between skills and US exports. The proportion of individuals with more than nine years of formal education was higher in US export industries than in import-competing sectors. It was even higher when only those with over thirteen years of education were included. Those with eight

Table 5.4 US export destinations and US economic characteristics (selected countries)

	Scientists and engineers	Percentage of labour force by skill group						K/L	Unionisation index	Scale index	R^2
		Rest of I	II	III	IV	V	VI				
United Kingdom	−4,343	−252	−282	815	−300	31	−574[a]	−0.77[b]	−126	660	0.41
Canada	1,239	−533	−830	−623	23	968	−30	0.63[b]	367	−251	0.23
West Germany	−4,168	901	−634	694	−448	−95	−657[a]	−0.72[b]	75	446	0.44
Japan	−11,232[c]	−2,095	653	1,331	−430	1,034	−635[b]	−1.4[a]	−872[b]	1,835[a]	0.57
Denmark	−1,223	3,638	−688	65	−21	−1,971	1,104[a]	−0.70	774	−938	NR
Australia	1,013	2,097	−1,837	−943	−158	−2,046[b]	2,119[a]	0.21	1,667[a]	−1,314[a]	0.70
Korea	−3,985	1,264	−598	−2,386[b]	2,026[a]	−77	−275	−0.20	−467	306	0.37
Thailand	1,756	8,594[b]	−4,210[c]	−1,467	210	−326	2,028[a]	−0.15	1,142[c]	−1,560[b]	0.50
Ghana	3,416	1,327	−1,071	−803	−161	262	1,056	−0.18	1,551	−1,587	0.14
Malawi	11,835	2,222	−2,039	1,651	287	−2,540	4,711[a]	−0.67	697	−1,746	0.37

Dependent variable: US net exports (US$). These are adjusted exports minus imports and are a representative per million dollar bundle of total commodity exports less a representative per million dollar bundle of total commodity imports.

Independent variables: Engineers and scientists, proportion of engineers and scientists in an industry; Rest of I, percentage of professional, technical and managerial employees less percentage of engineers and scientists; II, percentage of clerical and sales workers; III, percentage of craftsmen and foremen; IV, percentage of operatives; V, percentage of non-farm labourers and service workers; VI, percentage of farmers and farm labourers; K/L, capital per person in thousands of dollars; Unionisation index, percentage of industry's production workers in plants where a majority of workers are covered by collective bargaining contracts; Scale index, percentage of workers in plants of 250 or more employees.

b, c and d indicate 1%, 5% and 10% significance levels for the t-values of the regression coefficients, respectively.

NR, Not reported.

Source: Baldwin (1979).

and fewer years of education were highly concentrated in import-competing industries. One anomaly, however, was the presence of farmers and farm labour in the export category – although they were one of the least educated groups. In aggregate, nonetheless, the basic proposition held: exports were associated with highly educated and skilled labour whereas imports and import-competing industries were dominated by labour with a lower level of education and fewer skills.

In a similar study, Baldwin (1979) used data from twenty-eight countries which were US export destinations. These ranged from developed countries such as the UK and Canada to developing countries such as Malawi and Ghana. Using US net exports as the dependent variable, he employed ten independent variables in a multiple regression – seven labour skills categories, the capital–labour ratio, an index of unionisation and a proxy for economies of scale. The information was collected by industry. The results of these regressions are reported for a selection of Baldwin's countries in Table 5.4. They show that there was, in general, a positive and significant relationship between the proportion of engineers and scientists, craftsmen and farmers and US net exports. Typically, the percentage of operatives and non-farm labourers also had the expected sign, but the coefficients were not significant. In a separate regression Baldwin used the capital– labour ratio and the number of years of education as independent variables. Industries with a large proportion of workers with high-school education were positively and significantly related to net exports.

In the late 1960s and early 1970s Gruber, Mehta and Vernon (1967) and Gruber and Vernon (1970) examined the influence of technology on US exports. In addition to using the proportion of scientists and engineers employed in an industry as a proxy for technological superiority, they also used the proportion of total expenditure spent on research and development (R&D).

The results of Gruber, Mehta and Vernon's (1967) study are summarised in Table 5.5. Industries with the highest research effort accounted for 89.4 per cent of total R&D expenditure, 78.2 per cent of company R&D, 85.3 per cent of the total scientists and engineers in R&D, 39.1 per cent of total US sales and 72.0 per cent of US exports. Industries – at least in the US – with a high research effort tended to export a high proportion of their output. Gruber and his colleagues

Table 5.5 Research effort, sales and exports for 19 US industries, 1962

Industries	Total R&D expenditure	Percentage distribution		Sales	Exports
		Company-financed R&D	Scientists and engineers in R&D		
Five industries with highest research effort	89.4	78.2	85.3	39.1	72.0
14 other industries	10.6	21.8	14.7	60.9	28.0

Source: Gruber, Mehta and Vernon (1967).

Table 5.6 Regressions derived from relating exports of 24 industries to selected industry characteristics

Exporting area	Independent variables						Multiple correlation
	Raw labour	Technology	Capital	Industry concentration	Intermediate goods	Crude material	
US	-0.804 (2.75)	0.169 (1.73)	-0.641 (2.59)	0.296 (1.07)	0.456 (1.76)	-0.017 (0.89)	0.85 (7.27)
Japan	1.983 (2.09)	0.414 (1.30)	0.254 (0.32)	-1.554 (1.73)	0.717 (0.85)	0.072 (1.16)	0.73 (3.18)
Mexico	-2.06 (1.74)	-0.420 (1.05)	-0.997 (0.99)	-2.54 (2.53)	-0.153 (0.15)	0.062 (0.79)	0.74 (3.33)
West Germany	0.029 (0.05)	0.119 (0.58)	0.206 (0.40)	-0.342 (0.59)	-0.056 (0.10)	-0.032 (0.80)	0.36 (0.43)
France	1.00 (0.23)	0.062 (0.43)	0.028 (0.07)	-0.507 (1.23)	0.021 (0.05)	0.004 (0.15)	0.36 (0.42)
Canada	1.065 (1.07)	-0.058 (0.17)	0.706 (0.84)	0.398 (0.42)	-0.002 (0.01)	-0.010 (0.15)	0.41 (0.56)
Brazil	-0.505 (0.28)	0.233 (0.39)	-0.945 (0.62)	-0.643 (0.38)	0.910 (0.57)	0.210 (1.77)	0.44 (0.68)

Dependent variable: industry-normalised exports.
Figures in parenthesis under regression coefficients are t values; those under the correlation coefficients are F values.
Source: Gruber and Vernon (1970).

found this to be true whether export performance was measured as the proportion of total sales accounted for by exports or as net exports taken as a proportion of total sales. Both these measures, however, have some drawbacks as indicators of comparative advantage. The ratio of exports to total sales, while a possible indicator of the US's competitive position, could also be affected by foreign demand patterns, transport costs and trade restrictions. The second measure – net exports as a proportion of total sales – takes these factors into account to some degree. Nevertheless, they may not be a true measure of competitiveness because demand patterns and tariff distortions in the US may well influence the level of imports.

Conscious of the fact that technology may be only one influence on countries' trade patterns, Gruber and Vernon (1970) set out to assess its importance relative to other factors that might influence competitiveness. Their approach consisted of regressing the export share of eight countries' (and two other geographical areas) industrial exports aggregated into twenty-six groups against six independent variables. The independent variables were: raw labour, measured by employees per dollar of value added; technological intensity, proxied by the ratio of scientists and engineers to total employment; capital intensity, shown by the proportion of fixed assets to sales; a measure of specialisation in intermediate goods, constructed by taking the output delivered to other businesses as a percentage of total output; an industry concentration measure based on the importance of the largest firms to the US economy; and, finally, a materials input measure, which was proxied by the input of crude materials as a percentage of total output, again based on US figures.

All of the variables were transformed into logarithmic form. The results of these regressions for the eight individual countries are reported in Table 5.6. Only three of the eight multiple regressions gave high R^2 values – those for the US, Japan and Mexico. Gruber and Vernon (1970) concluded that, at least for the US, there was a strong association between technology and exports and that technology's inclusion as a distinct trade variable was warranted.

A further, but more comprehensive, foray into technology-based theories of trade was carried out by Goodman and Ceyhun (1976). In contrast to Gruber and Vernon (1970), they concentrated exclusively on the US and opted to use both a time-series and a cross-section analysis. They used the technique of principal components, feeling that collinearity among the independent variables made the normal ordinary least-squares approach unsuitable.

Goodman and Ceyhun's approach consisted of regressing the export performance of twelve industries over the period 1958 to 1968 against a number of independent variables. The independent variables were technological innovation, industry concentration, industry growth, sales promotion, a labour skills ratio, unit labour costs, scale economies and the capital to labour ratio. On the basis of the amount spent on R&D as a proportion of total revenue, industries were split into two groups. The five industries that spent more than the national average on R&D were classed as 'new', while those that spent less were grouped as 'old' or 'standard' industries. The proxies adopted to measure the technology variable were either R&D expenditure as a proportion of total industry revenue or the ratio of scientists and engineers to the total labour force employed.

The inclusion of the additional independent variables and the proxies used to measure them require some further explanation. Market concentration was considered important for several reasons. Large firms with higher cash flows and lower risks than small firms would be better able to export because they could maintain extensive R&D facilities and marketing programmes as well as being able to finance export credits. Data limitations forced Goodman and Ceyhun to develop their own measure of market concentration. In the time-series analysis they used the ratio of a firm's revenue to total industry revenues as a proxy, while in their cross-section study the value of a plant's shipments as a proportion of total industry shipments was used as the proxy.

Industry growth and overseas sales promotion were considered important factors because the former implied an ability to supply goods that were in demand, while the latter would enable firms to overcome barriers in foreign markets and expand their export sales. Industrial growth was proxied by the growth in sales. Owing to a dearth of information, overseas advertising was measured by the ratio of total advertising outlays to total current sales – a weak proxy at best.

Skilled labour was included to take into account its influence on the process of innovation. The proportion of non-production workers to production workers was used as a proxy. Production workers were defined as the sum of operative and kindred workers plus labourers in the time-series studies but as labourers only in the cross-section analysis.

The effects of cost factors – scale economies, unit labour costs and the capital to labour ratio – are fairly self-evident. Economies of scale were modelled by taking the assets of each firm as a proportion of total industry assets in the time-series studies, whereas the ratio of employees per establishment to total industry employment was used in the cross-section analysis. Labour costs were taken as wages per unit of value added. The lower these costs, the greater the exports were expected to be. The capital–labour ratio was defined as the ratio of capital expenditure to the number of production workers.

A priori, Goodman and Ceyhun (1976) expected the influence of the independent variables to differ between new and old industries. The export performance of new industries, they felt, was critically dependent on product innovation and successful marketing. Thus, they expected the following variables to be positively associated with exports: the R&D sales ratio and/or the proportion of scientists and engineers in total employment; the degree of concentration; the growth of output; the ratio of advertising costs to sales revenue; the ratio of skilled to unskilled labour; and unit labour costs. Negative relationships were expected for scale economies and the capital–labour ratio.

As the older industries' international competitiveness was felt to be more dependent on cost factors, Goodman and Ceyhun expected the effect of the independent variables to be the opposite to that of the new industries with the exception of advertising expenditure. This variable was also expected to be positively related to exports because firms in older industries would attempt to maintain their advantage in international markets by differentiating their products.

The results of Goodman and Ceyhun's (1976) work are reported in Table 5.7. In the published results, for some industries independent variables were dropped to improve the fit. The equations estimated are given below.

For the time-series regressions:

$$Y_t = b_0 + b_1 X_{1t-2} + b_2 X_{2t-2} + b_3 X_{3t-1} + b_4 X_{4t-2} + b_5 X_{5t-2} +$$

$$+ b_6 X_{6t-1} + b_7 X_{7t-1} + b_8 X_{8t-1} + e_t \qquad (5.1)$$

For the cross-sectional regression:

$$Y_t = b_0 + b_1 X_{1t-8} + b_2 X_{2t-3} + b_3 X_{3t-4} + b_4 X_{4t-2} + b_5 X_{5t-2} +$$

$$+ b_6 X_{6t-5} + b_7 X_{7t-4} + b_8 X_{8t-4} + e_t \qquad (5.2)$$

The independent variables were incorporated in a lag structure. The actual lags used, however, were chosen more for the availability of the data than their basis in economic theory.

Overall, Goodman and Ceyhun's results appear to be quite strong as in all but three regressions the R^2 values were over 0.80. For the new industries, the R&D ratios and industrial concentration variables are significant and have the expected signs. Labour skills, wage costs, sales promotion and economies of scale also turned out to be significant determinants of export performance, although their signs differ from industry to industry. Generally, the results suggest that labour skills had a negative effect on exports while sales promotion had a positive effect. The frequency of the negative sign on the labour skills variable led Goodman and Ceyhun to doubt the validity of Keesing's earlier (1971) results. The wage-cost and economy of scale variables had mixed signs that were almost evenly distributed among industries. Neither the capital–labour ratio nor the growth of industrial output variables were statistically significant except in the machinery (non-electrical) industry. Goodman and Ceyhun did not find this result surprising given that the industry was both very highly capital-intensive and undergoing rapid growth.

The chemical industry gave rise to some unexpected results because its export performance was negatively related to technological innovations. Goodman and Ceyhun (1976) suggested that this could be explained by spill-over factors whereby chemical innovations find their commercial application in industries such as synthetic fibres, paints and plastics.

The regressions undertaken on the old industries also gave some interesting results. The capital–labour ratio and industry growth variables were not

Table 5.7 Principal component regression estimates

Explanatory variables	New industries					Time-series analysis — Old industries							Cross-section analysis
	N_1	N_2	N_3	N_4	N_5	O_1	O_2	O_3	O_4	O_5	O_6	O_7	
Technology (X_1)	5.174[b]	3.814[b]	7.717[b]	-3.020[b]	108.022[b]	1.009[b]	1.522[b]	0.041[b]	-22.894[b]	22.350[b]	122.628[b]	22.398[b]	0.741[b]
Market conc. (X_2)	0.059[a]	0.104[b]	0.525[b]	-0.201	46.029[b]		-0.044[a]	-0.003	-1.661[b]	0.244[b]	-0.246[a]		
Ind. growth (X_3)			0.023	0.001	21.510[b]		-0.37[a]	0.0003	0.104		0.006		0.332[b]
Scale econ. (X_4)	0.053	-0.204[b]	0.343[b]	0.343[b]	-81.157[b]	-0.022[b]	-0.188[b]	-0.003	1.102[b]		-0.051	-0.027[b]	
Advert./sales (X_5)	-1.263[b]	3.303[b]	-2.810[b]	1.612[b]	1256.170[a]		1.114[b]	-0.193[b]	60.476[b]	-14.409[b]	-1.949[b]	-0.559[b]	1.147[b]
Skilled labour (X_6)	-0.684[b]	-0.756[b]	-0.247[b]	0.484[b]	47.817[b]	-0.182[b]	-0.202[b]	0.001	-1.992[b]	0.626[b]	-1.041[b]	-0.027[a]	
Unit lab. cost (X_7)		0.903[b]	-0.868[b]	-0.782[b]	138.043[b]	0.174[b]	-0.570[b]	0.157[b]	1.767[b]	0.378[b]	7.246[b]	-0.017[a]	-0.144
Capital/labour (X_8)		-0.001		0.002	0.292[b]		-0.0002	0.002	-0.002		-0.001	-0.006	
R^2	0.82[b]	0.80[a]	0.96[b]	0.81[b]	0.95[b]	0.72[b]	0.84[b]	0.80[a]	0.60	0.94[b]	0.51	0.83[b]	0.45[b]

New industries: N_1, electrical equipment and communication; N_2, motor vehicles and other transportation equipment; N_3, professional and scientific instruments; N_4, chemicals and allied products; N_5, machinery, except electrical.

Old industries: O_1, rubber and plastics products; O_2, fabricated metal products; O_3, other manufacturing industries; O_4, primary metal industries; O_5, paper and allied products; O_6, food and kindred products; O_7, textiles and apparel.

a Significant at the 0.5% level.
b Significant at the 1% level.
Source: Goodman and Ceyhun (1976).

statistically significant in explaining export performance. The one exception was the fabricated metal products industry, where the industry growth variable was statistically significant.

Surprisingly, and contrary to expectations, the innovation variables were not only significant but had a positive effect on the export performance of the old industries except in the case of primary metal industries. By and large, the coefficients of the labour skills and wage cost variables had the expected signs, as did sales promotion. There was also some support for the influence of industry concentration and economies of scale on export performance.

The cross-section results showed that the export performance of US manufacturing industries was determined by technological, marketing and industry growth factors, while unit labour costs had no statistical significance. Although the R^2 was lower than those found in the time-series studies, this reduction in the explanatory power of the equation was not considered important as it is a common feature of cross-section estimations.

Goodman and Ceyhun's (1976) results tended to support the earlier findings of Leontief (1956), Branson and Junz (1971) and Baldwin (1979) that the capital–labour ratio is not an important factor in determining the export performance of the US manufacturing industry. They also confirmed Baldwin's findings with regard to industrial concentration and economies of scale and provided added support for Leamer's (1974) hypothesis concerning the importance of technological factors for export performance.

A limitation of the studies outlined thus far is that they are industry/country-specific. Leamer (1974) put forth the argument that, as trade theories are commodity-specific, any tests carried out should be on the same basis. Soete (1981) set out to accomplish this task with respect to the technological gap theory by examining the trade data for seventeen OECD countries.

A new feature of the work by Soete (1981) was the use of an output measure of R&D activity – in contrast to previous studies, which relied on input measures. He based his output measure on patents awarded rather than on R&D expenditure or the proportion of scientists and engineers employed in an industry. His reason for taking this approach was that it helped to contrast the approach of the technology gap theorists with that of the *neo-factor proportions* school – those economists who approached the resolution of the Leontief paradox by disaggregating and better defining the factors of production. Variables such as 'engineers and scientists' employed in an industry can be interpreted as a proxy for human capital rather than as producers of a technology gap. If input measures of R&D activity are used as an independent variable, it is not possible to distinguish between the technology gap theories and the neo-factor proportions approach. A country could export technologically advanced goods because it is well endowed with the appropriate factors, such as intellectual capital. In other words, there is no real need for it to be a leader in its product field; it merely has to have the right mix of factor endowments. By tying R&D activity to an output measure, Soete felt better able to account for the role of new products, product innovations and imitation and how they confer a time advantage over competing countries.

As the ratio of patents granted to those applied for differs widely among countries, largely owing to divergent legal systems, Soete was forced to adopt another measure of innovativeness. His proxy was the number of patents originating in foreign countries but awarded in one particular country – the US. By taking this approach, he argued that he was able to overcome difficulties with cross-national comparability because all patent applications would have undergone the same screening process. The only drawback was that using his measure precluded using the calculation for US patents originating in the US. This difficulty was overcome by estimating a figure for the success of US patents in foreign countries based on US patent sources.

Soete then proceeded to estimate the relationship between the share of exports from each country, i, produced by industry j in total OECD exports of industry j against the share of each country, i, in 1963–77 US patents in industry j. In addition, the capital–labour ratio, the population of each country and a distance variable were used as further explanatory variables. The distance variable was used as a proxy for the physical distance of individual countries from an assumed world centre. The additional variables were included to capture the effects of factor proportions, economies of scale and transport and other transaction costs associated with trade. Apart from the patents, all other variables were based on 1977 data. It is important to note that Soete did not include variables to capture the effects of factor endowments on trade.

Soete's (1981) results are presented in Table 5.8. Unsurprisingly, the results were not significant for the three industries in which factor endowments could be expected to play an important role in determining exports – food, agricultural chemicals, and petroleum and natural gas. They do, however, clearly show overwhelming support for the importance of the technology variable in explaining trade. Export performance was explained in a large number of industries by the patents proxy. The exceptions are the natural resource industries already mentioned, plus stone, clay and glass. Patents were also not significant in other industries where factor proportions might be expected to play an important role – textiles, paint, radio and television equipment, ship and boat building, railroad equipment and motorcycles and bicycles.

The scale and size effect factors, as proxied by the population variable, were significant in stone, clay and glass products, fabricated metal products, refrigeration and service machinery and the motor vehicle industry. One would expect these industries to be ones where economies of scale would be important. Examination of the distance variable showed that it was a significant factor in many industries, confirming Gruber and Vernon's (1970) findings.

Soete's (1981) static cross-section analysis indicates that, for most innovative industries, the international trade performance of the various OECD countries examined was strongly related to their technological performance.

As noted above, a major problem when attempting to test for the influence of technology on trade is distinguishing between research and development as a

Table 5.8 Estimates of regression equations explaining OECD countries' export shares for 40 industrial sectors

Industry	Intercept	ln (Share of patents$_{ij}$)	lnK/L_i	ln POP$_i$	Distance$_i$	R^2	$F(4,17)$
1. Food products	−5.01	0.099	0.402	0.368	0.004	0.32	3.52
	(2.69)	(0.147)	(0.588)	(0.255)	(0.003)		
2. Textile mill products	12.90*	0.145	−0.337	0.631**	0.011*	0.73	15.15*
	(2.19)	(0.117)	(0.551)	(0.230)	(0.003)		
3. Industrial inorganic chemicals	−8.10**	0.488**	−0.128	0.522	0.003	0.78	19.53*
	(2.97)	(0.197)	(0.849)	(0.393)	(0.004)		
4. Industrial organic chemicals	−8.66*	0.238	0.712	0.776**	0.013**	0.82	25.37*
	(2.63)	(0.114)	(0.539)	(0.262)	(0.003)		
5. Plastic materials, synthetics	−0.255	0.305*	1.148**	0.544**	0.008*	0.91	51.16*
	(1.99)	(0.098)	(0.477)	(0.235)	(0.002)		
6. Agricultural chemicals	−11.36	0.256	0.457	0.939	0.009	0.20	2.34
	(8.24)	(0.385)	(1.607)	(0.785)	(0.009)		
7. Soaps, cleaners, toilet goods	−0.49	0.325**	1.261	0.382	0.009**	0.69	12.67*
	(3.65)	(0.158)	(0.656)	(0.334)	(0.004)		
8. Paints and allied products	−0.069	0.214	1.585*	0.478	0.010**	0.68	12.15*
	(3.79)	(0.164)	(0.538)	(0.339)	(0.004)		
9. Misc. chemical products	−4.33	0.226	0.743	0.492	0.006**	0.67	11.61*
	(2.83)	(0.137)	(0.627)	(0.289)	(0.003)		
10. Drugs	−5.82**	0.340*	0.164	0.278	0.011*	0.77	18.41*
	(2.67)	(0.108)	(0.495)	(0.252)	(0.003)		
11. Petroleum, natural gas	3.22	−0.151	3.561**	1.071	0.009	0.36	3.96
	(7.76)	(0.362)	(1.363)	(0.827)	(0.008)		
12. Rubber and misc. plastic products	−7.63*	0.441	−0.039	0.424**	0.009*	0.86	33.38*
	(2.11)	(0.121)	(0.573)	(0.210)	(0.002)		
13. Stone, clay, glass & concrete products	−11.58*	0.220	−0.129	0.679*	0.009*	0.31	23.97*
	(1.88)	(0.113)	(0.489)	(0.191)	(0.002)		
14. Primary ferrous products	−4.71**	0.417**	0.577	0.514	0.005**	0.84	28.69*
	(2.32)	(0.146)	(0.642)	(0.265)	(0.003)		
15. Primary & secondary non-ferrous metals	0.94	0.262**	1.154**	0.316	0.001	0.81	23.36*
	(2.02)	(0.118)	(0.533)	(0.234)	(0.002)		
16. Fabricated metal products	−7.66*	0.346*	0.107	0.502*	0.008*	0.88	40.34*
	(1.81)	(0.090)	(0.468)	(0.160)	(0.002)		
17. Engines and turbines	−4.71	0.473**	1.250	0.843**	0.008**	0.81	23.52*
	(3.32)	(0.213)	(0.765)	(0.382)	(0.004)		
18. Farm and garden machinery and eq.	−3.37	0.657*	0.704	0.530	0.005	0.78	19.52*
	(3.98)	(0.223)	(1.022)	(0.349)	(0.004)		
19. Construction, mining & material handling machinery and eq.	−7.44**	0.512*	0.117	0.527	0.007**	0.84	28.31*
	(2.74)	(0.154)	(0.749)	(0.257)	(0.003)		
20. Metalworking machinery and eq.	−8.93*	0.569*	−0.562	0.287	0.009*	0.84	28.35*
	(2.74)	(0.133)	(0.709)	(0.293)	(0.003)		

(Table continues on next page)

The figures in parentheses are the estimated standard errors of the coefficients.
*Significant at the 1% level (*t*-statistic).
**Significant at the 5% level (*t*-statistic).
Source: Soete (1981).

Table 5.8 (*cont.*) Estimates of regression equations explaining OECD countries' export shares for 40 industrial sectors

Industry	Intercept	ln (Share of patents$_{ij}$)	lnK/L_i	ln POP$_i$	Distance$_i$	R^2	$F(4,17)$
21. Office, computing & accounting machines	−7.95 (6.36)	0.892** (0.320)	−0.509 (1.591)	0.238 (0.630)	0.014** (0.007)	0.65	10.90*
22. Special industry machinery	−4.49 (2.80)	0.676* (0.146)	−0.51 (0.729)	0.191 (0.264)	0.007** (0.003)	0.86	33.60*
23. General industrial machinery	−6.09** (2.67)	0.494* (0.112)	0.340 (0.642)	0.494** (0.232)	0.009* (0.003)	0.87	36.72*
24. Refrigeration and service machinery	−8.30** (2.94)	0.513* (0.146)	0.618 (0.629)	0.858* (0.271)	0.006 (0.003)	0.84	28.46*
25. Misc. machinery excl. electrical	−0.37 (2.97)	0.930* (0.166)	−0.248 (0.768)	−0.211 (0.301)	0.007** (0.003)	0.87	36.67*
26. Electrical transmission and distributing eq.	−3.14 (2.93)	0.672* (0.174)	−0.230 (0.797)	−0.023 (0.334)	0.008** (0.003)	0.81	23.03*
27. Electrical industrial apparatus	−1.39 (3.32)	0.615* (0.190)	0.134 (0.878)	0.040 (0.401)	0.004 (0.004)	0.78	19.18*
28. Household appliances	−4.68 (2.46)	0.501* (0.132)	0.109 (0.618)	0.184 (0.248)	0.004 (0.003)	0.78	20.09*
29. Electrical lighting, wiring eq.	−3.37 (3.47)	0.509** (0.219)	0.373 (0.992)	0.245 (0.488)	0.009** (0.004)	0.77	19.05*
30. Misc. electrical equipment supplies	−4.71 (2.27)	0.412* (0.119)	0.702 (0.551)	0.578** (0.264)	0.006** (0.003)	0.88	40.76*
31. Radio, TV receiving eq.	−5.58 (4.48)	0.503 (0.254)	−0.097 (1.185)	0.170 (0.580)	0.009 (0.005)	0.61	9.13*
32. Communications eq. and electronic comp. & access.	−8.29** (2.99)	0.463** (0.172)	0.009 (0.862)	0.499 (0.343)	0.010* (0.003)	0.80	22.36*
33. Motor vehicles and equipment	−9.45* (2.88)	0.456** (0.162)	0.732 (0.724)	1.027* (0.310)	0.007** (0.003)	0.86	32.85*
34. Ship, boat building, repairing	1.15 (5.68)	0.529 (0.348)	0.808 (1.388)	0.089 (0.582)	0.003 (0.006)	0.38	4.21**
35. Railroad equipment	−14.95** (5.49)	0.133 (0.239)	1.154 (0.988)	1.557** (0.542)	0.015** (0.006)	0.62	9.71*
36. Motorcycles, bicycles and parts	0.54 (6.63)	0.530 (0.282)	1.898 (0.998)	0.575 (0.599)	0.012 (0.007)	0.60	8.87*
37. Misc. transportation equip.	6.29 (4.12)	0.799* (0.199)	1.186 (0.764)	−0.189 (0.404)	0.011** (0.004)	0.80	21.51*
38. Ordnance guided missiles, space vehicles and parts	−5.09 (5.79)	0.900* (0.277)	−0.982 (1.118)	−0.108 (0.570)	−0.001 (0.006)	0.53	6.88*
39. Aircraft and parts	1.09 (4.50)	1.262* (0.242)	−0.206 (0.891)	−0.307 (0.449)	0.009 (0.005)	0.81	22.67*
40. Professional and scientific instruments	−6.94 (3.53)	0.743* (0.184)	−0.611 (0.944)	0.109 (0.343)	0.010** (0.004)	0.80	22.62*

The figures in parentheses are the estimated standard errors of the coefficients.
*Significant at the 1% level (*t*-statistic).
**Significant at the 5% level (*t*-statistic).
Source: Soete (1981).

factor endowment and as a measure of a country's innovativeness and technological superiority. If research and development (however it was measured) were
treated as a factor of production, a country's trade pattern could be predicted by
using a modified Heckscher–Ohlin model which included this variable. A country abundant in R&D factors will export R&D-intensive goods. The technology
gap theory is based on a different hypothesis. It suggests that having a lead or
being more advanced than competitors in research and development determines
the level of a country's exports.

A number of authors have attempted to unravel the dual influence of
research and development on trade patterns. They include Katrak (1973, 1982),
Hughes (1983) and Smith *et al.* (1982). We will not examine the findings of the
last two studies in detail here as they will be examined in Chapter 7, which deals
with the comparative testing of different trade models.

In his earlier (1973) paper, Katrak's aim was twofold. First, he wanted to
test the relative performance of US and UK exports with respect to R&D, human
skills and economies of scale. Second, he wished to re-examine Gruber, Mehta
and Vernon's (1976) unsatisfactory explanation of US versus UK exports by
including an R&D variable.

To reflect R&D activity Katrak (1973) used an industry's outlay per unit of
sales. Human skills were proxied by the ratio of skilled to unskilled employees
in particular industries. Although Katrak knew that this was not an ideal measure
– since some skilled workers would be used in R&D activities – he was forced
to use this variable because of a lack of more appropriate data. He believed that
the measure was an acceptable proxy because Keesing (1971) had found that
only a small proportion of scientists and engineers (skilled workers) were used
in R&D activities.

Katrak was prevented from using plant size as a measure of economies of
scale due to a dearth of data for the UK. He dismissed national output measures
such as GDP and GDP per capita because they do not take into account minimum economic size. Instead, he turned to an alternative measure, using employment by industry to represent the relative size of US and UK industries.

Katrak tested his hypothesis for two aggregated groups of fourteen and
seventeen industries utilising both rank correlation and regression analysis.
The regression results are reported in Table 5.9. Taken overall, the regressions
performed well, with adjusted R^2 values ranging from 0.61 to 0.91, and all
the F ratios were significant at the 5 per cent level. As in previous studies, the
human skills variable performed well, with six of the coefficients significant.
The measure of scale economies was significant in all equations. The research
and development coefficient, however, did not appear to be significant in any of
the equations.

In his later (1982) study examining the changes in the composition of the
UK's trade relative to technological developments, Katrak found that the skill
and R&D intensities of UK exports had decreased while capital increased in
importance. He used the number of scientists and engineers employed in research

and development as an indicator of R&D activity in contrast to his previous monetary measure – industry expenditure on R&D per unit of sales revenue.

Smith *et al.* (1982) also distinguished between technology and skills by taking the expenditure on R&D as a proportion of total sales as an indication of the former and the percentage of skilled workers as a proxy for the latter. Skills were found to be an important variable in determining the UK's trade, while technological factors appeared to be less important.

Hughes (1983) differed from Katrak (1973) and Smith *et al.* (1982) by using a simultaneous equation system. Further, his study was carried out at a greater level of disaggregation. He used a sample of forty-six manufacturing

Table 5.9 Regression equations relating US/UK exports to R&D, skill intensities and scale effects

Seventeen-industry classification[a]

Linear equations

$$X_{62} = -1711.94 + 0.17R + 1.36H + 17.23N \qquad R^2 = 0.896$$
$$\phantom{X_{62} = -1711.94 + } (0.26) \quad (0.74)^* \quad (2.90)^*$$

$$X_{64} = -1275.00 + 0.07R + 1.30H + 13.20N \qquad R^2 = 0.906$$
$$\phantom{X_{64} = -1275.00 + } (0.19) \quad (0.54)^* \quad (2.19)^*$$

$$X_{66} = -165.45 + 0.09R + 0.47H + 2.73N \qquad R^2 = 0.645$$
$$\phantom{X_{66} = -165.45 + } (0.13) \quad (0.38) \quad (1.51)^*$$

Log linear equations

$$X_{62} = -9.73 + 0.02R + 0.17H + 5.75N \qquad R^2 = 0.842$$
$$\phantom{X_{62} = -9.73 + } (0.06) \quad (0.07)^* \quad (1.00)^*$$

$$X_{64} = -7.71 + 0.0004R + 0.19H + 4.76N \qquad R^2 = 0.840$$
$$\phantom{X_{64} = -7.71 + } (0.05) \quad (0.06)^* \quad (0.89)^*$$

$$X_{66} = -2.27 + 0.04R + 0.16H + 2.03N \qquad R^2 = 0.609$$
$$\phantom{X_{66} = -2.27 + } (0.06) \quad (0.07)^* \quad (1.02)^*$$

Fourteen-industry classification[b]

Linear equation

$$X_{62} = -6200.32 - 0.07R + 3.97H + 71.39N \qquad R^2 = 0.700$$
$$\phantom{X_{62} = -6200.32 - } (0.81) \quad (2.26) \quad (17.99)^*$$

Log linear equation

$$X_{62} = -915 - 0.02R + 0.12H + 6.02N \qquad R^2 = 0.707$$
$$\phantom{X_{62} = -915 - } (0.04) \quad (0.06)^* \quad (1.47)^*$$

The term R in the equations denotes the measure $R_j^{US} - R_j^{UK}$, i.e. the R&D gap between the United States and the United Kingdom; H denotes the skill intensity; N denotes the relative size of employment $(N_j^{US}/N_j^{UK})^{aj}$; and X_{62} denotes US/UK exports in 1962, etc.
The standard errors of the coefficients are shown in parentheses.
*Indicates *t*-values significant at the 5% level.
a United States skill intensities were used in these regressions.
b United Kingdom skill intensities were used in these regressions.
Source: Katrak (1973).

industries. Hughes proxied technology by taking the amount spent on R&D as a proportion of value added, and the ratio of skilled manual labour to total labour employed by industry to indicate the level of human skills. He found that, for the UK, both technology and skill factors played a role in determining the pattern of trade.

On aggregate, the tests of the technology gap theory appear to support the proposition that differences in technology have a positive role in the determination of trade patterns. This conclusion was supported by both the case study approach and the broader industry–country approach. Some authors have, moreover, differentiated between the human skill endowments approach of the neo-factor proportions and the technology gap theory by more carefully specifying their independent variables.

5.3 Testing product cycle theories

As with tests of the technology gap theory, empirical work on the product cycle hypothesis was initially concerned with case studies of products developed in the US or other advanced countries. A collection of these case studies can be found in Wells (1972). Again, we will examine only a few of the industry case studies before moving on to examine in greater detail the more broadly based industry–country studies. From the large number of case studies we have selected three: two older studies on electronics and petrochemicals and one more recent study on telecommunications.

5.3.1 Case studies of the product cycle

Hirsch's (1972) study of the US electronics industry models the product life cycle hypothesis. Identifying six major product groups within the electronics sector that had high value-added growth rates in the early stage of the product cycle, he found, first, that the sectors that grew fastest were also those in which the US possessed a comparative advantage. Second, he observed that as the sector became older its trade balance deteriorated. Finally, the fastest-growing and, therefore, younger sectors tended to be more labour- and skill-intensive than the more slowly growing, older sectors. Hirsch's results suggest that the comparative advantage of the US in the electronics industry was dynamic, meaning that the advantage dissipated over time. As the specific product groups aged and the production process became more mature and standardised, the importance of skilled labour declined. A lower skill component in production enabled foreign countries to acquire the necessary technology and establish industries in competition with US manufacturers.

Wells' (1969) study of twenty consumer goods industries also lent support to the product cycle theory. He took as his measure of export performance the ratio of 1962–63 export growth rates to 1952–53 export growth rates. He used income elasticities for product ownership as the independent variable. This measure was calculated using US data, but he was able to show that the rankings of various consumer products owned by households were quite similar between the US and countries of the European Economic Community and Israel. His preferred independent variable, income elasticities of demand, could not be used because of data limitations. His hypothesis was that the US would export high-income products, with the underlying assumption that, over time, as high-income products become standardised, their cost falls. Foreign competitors can then take advantage of their cost advantage to begin their own production. A high correlation coefficient of 0.896 between the dependent and independent variables led Wells to claim that his results supported the product cycle theory. He believed they showed that the US had a strong propensity to innovate and produce goods that satisfied the demands of high-income consumers.

There are two criticisms of Wells' (1969) approach. First, he used the growth rate of exports as his dependent variable on the assumption that high growth rates reflect the newness of a product. This need not necessarily be the case – high levels of value added, such as those used by Hirsch (1972), are a better indicator of newness. The second criticism of Wells' approach is that innovations were assumed to be devised solely to meet the demands of wealthier consumers. This is certainly not the only motivation for new product development. Wells also found some evidence that economies of scale influence trade patterns. Given these limitations, Wells' results do, however, lend support to the product cycle hypothesis.

Support for the product cycle is also provided by a study of the UK electronics industry. Poh (1987) measured export performance by the export/sales ratio of five sub-sectors of the electronics industry: components, computers, electronic capital goods, telephone and telegraph apparatus and, finally, consumer electronics, over the period 1970–79. Export performance was related to product maturity. An indicator of product maturity was constructed by fitting a logistic growth curve to the consumption data for each sub-sector and estimating the size of the saturation gap, which is the difference between the potential market and actual consumption. The younger the industry, the larger this gap is. Electronic components, computers and electronic capital goods were found to be in the growth stage of the product cycle, while telephone/telegram apparatus and consumer electronics had reached the mature phase. The product cycle hypothesis would suggest that the UK should have a comparative advantage in the newer and growing sub-sectors. A positive correlation coefficient of 0.9 was found between the ranking of export performance and the ranking of the saturation gap.

5.3.2 Country–industry studies of the product cycle

One criticism of the case studies approach is that it concentrates on particular industries or particular industry groups at specific times and, hence, may represent only special cases that cannot provide a generalised explanation for trade patterns. In an attempt to provide broader-based evidence to support the product cycle hypothesis, Morrall (1972) examined all twenty-two two-digit SIC industries in the US over a period of four years. Two measures of export performance – exports minus imports, X_1, and exports minus imports taken as a percentage of total industry shipments, X_2 – were related to variables that characterise the product cycle.

Morrall suggested that four variables were distinctive of the product cycle. The first two were: scientists and engineers employed in research and development, S&E, as a proxy for the propensity of the US to develop new products; and the industries' growth rates as shown by the growth of value added, VA, proxying product maturity as well as product and process innovation. The logic behind using the latter proxy is that new products should have faster growth rates than older products. Furthermore, as the US had the highest per capita income and labour costs in the world, US firms would develop products that were highly income elastic and labour-saving. Products with high income elasticities should, in addition, have the highest growth rates. In so far as long-run industry supply curves were elastic, the VA index would reflect income elasticities.

Following Vernon's (1966) premise that the US was a high labour cost country, Morrall expected to find that technological progress in labour-saving processes was more likely to originate there than elsewhere. Thus, the US was likely to have a comparative advantage in the development of processes that increased labour productivity, whereas its rivals, who were not so well endowed with capital, would be expected to have an advantage in capital-saving processes. In order to relate export performance to developments in new labour-saving technology, Morrall utilised an index of the growth of labour efficiency less the growth of physical capital efficiency, L–C, as his third distinctive product cycle variable. This measure had previously been suggested by Ferguson and Moroney (1969).

In accordance with the product cycle theory, rapidly growing firms and industries would exhibit other characteristics in addition to those listed above. Their temporary monopoly position would be reflected in higher profit to sales ratios, while rapid change would be revealed by higher than average depreciation rates. They would also rely more heavily on the services of specialists, such as consultants, research and development agencies, legal advisors and marketing and communications experts. Finally, intent on maximising growth rates, they would also be expected to receive higher royalty payments and patent fees and have proportionally greater sales-promotion budgets. To capture these additional variables, Morrall utilised an index of payroll and materials costs developed by the US Department of Commerce – the O/S index. As total shipments are equal to material costs plus payroll value-added, one minus the O/S index will give non-payroll value-added, which is used as a proxy for the residual variables listed above. Unlike the other three variables, therefore, the O/S index would be negatively related to measures of export performance.

Table 5.10 Spearman and linear correlation coefficients between product cycle variables and indices of export performance

	1958 (Spearman)		1960 (Spearman)		1960 (linear)		1965 (Spearman)		1965 (linear)		1966 (Spearman)	
	X_1	X_2	X_1	X_2	X_1	X_2	X_1	X_2	X_1	X_2	X_1	X_2
S&E	0.552**	0.605**	0.537**	0.613**	0.627**	0.619**	0.492*	0.602**	0.533**	0.573**	0.433**	0.531*
VA	0.657**	0.695**	0.632**	0.705**	0.473**	0.543**	0.559**	0.656**	0.396	0.577**	0.556**	0.635**
L–C	0.194	0.298	0.215	0.283	0.181	0.186	0.298	0.356	0.250	0.298	0.286	0.369
O/S				−0.588**				−0.533**	−0.380	−0.554**		−0.613**

*Significant at the 0.05 level.
**Significant at the 0.01 level.
Source: Morrall (1972).

Morrall's (1972) correlation analyses are summarised in Table 5.10. The results show clearly that the product cycle variables relate to the export performance indicators in the expected way. When he compared the Spearman coefficients and the standard (referred to as 'linear' by Morrall) correlation coefficients, he was surprised to find that there was a reversal in the relative size of the S&E and VA correlation coefficients between these two tests. In the Spearman rank correlation, the VA coefficients were larger than the S&E coefficients while the opposite was the case in the linear case. This, he suggested, could arise because the relationships between the variables were non-linear, contrary to standard assumptions. Nevertheless, Morrall accepted the 1965 linear evidence that the rate of growth of industry, as proxied by the VA variable, was a better indicator of export performance than the percentage of scientists and engineers engaged in R&D.

The L–C variable, despite having the correct sign in all the cases in which it was included, did not appear to be significant. Morrall felt that the positive correlations still provided some evidence to indicate that the US had an advantage in industries using labour-saving technology.

Finally the somewhat catch-all variable, O/S, performed as expected and was significant in all but one case. This suggests that the items captured by it were related to export performance and consistent with the product cycle model.

Morrall also regressed X_2 – exports minus imports as a percentage of total industry shipments – against various combinations of the same four variables for 1965. The results are presented in Table 5.11.

Interestingly, the equation with the best fit (in terms of having the smallest standard error) was not the model which included all four independent variables – equation (1) – but equation (2). Equation (2) excludes VA, which was not significant in equation (1). From his examination of the remaining equations, Morrall concluded that there was probably a high degree of multicollinearity between S&E and VA. This multicollinearity was bound to arise, Morrall suggested, because of the feedback between rapid growth and research and development effort. As the preferred variable, he chose VA over S&E because it was available at a more disaggregated level and for a greater number of years. Both the L–C and O/S variables had the correct signs and were significant in the equations in which they appeared. The significance of the L–C variable gave further support to Morrall's proposition that the US had a comparative advantage in labour-saving capital goods industries.

In summary, Morrall's (1972) results suggested that at least three factors influenced US export performance: VA, L–C and O/S. As a result, the US enjoyed a comparative advantage in both new consumer and capital goods, a conclusion that appeared to support the hypotheses of the product cycle model.

Other country–industry studies which offer support for the product cycle hypothesis, though using less formal methodology, can be found in Wells (1972). For example, Tsurumi's (1972) paper dealing with R&D factors found a distinct product cycle in the pattern of Japan's exports. In his study he attempted

Table 5.11 Regression results for the product cycle model, 1965

Equation	Dependent variable	Intercept	S&E	VA	L–C	O/S	$\bar{R}^2$	$\bar{S}$	F
1	Exports–imports as percentage of total Industry shipments (X_2)	12.79	0.8845 (0.5766) 0.15	0.005694 (0.008941) 7.25	23.59 (15.22) 0.10	−19.76 (12.36) 0.10	0.740	2.83	4.54 0.05
2	X_2	16.23	1.169 (0.4979) 0.025		23.84 (14.93) 0.10	−22.45 (11.40) 0.05	0.732	2.78	6.15 0.01
3	X_2	−3.704	0.9388 (0.7082) 0.15	0.01058 (0.008809) 0.15	25.75 (15.90) 0.10		0.686	2.97	4.75 0.05
4	X_2	17.59	1.125 (0.5193)			−24.31 (11.85) 0.05	0.680	2.90	7.29 0.01
5	X_2	−5.238		−0.01903 (0.006213) 0.005	24.61 (16.22) 0.10		0.643	3.03	5.98 0.05
6	X_2	−1.192	1.554 (0.4951) 0.005		26.88 (16.08) 0.10		0.650	3.01	6.24 0.01

$\bar{S}$, Standard error of the estimate
The numbers in parenthesis below the regression coefficients are standard errors. The number below the standard errors and the F-statistic are levels of significance.
Source: Morrall (1972).

to distinguish between distinctively new products and processes and those which were old or owed their production in Japan to licensing agreements with foreign firms. Using this method of classifying industries, he was able to establish the rate at which new products and processes came on stream – which he termed the 'renovations rate'. Relating the export profile of Japanese manufacturing to the renovations rate for 1966 gave a Spearman rank correlation coefficient and a simple logarithmic correlation of +0.550 and +0.502, respectively. As both of these were significant at the 5 per cent level, Tsurumi suggested that the product cycle hypothesis appeared to be confirmed. He did ascribe some importance to other variables, such as the growth of the home market, protection from overseas competition and a competitive domestic environment, although he did not attempt to quantify their importance.

The empirical evidence on the product cycle appears to give it considerable validity despite the fact that the evidence draws largely on the US experience. Two studies do, however, caution against accepting the theory's predictions without qualification. The first, a study by Mansfield, Romeo and Wagner (1979), began by attempting to discern the effect of foreign trade on research and development in the US. In a later section of their study, however, they analysed the responses of twenty-three firms to questions inquiring how they channelled their international transfers of technology. The questions focused on transfers initiated in the first five years after commercialisation. Their results for 1974, which appear in Table 5.12, show clearly that the most frequently used method of technological transfer was via a foreign-owned subsidiary. This was followed, in order, by exports, licensing and joint ventures. The preponderance of the foreign subsidiary channel during the first five years is noteworthy because it is contrary to the premise on which the product cycle hypothesis is built. Central to the hypothesis was the proposition that only after an overseas

Table 5.12 Percentage distribution of R&D projects by expected channel of technological transfer

| Category | Channel of technological transfer | | | |
	Foreign subsidiary	Exports	Licensing	Joint venture
All R&D projects				
16 industrial firms	85	9	5	0
7 major chemical firms	62	21	12	5
Projects aimed at[a]				
Entirely new product	72	4	24	0
Product improvement	69	9	23	0
Entirely new process	17	83	0	0
Process improvement	45	53	2	1

a Only six chemical firms could be included.
Source: Mansfield, Romeo and Wagner (1979).

market had been established via direct exports would technology be transferred overseas via foreign subsidiaries.

The results presented in Table 5.12 also suggested that product innovations are more likely to be transferred abroad via foreign subsidiaries than process innovations – process information is more likely to be transferred via exports than via product innovations. Mansfield and his co-authors suggested that the unwillingness of firms to have technology transferred to independent firms in countries where it can be imitated and produced at lower cost could account for these differences in the preferred transfer mechanism.

The conclusion that one draws from the work of Mansfield, Romeo and Wagner (1979) is that the influence of product innovation in determining the pattern of trade in goods may have been exaggerated. As long as the innovator can maintain a flow of improvements to his processes, the transfer of technology abroad can be postponed. This dynamic aspect of innovation will, as a result, inhibit the expected shift in the source of exports and prevent the product cycle model from being fulfilled.

A second critical paper by Dunning and Buckley (1977) lends support to the observations of Mansfield, Romeo and Wagner. They attempted to discover the relative importance of a country's location-specific endowments and industry-ownership characteristics in determining trade flows. Their proposition was that the existence of multinational companies weakens the Ricardian and neoclassical assumption of factor immobility. A transnational institutional structure for firms means that technology can be freely transferred from the centre to subsidiaries. Thus, a country's comparative advantage can be affected when technology is transferred between countries but within the same company. For example, the US might have an advantage in the production of knowledge, but if this information was transferred to other countries within the company structure of US multi-nationals, what would normally be classed as a locational advantage would become an ownership advantage. In other words, they argued, product cycle theories would be less successful in explaining trade patterns when international production (i.e. technology transfer) is a profitable alternative to exporting goods directly from the home country.

To test their proposition, Dunning and Buckley compared the influence of industry characteristics on the production and export performance of US subsidiaries operating in the UK. Their first measure was the value of production of subsidiaries as a proportion of the value of production of indigenous firms. The value of exports generated by subsidiaries as a proportion of the value of exports generated by indigenous firms was their second measure. The industry characteristics employed were: research intensity, measured by the difference between the percentage of an industry's sales that can be accounted for by R&D activity in the US and the UK ($R_{US} - R_{UK}$) and the ratio of these two percentages (R_{US}/R_{UK}); human capital, as represented by the proportion of skilled to unskilled labour; and a scale economies variable derived from US data on plant sizes by industry.

The results, presented in Table 5.13, show the extent to which the industry characteristics are correlated with the share of US subsidiaries' production in UK industrial output. What they show is that both R&D and human skills are positively and significantly correlated with US involvement in UK industry. The scale variable was positively correlated but not significant.

These industry characteristics were also correlated with the share of US subsidiaries' exports in total UK exports. As total exports were made up of the exports of indigenous UK firms plus those of the US subsidiaries, both the location- and the ownership-specific effects were combined. By deducting the US subsidiaries' exports from total exports but taking them as a proportion of the net figure, the influence of location was removed. Taken together, these results show that R&D was better at explaining the pattern of international production than that of trade, while the existence of technology-intensive international firms weakened the explanatory power of theories based only on location-specific factors.

Vernon (1979) reached the same conclusion almost simultaneously. Aware that the growth of multinationals had transformed the rate at which production could be moved abroad, he hypothesised that the growing similarity of advanced countries' economies would also weaken the ability of the product cycle theory to predict trade patterns. Vernon drew on factual evidence to support his view. Examining the behaviour of 180 US multinationals prior to 1946, he found that when planning their overseas operations for new products the probability of setting up a plant first in Canada was 79 per cent higher than it was in Asia. After 1960 the same probability had fallen to 59 per cent. The geographic dispersion of subsidiaries also increased between 1950 and 1975. At the beginning of the period only forty-three of the 180 leading US companies had subsidiaries in more than six but not more than twenty countries. By the end of

Table 5.13 Spearman rank correlation between selected industry characteristics and production and exports generated by US subsidiaries in the UK

Independent variable	$R_{US} - R_{UK}$	R_{US}/R_{UK}	Skill intensity	Scale elasticity
US/UK production				
17 industries (1970)	0.551*	0.718*	0.524*	0.036
16 industries (1970)	0.754***	0.776***	0.755**	0.032
US/UK exports				
17 industries (1970)	0.615**	0.328	0.697**	0.535*
17 industries (1962)	0.42*	0.11	0.56*	0.59*
16 industries (1970)	0.607**	0.474*	0.684**	0.440*

*Significant at 5%.
**Significant at 1%.
***Significant at 0.1%.
Source: Dunning and Buckley (1977).

the period, 128 companies were in this category, while forty-four had subsidiaries in over twenty countries.

Data on the time elapsed between the introduction of products in the US and their first overseas production via subsidiaries showed that whereas, between 1946 and 1950, only 8.1 per cent of new products were produced by subsidiaries abroad, this figure had grown to 35.4 per cent by 1971–75. Companies that had experience in transferring production to foreign subsidiaries were also found to be quicker in setting up production abroad than those that did not.

Vernon (1979) validated his second proposition – the convergence of advanced countries' economies – by examining trends in per capita income. From having per capita incomes of approximately one-third of those in the US in 1949, France and Germany were nearing equality with the US by 1970. Per capita income in Japan increased from 6 per cent of the US level to almost 70 per cent over the same period. He also felt that market size was important. In particular, the expansion of the European Economic Community had led to a community market that rivalled the size of the US market.

According to Vernon, the growth of multinationals and the convergence of the advanced economies in terms of per capita income and market size meant that innovating firms were no longer ignorant of foreign conditions. It could no longer be assumed that US firms faced a home business environment different from that of European and Japanese firms. Hence, with some of the main assumptions of the product cycle in doubt, Vernon had to reassess the relevance of the theory he had helped to develop. He began by accepting that the relevance of the product cycle theory for explaining trade patterns between advanced countries dominated by large multinationals was now minimal. There were, however, several reasons for not dismissing the product cycle theory entirely.

First, even large multinationals that were closely in tune with the characteristics of many countries might not be able to identify the best locations for plants when the product or process was still in its early stage of development. Second, smaller innovating firms might not have acquired the global view of the larger multinationals, so for them the product cycle hypothesis would still apply.

Third, the innovative activity of European and Japanese firms could be concentrated in different product areas than those of US firms. In contrast to the latter, their efforts would be concentrated in capital-saving and natural resource-saving activities. This hypothesis was based on the relative scarcity of these factors. Vernon (1979) speculated that, as the price of capital and natural resources rose, world demand for European and Japanese innovations would rise while demand for those of the US would decline. He noted that the increased exports of Japanese and European cars and steel were in agreement with product cycle theory predictions. The theory also predicted that their advantage would be short-lived as US firms responded to the competitive threat with their own innovations. General Motors' global car strategy was cited as evidence supporting these conclusions.

Fourth, although multinationals had established subsidiaries in both advanced and developing countries, subsidiaries in the latter rarely manufactured the same range of products as those in the advanced countries. Most developing countries were, therefore, still in the process of absorbing the products and innovations that had been produced earlier in other countries. Again, this pattern of technological diffusion was consistent with the product cycle.

Fifth, firms operating in the more rapidly industrialising developing countries invented and promoted their own range of products in response to their own special conditions. These products could subsequently be adapted and exported to other developing countries that lagged behind them in innovative ability. Vernon (1979) was thus led to conclude that, although weakened, the product cycle still possessed a high degree of explanatory power.

Giddy (1978), however, was more damning in his conclusions regarding the product cycle, reserving for it the role of a special case in a theory of trade that was anchored in industrial organisation. He surmised that the product cycle theory could not explain the behaviour of some multinationals, such as raw materials producers, nor could it account for direct investment as opposed to licensing agreements. This particular industrial organisation approach to international commercial relations is based on the benefits arising from the internalisation of factor markets and barriers to entry.

According to Giddy (1978), whether a firm sets up a subsidiary or enters into licensing agreements with overseas producers depends on which approach is expected to give it the greatest benefit. In the international context, he suggested that geographical distance between countries, cultural information and economic differences as well as regulations and political uncertainties give rise to serious market imperfections that raise the costs of undertaking international transactions. Thus, whenever a firm wants to exert effective control over foreign production, extraction, transportation or marketing, direct investment would be the preferred method of overseas production. These reasons, Giddy suggested, could explain the behaviour of both resource-based multinationals and those specialising in R&D-intensive products.

Whereas the product cycle hypothesis suggests that changing barriers to entry encourages firms to invest directly abroad, the industrial organisation approach argues that all forms of direct investment are the result of firms trying to extend abroad their domestic barriers to entry into factor and product markets.

Innovation-based oligopolies, which are characterised by high R&D expenditure or a high ratio of specialists to total employees, create barriers to entry through the continuous introduction of new products and/or a high degree of differentiation in existing products. Their products are not necessarily designed for high-income markets but are ones that cater to a range of domestic requirements as well as those found in other countries. Firms in this category appear to behave in a fashion consistent with the predictions of the product cycle theory but have a different motivation. For example, research and development will take place near the company head office and the firm's leading market. Production is transferred abroad to maintain a firm's competitive advantages.

Mature oligopolies, on the other hand, adopt a different strategy. Concentrating either on fairly standard products – such as automobiles or pulp and paper – or resource-based oil, aluminium, copper or nickel production, they depend on high fixed costs to provide barriers to entry. The corollary, however, is that they exhibit elastic marginal costs which can have a destabilising effect when demand slackens. The tactics of firms in mature oligopolies include follow-the-leader behaviour in entering new countries or product lines. In addition, they practise mutual hostage and alliance policies. The former is indicated by toleration for competitors' subsidiaries in their own territory when reciprocal agreements exist, and the latter by the establishment of multi-firm, joint-product subsidiaries. Firms in mature oligopolies may also use pricing conventions whereby, for example, they do not compete on price in order to maintain market share. The major element determining the strategy of mature oligopolies, however, is the benefits arising from reducing costs, be it through standard economies of scale or those of a more dynamic nature outlined above. According to Giddy (1978), as long as profits can be increased, or losses minimised, mature oligopolies will follow strategies similar to those just described.

The consequence of strategies to internalise markets and maintain barriers to entry is that firms will set up foreign subsidiaries and supply their home and third markets much more rapidly than is suggested by the product cycle. Thus, the transfer of production rather than goods will occur far sooner than was previously thought possible and will, moreover, be the norm. Trade patterns will then be less influenced by the product cycle except in the special case where innovative oligopolies exist. As this type of oligopoly represents only a small proportion of the total business community, its effect on overall trade patterns will be limited.

Recent empirical work on the product cycle has tended to concentrate on trade relations between developed and developing countries, where the theory is still expected to have considerable explanatory power. The emphasis, however, has shifted away from its explanatory potential for trade patterns to the effects of the cycle on economic development and the distribution of income among countries (see for example Helpman, 1993).

Notwithstanding the empirical evidence in its favour, there does appear to be a body of evidence of both an empirical and a theoretical nature that tends to downgrade the importance of the product cycle hypothesis in explaining trade patterns. Whether the product cycle has reached a mature phase in the cycle of trade theories is, however, a subject that requires a more formal discussion of the role of models in international trade. This issue will be examined in the final chapter. In the meantime, we turn to the empirical evidence pertaining to Linder's (1961) explanation of trade patterns based on similarities in demand.

5.4 Tests of theories based on similarities in demand

Linder's (1961) hypothesis that countries with similar income levels would tend to trade more intensively with one another has been subjected to a number of empirical investigations. In his book, Linder calculated an average propensity to import (APM) for each country by expressing its imports from a trading partner as a proportion of GNP. He then correlated the APMs with income similarity and found a positive relationship. In reviewing Linder's book, Johnson (1964) argued that the observed positive correlation was really due to the geographical proximity of trading partners. Countries with similar income levels tended to be grouped in geographical proximity to one another. Proximity also meant that countries tended to trade more easily with one another; hence the correlation between APMs and income similarity. A number of economists set out to resolve these issues empirically.

Fortune (1971) undertook an econometric study based on the 1967 trade flows between twenty-three countries. He regressed the average propensity to import the manufactured goods of country j into country i against the differences between the countries' per capita incomes and a distance variable based on the mileage between the principal cities of the trading partners.

The cross-national regressions took the following form:

$$\text{AMP} = a + b \left(\frac{Y_j}{N_j} - \frac{Y_i}{N_i} \right) + c D_{ij}$$

where Y_i is country i's GNP, Y_j is country j's GNP, N_i is country i's population, N_j is country j's population, D_{ij} is the physical distance between the trading partners' closest principal cities, and

$$\text{AMP} = \frac{M_{ij}}{Y_i}$$

where M_{ij} is the value of country i's imports of finished manufactured goods from country j.

Fortune's hypothesis was that the greater the difference between the per capita GNP of the exporting and importing countries, the smaller would be the APM. For countries with similar per capita GNPs the APM would be larger. This implied that the b coefficient would have a negative sign. In addition, he expected that the greater the distance between countries, the smaller would be the average APM and, hence, the c coefficient would also be negative. The reason for this negative relationship is that distance is expected to impose increased transport costs and reduce entrepreneurs' awareness of market opportunities in other countries.

A summary of Fortune's (1971) results is presented in Table 5.14. It is obvious, given the low coefficients of determination, that some important explanatory factors were omitted. He suggested that the omitted variable(s) could relate to tariffs, exchange restrictions and political factors such as customs unions. As his purpose was to determine whether the two variables tested contributed to trade and was not to provide a complete analysis of the determinants of bilateral trade, he did not place a great deal of emphasis on the low explanatory power of his estimating equation.

The difference in per capita income was a significant explanatory variable (at the 5 per cent level) for nine countries. In seven of these cases the variable possessed the expected negative sign. The distance variable was also significant in eleven of the twenty-three regressions. When the level of significance was reduced to 10 per cent, distance was significant in seventeen equations.

Table 5.14 Regressions of average propensity to import against difference in per capita income and distance

Exporting country	Differences in per capita income	Distance	R^2	F
United States	9.82 (0.36)	−21.95 (1.87)	0.07	1.86
Sweden	−24.66 (2.17)	−5.73 (1.56)	0.18	5.05
Canada	−1.25 (0.85)	−0.41 (1.12)	0.03	0.77
Switzerland	−5.21 (2.45)	−1.12 (1.89)	0.18	5.16
Denmark	−11.34 (2.32)	−2.13 (1.49)	0.19	5.35
Australia	−5.54 (2.68)	−3.24 (4.93)	0.36	13.48
France	22.00 (1.07)	−14.38 (2.94)	0.14	3.81
New Zealand	−0.18 (2.81)	−0.10 (5.20)	0.38	14.55
Norway	−3.83 (0.86)	−1.79 (1.53)	0.08	2.12
West Germany	−65.75 (2.91)	−21.57 (3.86)	0.41	16.32
Belgium–Luxemburg	−14.20 (1.56)	−2.13 (0.98)	0.09	2.31
United Kingdom	−19.89 (0.62)	−1.37 (0.18)	0.01	0.26
Finland	−1.48 (1.33)	−0.44 (1.71)	0.13	3.36
Netherlands	−14.82 (2.14)	−3.00 (2.33)	0.23	6.85
Austria	0.07 (0.03)	−1.25 (3.41)	0.20	5.96
Italy	−18.23 (1.46)	−5.04 (2.79)	0.17	4.92
Japan	−16.60 (0.67)	−17.35 (3.27)	0.19	5.36
Greece	−0.87 (1.40)	−0.20 (1.40)	0.07	1.76
Portugal	0.42 (2.68)	−0.05 (1.08)	0.17	4.87
Colombia	−0.23 (1.51)	−0.16 (2.82)	0.16	4.55
Brazil	−0.25 (0.93)	−0.46 (4.42)	0.31	10.69
Taiwan	−0.23 (0.60)	−0.33 (2.37)	0.11	2.92
Korea	0.36 (3.70)	−0.04 (1.07)	0.25	7.75

t-values in parenthesis.
$t = 1.96$ significant at 5% level.
$t = 1.67$ significant at 10% level.
$F = 2.80$ significant at 5% level.
Source: Fortune (1971).

Fortune's results, however, warrant further comment. For example, income similarity had very little effect on US trade and physical distance was only significant at the 10 per cent level. He suggested that tied aid and other politically motivated distortions of trade patterns could explain the US case. Some countries that were members of the (British) Commonwealth exhibited considerable differences in per capita income and a high degree of geographical dispersion as well as high APMs. Extra-economic ties such as cultural similarity and long-established trade links might account for this anomaly. A similar explanation was put forward for France. Fortune noted that France traded heavily with its Common Market neighbours and, as a result, the distance variable proved to be significant. France's heavy involvement with its ex-colonies, however, probably prevented the per capita income variable from becoming an important factor in its trade. In West Germany, Sweden, Italy and the Netherlands political factors did not appear to play an important role and trade seemed to be influenced more directly by income and distance. Distance was considered important in explaining Japan's trade with its Asian partners. The importance of both income and distance in the regressions for Australia and New Zealand was put down to the high degree of bilateral trade between them. Income levels were similar and the two countries were in relatively close proximity to one another.

Fortune (1971) concluded that the distance factor was an important force in limiting trading activities and was, for many countries, a more powerful influence than the trade-creating influence of income similarity. Nevertheless, he believed that his results gave some support to Linder's (1961) hypothesis, although, where per capita income variables were significant, the low coefficients of determination suggested that other factors were also likely to be important in determining trade patterns. As a result, Fortune ascribed a supplementary role to the similar demands hypothesis rather than suggesting that it was an alternative to other trade theories.

Sailors, Qureshi and Cross (1973) tested the relationship between per capital income and bilateral trade intensity using a different approach. Arguing that the data employed by Fortune (1971) were not sufficiently precise to use regression analysis because both GNP and population data were subject to errors of up to 20 per cent, they chose instead rank correlation techniques. The authors based their work on 1958 data for thirty-one countries and provided correlations of ranked income differences and import propensities. In other words, each correlation matched one country and its relationships with its trading partners. Taking the illustrative example of Sweden, their procedures involved calculating the income difference between Sweden and all the countries with which it was trading. These differences were then ranked. In a similar way, the propensities to import from Sweden were also calculated and ranked, and the two rankings were then correlated. The results of these calculations are presented in Table 5.15. The left-hand column shows that sixteen of the correlations were significant at the 5 per cent level. Correlations were also calculated for a sub-sample of twenty-five countries. Six countries were excluded that either relied heavily on non-transportable natural-resource inputs (Finland, Chile and South Africa) or whose manufactures were a small proportion of total exports (Brazil, Ghana and Greece). These correlations are presented in the right-hand column of the table and show that fourteen of these twenty-five correlations were significant at the 5 per cent level and six at the 1 per cent level.

Table 5.15 Rank correlations between trade in manufactures and differences in income

Country	Rank correlation	
	31 nations	25 nations
United States	−0.01	−0.00
Canada	−0.36*	−0.35*
New Zealand	−0.33*	−0.37*
Switzerland	−0.35*	−0.29
Australia	−0.24	−0.18
Sweden	−0.54**	−0.50**
France	−0.36*	−0.42*
Belgium–Luxemburg	−0.48**	−0.56**
United Kingdom	−0.23	−0.43*
Norway	−0.53**	−0.69**
Finland	−0.59**	ni
Denmark	−0.60**	−0.63**
West Germany	−0.60**	−0.67**
Netherlands	−0.50**	−0.68**
Israel	+0.13	+0.06
Austria	−0.34*	−0.38*
Italy	−0.35*	−0.44*
Union of South Africa	+0.05	ni
Argentina	−0.32*	−0.29
Brazil	−0.19	ni
Japan	−0.24	−0.05
Greece	−0.02	ni
Portugal	+0.01	+0.13
Mexico	−0.09	−0.12
Chile	−0.11	ni
Ghana	+0.06	ni
Tunisia	−0.39*	−0.47*
United Arab Republic	−0.13	−0.23
Thailand	−0.15	−0.12
India	−0.22	−0.23
Pakistan	−0.35*	−0.40*

ni, not included.
*Significant at the 0.05 level.
**Significant at the 0.01 level.
Source: Sailors, Qureshi and Cross (1973).

Commenting on their results, Sailors, Qureshi and Cross suggested that those results which were not significant could be explained by fundamental economic changes taking place in the countries concerned. For example Greece, Ghana and South Africa were, during this period, experiencing substantial changes in their economic relationships with their trading partners. Greece was in the process of joining the European Economic Community as an associate member, Ghana was gaining independence and South Africa was breaking its links with the Commonwealth. The reason put forward to explain the poor correlation of Portugal and Israel was that, given their general underdevelopment, these countries were slower than others in reallocating resources. Similar arguments applied to Greece, Ghana and South Africa. According to the authors, in the dynamic world of international commerce technological advances caused relative prices to change continually, which in turn had an impact on trading opportunities. To avail themselves of such opportunities, countries would not only have to respond to these changes but would have to do so quickly. In countries whose markets were either underdeveloped or characterised by rigidities, swift changes could not be expected and statistical outcomes contrary to theoretical expectations could result.

The authors suggested a number of ideas to account for the failure of the United States to conform with Linder's (1961) thesis. First, the year on which the correlations were based could have had a major effect. Currency convertibility had returned to the major European economies, the European Economic Community was reducing intra-European trade barriers and the closure of the Suez Canal had all had an impact on world trading relationships by 1958. Second, the structural transformation of the western European and Japanese economies – caused by their absorption of US technology combined with the interventionist policies of their governments – was having a major influence on their trade with the US.

On balance, Sailors, Qureshi and Cross (1973) believed that their empirical evidence lent support to Linder's (1961) thesis that trade in manufactures would be more intensive when the internal demand structures of countries were similar. They emphasised, nevertheless, that other factors such as exchange restrictions, tariff barriers, transport costs and the distance from markets also had a role to play in explaining trade patterns.

In a critical comment on their work, Hoftyzer (1975) expressed scepticism about the conclusions they had reached. He felt that their failure to include a distance variable was a serious omission and was unconvinced by the justifications advanced by the authors for those results which were most in line with *a priori* expectations.

Hoftyzer felt that physical distance acted as a proxy for both transport costs and market information. Thus, the shorter the distance between two countries, the more intensive trade would be between them. The only justification he could accept for ignoring the distance variable was if rich and poor countries were distributed uniformly over the earth's surface. As this was not the case, the distance variable should not have been ignored. In his view it was no accident that the best results were obtained for European countries, which were not only rich but were also in geographical proximity to one another.

Hoftyzer (1975) tested for the influence of distance by undertaking a multiple regression analysis for West Germany and Denmark – the two countries with the highest Spearman rank correlation in the study by Sailors, Qureshi and Cross. Distance was measured by taking the nautical mileage between the country's major port and those of its partners. Landlocked trading partners were dealt with by using the land distance between their main city and the nearest important port.

When the model was respecified the income variable was no longer significant at the 5 per cent level. This occurred in both the West German and Danish cases. In contrast, the distance variable was significant at the 5 per cent level for West Germany and at the 1 per cent level for Denmark. In both regressions there was a high degree of multicollinearity between the income and the distance variables.

To forestall the possible objection that the inclusion of distance undermined the true contribution of per capita incomes, Hoftyzer also estimated his model for the United States, where the income variable performed poorly. Once again, the distance variable performed well, and he concluded that very little of the explanatory power attributed to distance actually belonged to the income variable.

From his results, Hoftyzer concluded that the favourable results derived by Sailors, Qureshi and Cross were due more to geographical proximity than similarity of income. This view was strengthened further, he argued, if one considered that Canada and New Zealand were closely associated with Europe on the basis of culture and historical economic linkages. He questioned the authors' favourable results for Argentina, Tunisia and Pakistan because the data used for these countries had consisted of both manufactured and non-manufactured exports when only the former should have been included.

Hoftyzer's second criticism was that the economic and political reasons suggested by Sailors, Qureshi and Cross to explain their unfavourable results could also have been used to support the favourable outcomes. For example, the establishment of the European Economic Community had been advanced by the authors to account for the heavy propensity to import among its member countries. Hoftyzer suggested that Portugal's results could also be explained by its proximity to the wealthy economies of Western Europe. On the one hand, proximity would lead to Portugal importing heavily from those countries, while, on the other hand, its relative poverty would prevent close trade ties.

Reworking their results, but using 1955 data for nineteen countries and 1970 data for sixty countries, Hoftyzer (1975) attempted to question the conclusions relating to the United States. Once again, however, the Spearman rank correlation coefficients were insignificant. Unless one accepted that these two years were also unrepresentative, it was clear that Linder's (1961) hypothesis did not apply to the US.

In summary, Hoftyzer (1975) was sceptical of the conclusions reached by Sailors, Qureshi and Cross (1973) for the following reasons. First, they ignored distance, which appeared to explain the majority of the results obtained. Second, they used a data set that was too aggregated. Finally, he found their explanations for the inconsistent results weak.

Needless to say, in their reply to Hoftyzer's (1975) comments, Sailors, Qureshi and Cross (1975) disagreed with him on all three points. The second criticism was met by stating that they were testing Linder's proposal and so use of his data set, although highly aggregated, was consistent with this aim. The third objection was questioned on the grounds that their results could not be dismissed because alternative explanations were found to account for the inconsistent results. They felt that the important question was whether the inconsistent results were so great as to damage their findings and render their conclusions unacceptable.

However, they considered Hoftyzer's first argument to be a more substantive criticism and dealt with it in greater depth. The results he had presented for the United Sates were, they suggested, questionable because both regression and correlation have difficulty in dealing with the extremes in large data sets and truncated data. As the US per capita income was the highest in the study – 50 per cent higher than its nearest rival, Canada, and fifty times higher than that of Pakistan – the results were only to be expected.

Sailors, Qureshi and Cross disagreed with two of Hoftyzer's arguments concerning Denmark and Germany. The first, relating to the magnitude of the regression coefficient and the statistical significance of the distance variable, was discounted on the grounds that, in small data sets, these can be influenced greatly by the inclusion of extra variables. As for Hoftyzer's point that the inclusion of the distance variable reduced the significance of the partial correlation coefficient for income, they claimed that this was only to be expected when an extra variable is included in a regression. Hoftyzer was, moreover, comparing the first-order coefficient for the distance variable with the partial coefficient for the income variable – an incorrect comparison.

In defending their results and approach, Sailors, Qureshi and Cross (1975) put forward two further arguments to refute Hoftyzer's (1975) views. The first was that even if one accepted his results for the US, Denmark and West Germany, these cases would not be enough, on statistical grounds, to warrant a change in the general conclusions of their study. Second, they suggested that if there was a positive correlation between geographical proximity and income per head, it was just as likely that income per capita was the operative variable as distance. This was corroborated by the statistical evidence showing that income was a useful predictor in many cases but that distance was important in only a few cases. Hence, Sailors and his colleagues felt that the case in favour of the distance variable had not been proved.

In an effort to overcome the shortcomings of both the Sailors, Qureshi and Cross (1973) and Hoftyzer (1975) studies, Greytak and McHugh (1977) proposed a different approach. In contrast to the previous studies, their data set included only manufactured goods. An even more novel departure was the focus on trade between seven regions within the US as opposed to inter-country trade. The reason behind their use of this line of enquiry was that the distance would be more likely to reflect trade-retarding forces such as transport costs because trade patterns would not be influenced by artificial barriers such as tariffs. As the social, political and cultural background is less likely to vary within a country than between countries, their use of regional data would mitigate the effect of these factors.

Spearman rank correlation tests on data for 1963 showed that the income variables had the correct sign in five out of the seven cases, but in only three were they significant and then only at the 0.10 level. This was in stark contrast to the apparently strong results of Sailors, Qureshi and Cross (1973). For the distance variable a different picture emerged: all correlation coefficients were positive and significant.

As Spearman rank tests are of the *mutatis mutandis* variety and not the more appropriate *ceteris paribus* type, two analyses using Kendall partial rank correlation coefficients were performed. Greytak and McHugh's first analysis attempted to quantify the influence of the income variable by keeping the distance factor constant. Their second analysis tried to isolate the effect of distance by keeping the income variable constant. The results of these tests were not favourable to the income variable, with only two correlation coefficients above 0.50. In contrast, the distance variable performed well, exceeding 0.50 in five cases and 0.70 in three. This confirmed the simple correlation analysis, which indicated that distance rather than per capita income was an important influence on trade patterns. How much weight one attributes to Greytak and McHugh's (1977) findings depends on whether one accepts their use of inter-regional data to test international trade theory.

As empirical investigations had tended to concentrate on data for a single period, but with mixed results, a number of researchers tried to circumvent the difficulties caused by the correlation between income differences and distance by formulating time-series tests. Conceptually, the purpose was to see if changes in income similarity through time could account for changes in trade intensity. The studies by Ahmad and Simos (1979) and Kennedy and McHugh (1983) are representative of this approach to testing Linder's (1961) theory.

Ahmad and Simos's (1979) study, apart from using regression analysis and time-series data, differed from the previous studies by taking the ratio of countries' per capita incomes as a measure of similarity. They examined the bilateral trade of the US with twenty-one OECD countries both at an aggregate level of manufactures and in the case of four sub-groups of manufacturing industries. These sub-groups were chemicals, manufactures classified by material, machinery and transport equipment and miscellaneous manufacturers. Another departure from previous studies was their use of trade volumes instead of the average propensity to import (AMP) as a measure of trade intensity. Originally, Linder (1961) had used APM to control the effect of a country's size on trade volumes when using cross-section data. Time-series data removed this difficulty and allowed the use of actual trade volumes.

The relationship Ahmad and Simos tested was

$$X_{ij}^s E = F\left[\left(\frac{y_j}{y_i}\right) t, \, u_c\right]$$

where X_{ij} is the export volume from country i to country j, s is an index of the type of export (i.e. chemicals etc.), t is time, y_i is per capita income of the ith exporting country, y_j is per capita income of the jth importing country and u_c is a random disturbance term.

The relationship was expressed in logarithmic form so that Linder's (1961) hypothesis – that there is an exponential relationship between X_{ij} and y_j/y_i – could be taken more explicitly into account. The implication of this postulated relationship is that as y_j and y_i become closer, X_{ij} should rise more rapidly than the ratio itself because the import capacity of the jth country would rise as a result of the improvement in per capita income. The income ratio coefficient, thus, becomes the constant elasticity of exports from country i to country j with respect to the ratio of their per capita incomes.

Ahmad and Simos' (1979) results for aggregated bilateral trade are given in Table 5.16. For eighteen out of twenty-one countries the coefficient for per capita income has the expected positive sign, and in sixteen cases it is significant at the 5 per cent level. In only one case, the UK – where the estimated slope has the wrong sign – is the coefficient significant.

Further support for the Linder (1961) hypothesis came from an examination of the magnitude of the income coefficients. Linder had suggested that the closer any two countries' per capita incomes were, the more intensive would be their trade. The coefficients were, as expected, higher for the developed countries in Ahmad and Simos's sample – e.g. Belgium, Denmark, France and Germany – than for the less developed countries such as Greece, Portugal, Spain and Turkey.

Other favourable results came from the regressions on machinery and transport equipment and miscellaneous manufactures. Here, for all countries except New Zealand, Switzerland and the UK, the income coefficient had the correct slope and the values were statistically significant. In the case of chemicals and manufactures classified by material, however, only twelve countries showed significant results in the former industry and only ten in the latter. Ahmad and Simos's explanation for these somewhat poorer findings was that the capital-intensive nature of these industries made them more susceptible to the effects of factor proportions on trade, as suggested by the Heckscher–Ohlin model.

Table 5.16 Regressions of US manufacturing exports on the ratio of per capita income of OECD countries, 1960–75

Country	Intercept	Income ratio	R^2	F	SEE
Canada	10.802 (31.28)*	9.230 (6.06)*	0.724	36.71	0.248
Japan	8.887 (26.14)*	1.475 (5.00)*	0.642	25.05	0.290
Australia	9.099 (4.87)*	4.472 (1.38)	0.121	1.92	0.377
New Zealand	0.906 (0.50)	−4.879 −(2.06)	0.232	4.24	0.410
Austria	7.664 (14.16)*	3.963 (7.02)*	0.778	49.29	0.181
Belgium	9.718 (20.51)*	5.306 (7.18)*	0.786	51.49	0.214
Denmark	7.554 (10.66)*	6.221 (4.09)*	0.545	16.79	0.249
Finland	6.745 (18.81)*	3.138 (7.33)*	0.793	53.82	0.160
France	9.473 (24.00)*	4.561 (6.95)*	0.775	48.37	0.192
Germany	10.450 (14.78)*	6.844 (4.82)*	0.624	23.28	0.251
Greece	7.879 (17.24)*	2.129 (7.34)*	0.793	53.88	0.196
Ireland	15.905 (3.78)*	9.012 (2.85)*	0.367	8.1	0.540
Italy	11.700 (27.74)*	4.748 (12.44)*	0.917	154.87	0.087
Netherlands	11.250 (13.34)*	6.346 (5.61)*	0.692	31.55	0.249
Norway	7.972 (18.41)*	6.194 (7.82)*	0.813	61.23	0.188
Portugal	9.992 (16.12)*	2.940 (9.58)	0.867	91.94	0.198
Spain	12.780 (17.25)*	4.252 (9.88)*	0.870	93.76	0.231
Sweden	6.406 (16.81)*	3.198 (1.70)	0.171	2.89	0.241
Switzerland	4.124 (4.79)*	−4.851 −(2.11)	0.242	4.88	0.294
Turkey	12.841 (5.88)*	3.058 (3.52)*	0.469	12.39	0.208
United Kingdom	1.188 (0.71)	−7.761 −(3.60)*	0.481	13.00	0.304

SEE, Standard error of the estimate.
t-ratios in parenthesis.
*Significant at 5%.
Source: Ahmad and Simos (1979).

Despite some favourable results, one of the drawbacks of Ahmad and Simos's (1979) work was their neglect of distance and political factors such as trade groupings. Kennedy and McHugh's (1983) study attempted to take these factors into account by using regressions for different periods: 1963–76, 1963–70 and 1970–76. They regressed changes in trade propensities against changes in differences in per capita income. Data on US exports to fifty-seven nations – exports that accounted for 90 per cent of total US exports – were used. Hence, exports to both developed and underdeveloped nation were included. The data were disaggregated by industry to one-digit Standard International Trade Classifications (SITC). In addition to aggregate (fifty-seven country) estimates, separate regressions were undertaken for thirteen industrial countries, less industrialised countries and Latin American countries as a group.

Kennedy and McHugh's results provided no evidence to support the Linder (1961) hypothesis. In the sixty regressions estimated, the expected sign was found in only twenty-two cases. None were significant below the 10 per cent level. The Durbin–Watson statistics suggested that the poor results were not caused by model misspecification and that the assumed linear relationship was the correct one.

The authors concluded that, at least in the case of the US, the Linder hypothesis received little support. They did suggest, however, that proponents of the Heckscher–Ohlin theory should not take the results as support for their explanation of trade patterns. They proposed instead that some combination of the two approaches might provide a more plausible explanation of US trade patterns.

The time-series approach used by Kennedy and McHugh (1983) gave rise to additional problems and conflicting conclusions. Consistently low R^2 values suggest that important factors were excluded from the model, although it was not obvious which additional variables should have been included. Some later authors experimented by adding a large range of plausible variables – whose most common effect was to change the sign of the income coefficient. Omitted variables and multicollinearity among the variables that have been included in subsequent studies make it difficult for firm conclusions to be drawn with respect to Linder's (1961) hypothesis. However, an alternative test was suggested by Shelburne (1987).

Shelburne's (1987) ratio approach was based on Linder's hypothesis – if countries are listed in order of their per capita incomes from A (the richest) to Z (the poorest), then country A's average propensity to import (APM) falls continuously as one moves down the alphabet. In a similar way, the APM of Z from each source of imports increases as one progresses down the alphabet. A ratio can then be calculated by dividing the imports from country A by the imports from Z for each country B through to Y. This ratio should fall as one moves down the income ranking since the numerator (the APM from A) declines and the denominator (the APM from Z) increases. As both APMs are calculated using the GNP of the importer, this term cancels out and one can use the actual trade flows instead of APMs. Thus, a whole host of extraneous factors that affect trade flows cancel one another out because they affect both exporters and importers equally..

Shelburne (1987) formalised this approach by using a gravity model framework. The bilateral trade equation for country A's exports to each importer, j, is

$$X_{aj} = A_1 Y_a^b N_a^{-c} Y_j^d N_j^{-e} D_{aj}^{-f} P_{aj}^k L_{aj}^k O_1^n O_2^m$$

where a refers to country A, X_{aj} is the dollar volume of exports from A to j, Y is GNP, N is population, D_{aj} is geographical distance from A to j measured in kilometres between the major centres, P is a preferred trader factor (e.g. for members of the same trading bloc/customs union), L_{aj} is per capita income similarity, which is defined as the per capita income of country j (PCI$_j$) divided by the per capita income of country A (PCI$_a$), and O_1 and O_2 are omitted variables such as tariff structures and levels, climate, natural resources, etc.

The bilateral trading equation for country Z can be constructed in the same way, giving

$$X_{zj} = A_2 Y_z^b N_z^{-c} Y_j^{-d} N_j^{-e} D_{zj}^{-f} P_{zj}^h L_{zj}^k O_1^n O_2^m$$

Taking the ratio of these two equations and cancelling out similar terms, the log ratio of A's exports to the jth country to Z's export to the jth country would be

$$\ln\left(\frac{X_{aj}}{X_{zj}}\right) =$$

$$\ln\left(\frac{A_1}{A_2}\right) + b\ln\left(\frac{Y_a}{Y_z}\right) - c\ln\left(\frac{N_a}{N_z}\right) - j\ln\left(\frac{D_{aj}}{D_{zj}}\right) +$$

$$+ h\ln\left(\frac{P_{aj}}{P_{zj}}\right) + 2k\ln\left(\text{PCI}_j\right) - K\ln\left(\frac{\text{PCI}_a}{\text{PCI}_z}\right)$$

As Y_a/Y_z and PCI$_a$/PCI$_z$ are constants irrespective of which jth country is being considered, these can be aggregated into the constant term $\ln(A_1/A_2)$. If countries A and Z have no advantage, such as tariffs, etc., over one another when exporting to other countries, the preferred trader would equal zero and can be dropped from the equation. The model then becomes

$$\ln\left(\frac{X_{aj}}{X_{zj}}\right) = c_1 + c_2 \ln\left(\text{PCI}_j\right) + c_3 \ln\left(\frac{D_{aj}}{D_{zj}}\right)$$

This specification can then be tested empirically across all countries, j, where the per capita income of Z is less than j's, which, in turn, is less than that of A.

If two exporters are relatively close to one another geographically, they will be, for all intents and purposes, equidistant from all their importers, so for them the distance variables will equal zero. As a result, the correlation between the distance and income-similarity variables is reduced when this specification is compared to the previous models. It is still possible, however, for the trade horizons of countries to differ according to their stage of development. Shelburne tried to test for this phenomenon by including not only the relative distance (D_{aj}/D_{zj}) in his equation but the absolute distance (D_{aj}) as well. His estimating equation thus became

$$\ln\left(\frac{X_{aj}}{X_{zj}}\right) =$$

$$c_1 + c_2 \ln\left(\text{PCI}_j\right) + c_3 \ln\left(\frac{D_{aj}}{D_{zj}}\right) + c_4 \ln\left(D_{aj}\right)$$

Shelburne's (1987) approach clearly possesses a number of advantages when compared to the earlier attempts to test the Linder (1961) hypothesis – i.e., the problem of correlation between geographical proximity and income similarity was reduced and many previously omitted variables, while taken into account, conveniently cancel out. By using a gravity model he was able to keep the form of his equation simple – even though the 'true' model may well be complicated, with large numbers of variables interacting in complex ways.

To ensure that the requirements of the ratio test were satisfied, considerable care had to be taken when choosing exporting countries. A sufficient sample of importers could only be guaranteed by selecting pairs of exporters that had large differences in per capita incomes. As the discussion of demand similarity revolves primarily around manufactured goods, the exporting pair had to have a large proportion of manufacturing exports. As countries of unequal size would have given rise to issues of economies of scale, those with similar populations were chosen. Furthermore, to neutralise the effect of trade agreements, countries had to be in the same trading group and either use the same language or different languages than those used by importers. In other words, the US and Australia could be paired because they are both English-speaking – no restrictions would have to be placed on importers. On the other hand, Japan and Portuguese-speaking Brazil could only be chosen so long as Portugal, Angola, Mozambique and any other Portuguese-speaking countries were excluded from the list of importers. In that way, any bias arising from language affinity would be reduced. To minimise the influence of distance, exporting countries had to be near one another so that they would be equally distant from their importers. Although no set of countries chosen fulfilled all the criteria, those listed in Table 5.17 were considered by Shelburne to be the most appropriate examples.

Table 5.17 Regressions relating exports to per capita income and distance

	Independent variables			
Trade category	$\ln PCI_j$ c_2	$\ln D_{ij}/D_{zj}$ c_3	$\ln(D_{aj})$ c_4	R^2
Germany–Italy (1977)				
Total exports	0.1712	−1.2950	0.1168	0.815
	(0.91)	(5.16)*	(1.77)	
Manufactured exports	0.0257	−0.2872	0.0346	0.879
	(0.85)	(7.11)**	(3.26)**	
Non-manufactured exports	0.0755	−1.1008	0.0618	0.354
	(0.17)	(1.81)	(0.39)	
Machinery and transport	0.7635	−0.8753	0.1017	0.822
equipment (SITC7)	(3.72)**	(3.18)**	(1.41)	
Miscellaneous manufactures	−0.7501	−1.5237	0.1399	0.480
(SITC8)	(2.15)*	(3.26)**	(1.14)	
Austria–Switzerland (1970)				
Total exports	−1.0705	−1.5720	0.5333	0.906
	(4.63)*	(6.72)**	(9.51)**	
Manufactured exports	−1.3259	−1.5329	0.5094	0.823
	(4.18)**	(4.78)**	(6.17)**	
Non-manufactured exports	−0.8839	−1.967	0.1831	0.044
	(0.48)	(0.64)	(0.38)	
Machinery and transport	−0.17498	−1.7170	0.4364	0.662
equipment (SITC7)	(3.44)**	(3.34)**	(3.29)**	
Miscellaneous manufactures	−1.9194	−1.9251	0.4572	0.611
(SITC8)	(3.11)**	(3.08)**	(2.48)*	
Sweden–Greece (1981)				
Total exports	−1.8779	−1.7698	0.5597	0.829
	(4.59)**	(9.62)**	(3.14)**	
Manufactured exports	−1.6577	−1.7262	0.7978	0.779
	(2.86)**	(7.45)**	(3.37)**	
Non-manufactured exports	−2.2251	−1.8959	−0.1961	0.725
	(3.03)**	(6.46)**	(0.65)	
Machinery and transport	−1.1994	−2.3050	1.3078	0.758
equipment (SITC7)	(1.39)	(6.71)**	(3.72)**	
Miscellaneous manufactures	−1.7996	−1.7970	0.7453	0.597
(SITC8)	(2.35)*	(5.21)**	(2.23)*	

(Table continues on next page)

Out of the twenty-three income-similarity coefficients, c_2, estimated for manufactured goods, only two are significantly positive, while eleven are significantly negative and the remaining ten are not significant. These results did not give much support to the Linder (1961) hypothesis. There is, however, some variation in the results for commodity groups. In the miscellaneous manufactures group (SITC8), which is characterised by unsophisticated, low-

Table 5.17 (*cont.*) Regressions relating exports to per capita income and distance

| Trade category | Independent variables | | | R^2 |
	$\ln PCI_j$ c_2	$\ln D_{ij}/D_{zj}$ c_3	$\ln(D_{aj})$ c_4	
India–Australia (1979)				
Total exports	0.3196	−1.6017	−1.5918	0.410
	(1.56)	(3.16)**	(2.70)**	
Manufactured exports	−0.1957	−0.5159	−1.8997	0.745
	(0.73)	(0.67)	(2.69)*	
Non-manufactured exports	0.3892	−0.2935	−0.4944	0.104
	(0.87)	(0.26)	(0.48)	
Machinery and transport	1.2422	−2.2811	−2.3363	0.579
equipment (SITC7)	(4.65)**	(3.59)**	(3.20)**	
Miscellaneous manufactures	−0.6440	−1.1063	−2.9295	0.739
(SITC8)	(2.73)*	(2.01)	(3.34)**	
Japan–Korea (1981)				
Total exports	−0.2030	ni	0.1989	0.108
	(2.11)*		(0.99)	
Machinery and transport	−0.1217	ni	0.1247	0.022
equipment (SITC7)	(0.93)		(0.46)	
Miscellaneous manufactures	−0.4247	ni	−0.5494	0.367
(SITC8)	(3.12)**		(1.94)	
Sweden–Spain (1977)				
Total exports	−0.3634	−1.3189	0.0943	0.749
	(0.911)	(6.57)**	(0.51)	
Manufactured exports	−0.2107	−1.3049	0.2123	0.713
	(0.48)	(5.99)**	(1.06)	
Non-manufactured exports	−0.7903	−1.2906	−0.7781	0.831
	(1.99)	(6.48)**	(4.23)**	
Machinery and transport	−0.6009	−1.1513	0.0513	0.562
equipment (SITC7)	(0.97)	(3.72)**	(1.80)	
Miscellaneous manufactures	−0.6213	−2.0410	−0.2008	0.840
(SITC8)	(1.28)*	(8.41)**	(0.89)	

Dependent variable: $\ln(X_{aj}/X_{zj})$.
t-statistics in parenthesis.
*Significant at the 5% level.
**Significant at the 1% level.
ni, Not included
Source: Shelburne (1987).

technology goods that are not subject to economies of scale, the income coefficients are consistently negative. In contrast, in the machinery and transport equipment group (SITC7), whose products exhibit the opposite characteristics, two coefficients are significantly positive and one is negative and significant. Thus, these results gave some, albeit weak, support to Linder's theoretical expectations.

The relative distance variable has the expected sign and is significant at the 1 per cent level in all of the regressions with the exception of two of the Australia–India regressions. In half the regressions the absolute distance variable has a positive sign and is significant. A positive sign for this variable would appear to support the hypothesis that trade horizons increase with economic development – i.e. the larger the absolute distance, the larger the export ratio.

As the income coefficient was found to vary between SITC groupings, Shelburne (1987) decided to examine the effect of commodity characteristics more carefully. He disaggregated the industries of the 'Germany–Italy' exporter set into three-digit SITC categories and ascribed a set of commodity character-istics to each category. These characteristics were the commodity's physical and human capital intensity, level of differentiation, age, degree of scale economies, income elasticity and the degree to which the commodity could be classed as a consumer good. Each SITC category was then classified as being high, medium or low for each of these characteristics. Each commodity with similar charac-teristics was aggregated into one group and a regression using a ratio-based aggregation specification was performed on these three groups.

The results showed that the income coefficient was significantly and highly correlated with differentiated, new and human capital-intensive goods – characteristics that had been implied by Linder (1961). As this disaggregated approach was only applied to the Germany–Italy set of importers, the results could not be generalised. Shelburne (1987) concluded that his tests indicated that the relationship between income similarity and trade intensity bordered between being negative and insignificant.

In one final study considered here, Hunter and Markusen (1988) presented some additional evidence that appeared to contradict Linder's hypothesis. Their results showed that approximately 14 per cent of observed trade could be accounted for by differences, rather than similarities, in incomes.

The bulk of the empirical evidence pertaining to Linder's (1961) hypothesis provided little support for it as an important explanation of trade patterns. Income similarity may, however, explain trade in a limited set of commodities and for a few countries. As an alternative model of international trade, its usefulness seemed limited. It did, however, get a new lease on life as it appeared to provide a plausible explanation for intra-industry trade. We will examine both the theoretical development and empirical investigations of intra-industry trade in Chapter 6.

5.5 Summary

The empirical tests of the alternative theories can be judged to have been inconclusive. Although they did not appear to provide a comprehensive replacement for neoclassical trade theory, they could not be rejected entirely. The tests themselves were fraught with difficulties – particularly in the use of imperfect proxies, no matter how cleverly contrived. Thus, the empirical tests of trade theories both rejected the Heckscher–Ohlin hypothesis and failed to confirm any of the alternatives. The latter gave heart to Heckscher–Ohlin's proponents. On the other hand, the largely favourable results for some of the alternative theories, particularly those based on technology, provided the stimulus for research centred around the simultaneous testing of the Heckscher–Ohlin theory and its rivals. This approach was pioneered by Hufbauer (1970). His lead was followed by a large number of researchers who refined and extended his basic approach. The quest for a comprehensive theory to explain trade patterns will be discussed in Chapter 7, but first a diversion which captured the attention of many of those interested in alternatives to Heckscher–Ohlin – intra-industry trade – must be explored.

References

Ahmad, A., and Simos, E. O. (1979), 'Preference similarity and trade in manufactures: an alternative test of Linder's hypothesis', *Rivista Internazionale di Scienze Economiche e Commerciali*, 26(8), pp. 721–40.

Baldwin, R. E. (1971), 'Determinants of the commodity structure of U.S. trade', *American Economic Review*, 61(1), pp. 126–46.

Baldwin, R. E. (1979), 'Determinants of trade and foreign investment: further evidence', *The Review of Economics and Statistics*, 61(1), pp. 40–8.

Branson, W. H., and Junz, H. B. (1971), 'Trends in US comparative advantage', *Brookings Papers on Economic Activity*, 2, Washington: Brookings Institute, pp. 285–338.

Dunning, J. H., and Buckley, P. J. (1977), 'International production and alternative models of trade', *The Manchester School of Economic and Social Studies*, 45(4), pp. 392–403.

Ferguson, C. E., and Moroney, J. (1969), 'The sources of change in labour's relative share: a neoclassical analysis', *Southern Economic Journal*, 35, pp. 308–22.

Fortune, J. N. (1971), 'Some determinants of trade in finished manufactures', *Swedish Journal of Economics*, 73, pp. 311–17.

Giddy, I. H. (1978), 'The demise of the product cycle model in international business theory', *Columbia Journal of World Business*, 13(1), pp. 90–7.

Goodman, B., and Ceyhun, F. (1976), 'US export performance in manufacturing industries: an empirical investigation', *Weltwirtschaftliches Archiv*, 112, pp. 525–55.

Greytak, D., and McHugh, R. (1977), 'Linder's trade thesis: an empirical examination', *Southern Economic Journal*, 43(3), pp. 1386–9.

Gruber, W., Mehta, D., and Vernon, R. (1967), 'The R&D factor in international trade and international investment of United States industries', *Journal of Political Economy*, 75(1), pp. 20–37.

Gruber, W. H., and Vernon, R. (1970), 'The technology factor in a world trade matrix', in R. Vernon (ed.), *The Technology Factor in International Trade*, New York: National Bureau of Economic Research, pp. 233–72.

Helpman, E. (1993), 'Innovation, imitation and intellectual property rights', *Econometrica*, 61(6), pp. 1247–80.

Hirsch, S. (1972), 'The United States electronics industry in international trade', in L. T. Wells (ed.), *The Product Life Cycle and International Trade*, Boston: Harvard University Press, pp. 39–52.

Hoftyzer, J. (1975), 'Empirical verification of Linder's trade thesis: comment', *Southern Economic Journal*, 41(4), pp. 694–8.

Hufbauer, G. C. (1966), *Synthetic Materials and the Theory of International Trade*, Cambridge, Mass.: Harvard University Press.

Hufbauer, G. C. (1970), 'The impact of national characteristics and technology on the commodity composition of trade in manufactured goods', in R. Vernon (ed.), *The Technology Factor in International Trade*, New York: National Bureau of Economic Research, pp. 145–231.

Hughes, K. S. (1983), 'Exports and innovation: a simultaneous equation model', Economics discussion paper no. 83/141, University of Bristol.

Hunter, L., and Markusen, J. (1988), 'Per capita income as a determinant of trade', in J. Feenstra (ed.), *Empirical Methods for International Trade*, Cambridge, Mass.: MIT Press, pp. 89–109.

Johnson, H. G. (1964), 'Book review of Linder', *Economica*, 31(1), pp. 86–90.

Katrak, H. (1973), 'Human skills, R and D and scale economies in the exports of the United Kingdom and the United States', *Oxford Economic Papers*, 25(3), pp. 337–60.

Katrak, H. (1982), 'Labour-skills, R and D and capital requirements in the international trade and investment of the United Kingdom, 1968–78', *National Institute Economic Review*, 101, pp. 38–47.

Keesing, D. B. (1965), 'Labour skills and international trade: evaluating many trade flows with a single measuring device', *The Review of Economics and Statistics*, 47, pp. 287–94.

Keesing, D. B. (1966), 'Labour skills and comparative advantage', *American Economic Review*, 56(2), pp. 249–58.

Keesing, D. B. (1968), 'Labour skills and the structure of trade in manufactures', in D. B. Kenen and R. Lawrence (eds), *The Open Economy*, New York: Columbia University Press, pp. 3–18.

Keesing, D. B. (1971), 'Different countries' labour skill coefficients and the skills intensity of international trade flows', *Journal of International Economics*, 1, pp. 443–52.

Kennedy, T. E., and McHugh, R. (1983), 'Taste similarities and trade intensity: a test of the Linder hypothesis for United States exports', *Weltwirtschaftliches Archiv*, 119, pp. 84–96.

Leamer, E. E. (1974), 'The commodity composition of international trade in manufactures: an empirical analysis', *Oxford Economic Papers*, 26(3), pp. 350–74.

Leontief, W. (1956), 'Factor proportions and the structure of American trade: further theoretical and empirical analysis', *The Review of Economics and Statistics*, 38(4), pp. 386–407.

Linder, S. B. (1961), *An Essay on Trade and Transformation*, New York: John Wiley and Sons.

Mansfield, E., Romeo, A., and Wagner, S. (1979), 'Foreign trade and US research and development', *The Review of Economics and Statistics*, 61, pp. 49–57.

Morrall, J. F. (1972), *Human Capital, Technology and the Role of the United States in International Trade*, Gainsville: University of Florida Press.

Poh, L. Y. (1987), 'Product life cycle and export competitiveness of the UK electronics industry (1970–1979)', *The European Journal of Marketing*, 21(7), pp. 326–38.

Sailors, J. W., Qureshi, U. A., and Cross, E. M. (1973), 'Empirical verification of Linder's trade thesis', *Southern Economic Journal*, 40(2), pp. 262–8.

Sailors, J. W., Qureshi, U. A., and Cross, E. M. (1975), 'Empirical verification of Linder's trade thesis: reply', *Southern Economic Journal*, 41(4), pp. 698–700.

Shelburne, R. C. (1987), 'A ratio test of trade intensity and per-capita income similarity', *Weltwirtschaftliches Archiv*, 123, pp. 474–87.

Soete, L. L. G. (1981), 'A general test of technological gap trade theory', *Weltwirtschaftliches Archiv*, 117, pp. 638–60.

Smith, S. R., White, G. M., Owen, N. C., and Hill, M. R. (1982), 'UK trade in manufacturing: the pattern of specialization during the 1970s', Government Economic Service working paper no. 56, London: HMSO.

Tsurumi, Y. (1972), 'R&D factors and exports of manufactured goods of Japan', in L. T. Wells (ed.), *The Product Life Cycle and International Trade*, Boston: Harvard University Press, pp. 161–89.

Vernon, R. (1966), 'International investment and international trade in the product cycle', *Quarterly Journal of Economics*, 80(2), pp. 190–207.

Vernon, R. (1979), 'The product cycle hypothesis in a new international environment', *Oxford Bulletin of Economics and Statistics*, 41(4), pp. 255–67.

Wells, L. J. (1969), 'Test of a product cycle model of international trade: US exports of consumer durables', *Quarterly Journal of Economics*, 83(1), pp. 152–62.

Wells, L. T. (ed.) (1972), *The Product Life Cycle and International Trade*, Boston: Harvard University Press.

CHAPTER 6

Intra-industry trade theory and empirical evidence

6.1 Introduction

Thus far, we have outlined the theories and discussed the empirical evidence related to trade between countries in different products – for example, the exchange of cars for wheat. These types of trade flow are known as 'inter-industry' trade. We now turn our attention to theories that attempt to explain *intra*-industry trade and the empirical work which has been associated with them. 'Intra-industry' trade refers to trade in similar products. The simultaneous importation and exportation of cars by a country is one example.

The existence of intra-industry trade was first acknowledged by Ohlin (1933). However, intra-industry trade was not seriously studied until the mid-1960s, when economists began to assess the impact of the formation of the European Economic Community on the trade patterns of member countries. The standard trade theories based on trade in the products of different industries suggested that as trade barriers fell, countries would specialise on an inter-industry basis. In other words, some domestic industries would expand while others would contract. While some adjustments to changing competitiveness based on industry-wide expansion or contractions do occur, many industries experience simultaneous expansion in production, exports and imports. This observation provided the stimulus for a systematic documentation of intra-industry trade (Verdoorn, 1960; Balassa, 1965) and attempts to provide a theoretical structure to explain these trade patterns.

Along with the thorough documentation of the growing importance of intra-industry trade flows, attempts to both find theoretical explanations and to test the validity of these explanations have also grown apace. Trade in manufactures accounts for 60 per cent of world trade. Intra-industry trade is estimated to make up approximately half of the trade in manufacturing (Greenaway and Milner, 1986). It is growing most rapidly in manufactured goods (Hesse, 1974) and is more prevalent among developed than developing countries (Aquino, 1978).

In the history of intra-industry trade theory, Grubel and Lloyd's (1975) contribution was an important landmark. Their work incorporated a great deal of documentary evidence and attempted to develop a theoretical basis for the existence of intra-industry trade. For example, it provided evidence of the existence of intra-industry trade in both homogeneous and differentiated products. It also put forward a taxonomy of differentiation. This consisted of three groups. First, those products which are close substitutes but use different factor inputs – e.g. furniture, with factor inputs of wood and plastic. Second, goods that use similar inputs but are not substitutes in end use. Petrol and tar (factor input, crude oil), and cutlery and medical instruments (stainless steel) are examples. The third group comprises goods that have similar inputs and are highly substitutable in consumption but are differentiated from one another by style and/or quality. More recent formal theoretical work on intra-industry trade has taken Grubel and Lloyd's taxonomy as its starting point. In the following brief overview of intra-industry trade theory we will begin by outlining the hypotheses that attempt to explain intra-industry trade in homogeneous goods and then move on to discuss those that apply to differentiated products. Finally, we will examine the empirical work pertaining to the various theories.

6.2   Homogeneous goods and intra-industry trade

Grubel and Lloyd (1975) suggested that intra-industry trade is prevalent in entrepôt trade, seasonal trade and goods with high transport costs. Entrepôt trade – the reconstitution of goods from large to small consignments – is a labour-intensive activity. Hence, countries that have plentiful labour and are located on or near major trade routes will possess a comparative advantage in this activity. Typically, these economies act as transhipment points. The examples commonly used are Hong Kong – which acts as a transhipment point for China's trade with the world – and Singapore, which is a pivotal point for South East Asian commerce. An examination of the trade statistics of entrepôt nations should indicate the simultaneous importation and exportation of homogeneous goods.

Where a good's production is influenced by the seasons, as is the case with agricultural products, it is easy to envisage intra-industry trade. In one season a country may produce and export a good, whereas in another it might import it. Chile exports fruit during the northern hemisphere's winter and imports perishable fruit from the northern hemisphere during its winter.

High transport costs can give rise to intra-industry trade by making it cheaper to buy and import a good from a neighbouring country than to transport it from a much more distant region within the country. If the region in question were exporting its products across an adjacent border, intra-industry trade would result. For example, beef cattle are simultaneously exported from western Canada to the US Pacific states at the same time as beef is imported into eastern Canada from the US. The transport costs of moving Canadian beef 2,000 miles across Canada are simply too high.

Grubel and Lloyd (1975) also found that intra-industry trade could be the result of government policies and legal constraints. In the case of the former, a government might subsidise the domestic production of a good. This could give a domestic producer a comparative advantage which it might not otherwise enjoy. This would enable the firm to sell the product not only domestically but also abroad. If imports continued, intra-industry trade would appear in the trade statistics.

Intra-industry trade could also come about if a government undertook to buy foreign goods as part of an international agreement. If domestic producers were exporting similar goods, then intra-industry trade would again be evident in the trade statistics.

It is also possible to generate intra-industry trade when domestically produced goods are not allowed to be sold in the home market because of existing contractual arrangements. If they can be sold abroad and domestic demand is met by foreign imports, intra-industry trade will be manifest in the country's trade statistics as a result of this legal constraint.

Intra-industry trade can arise from differences in comparative costs as in the Heckscher–Ohlin model in the case of entrepôt trade and seasonal production. Hence, intra-industry trade in homogeneous goods can be compatible with a perfectly competitive market structure.

Oligopolistic market structures can also give rise to intra-industry trade (Brander, 1981; and Brander and Krugman, 1983). Assume two countries with one firm in each that supplies its domestic market under conditions of autarky. Further, assume that the countries have the same demand structures and that the firms experience the same cost structures and constant marginal costs. With identical demand patterns and cost structures, the prices and the quantities supplied are the same in the two countries before trade.

Once trade is opened up between the countries a duopolistic market structure is established. Market equilibrium is determined by the strategic interaction between the two firms. Assuming Cournot competition (Varian, 1990) – where one firm's output decisions are determined by taking the other firm's output as constant – an increase in output will increase marginal revenue. This will occur because the producer contemplating the increase knows that output increases and price declines will only have a partial impact on his revenues. The rival firm's revenues will also be affected. As trade is opened up each producer perceives marginal revenue to be above his marginal costs, and overall output will increase and prices fall. Some consumers will buy goods from the domestic producer, others will purchase their requirements from the foreign producer. Even allowing for the existence of transport costs does not invalidate the conclusions of the analysis. Relaxing the assumptions to allow one firm to anticipate the reaction of the other (non-zero conjectural variation) or allowing a range of behaviour situations to coexist (full competition to complete collusion) does not change the basic conclusion that intra-industry trade will arise (Brander and Krugman, 1983).

6.3   Intra-industry trade in differentiated goods

Although intra-industry trade in homogeneous goods can be explained in terms of the Heckscher–Ohlin framework (entrepôt and seasonal trade), transport costs and the strategic behaviour of oligopolists, trade in differentiated goods needs more sophisticated explanations. As international movements of differentiated goods account for a very high percentage of total intra-industry trade, theoreticians have been at pains to provide plausible explanations of this phenomenon.

Two sets of theories can be identified: those that deal with horizontally differentiated products and those that attempt to explain intra-industry trade in vertically differentiated goods. What is the difference between horizontal and vertical differentiation? The former implies that products are of the same quality but otherwise have different characteristics. For example, a consumer of ties is offered a selection of silk ties of the same quality but differing in colour and style. Vertically differentiated products are those that have the same characteristics but differ in quality. Keeping to the example of ties, our consumer is faced with an array of red ties made from different fabrics such as silk, wool, cotton, polyester. We will examine first the theories that purport to explain trade in horizontally differentiated products and then move on to outline those applying to vertically differentiated products.

6.4   Trade theories applying to horizontally differentiated goods

Two underlying consumer motives are utilised to develop intra-industry trade theories for horizontally differentiated goods. The first assumes that consumers have a particular view of the 'core properties' that make up their ideal product (Lancaster, 1979; 1980). It is hypothesised that consumers attempt to maximise these core properties when purchasing a product. The second motive is based on the assumption that consumers have a 'love for variety' (Dixit and Stiglitz 1977). When this motivation is assumed, consumers are expected to attempt to maximise the number of varieties they can purchase.

6.4.1 The core property model

In the core property model it is assumed that consumers differ with regard to a product's ideal characteristics. For example, when purchasing a vehicle some consumers may prefer fuel economy and low exhaust emissions whereas others may prefer power and speed. Each consumer will try to purchase the variant of the product that comes closest to his or her ideal.

In this model a product's characteristics (fuel consumption, exhaust emissions, colour, etc.) can be shown on a circle (Helpman, 1981). It is assumed that, because of economies of scale, it is impossible for manufacturers to produce every consumer's ideal variant, so firms offer only a few varieties. This is illus-

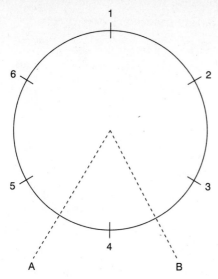

Figure 6.1

trated in Figure 6.1, which shows that firms supply only six variants – labelled 1 to 6 – to the market. Since consumers choose the variant that approximates their own ideal, those who occupy market segment A–B will choose variant 4. Assuming a market structure of monopolistic competition that includes free entry and exit, suppliers will position themselves in the market so as to max-imise their profits. This will lead to firms obtaining identical market shares, which results in the points 1–6 being evenly distributed around the circle.

In order to 'internationalise' the model, let us assume that we have two identical economies in which producers have identical cost structures and the price of all variants is equal in the pre-trade situation. Consumers in the two countries are also assumed to have identical preferences. We can illustrate a representative firm's output/pricing position as in Figure 6.2. In autarky, the firm experiences only the domestic demand curve *DH*. In equilibrium a firm would supply Q_1 and change P_1 and no supernormal profits would be earned because average costs, *AC*, would equal average revenue, *AR* – i.e. $P_1 = AC$.

What is the effect when trade is opened up between the two countries? Initially, firms produce the same number of variants (six) and all variants are produced in both countries. The doubling of the market available to each firm will, however, have important effects in the long run. Demand will increase from *DH* to *DH* + *F* (Figure 6.2), where *F* represents foreign demand for the partic-ular product variety. One of the producers will decide to expand output, gain economies of scale, undercut his rival on price and put him out of business. By implication, the firm that undertakes this strategy first will capture the market for this variant, so only one of the identical product variants will survive. The surviving firm will, of course, experience an increase in profits.

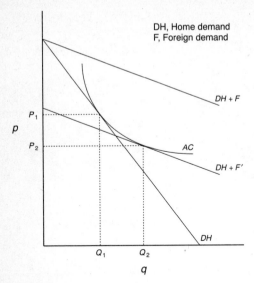

Figure 6.2

In the longer run this increase in profits will have an important effect on the number of variants offered. For example, because supernormal profits can be made, new entrants who will offer additional product varieties will be attracted into the industry. Those who are forced out of production may also switch to producing a new variant aimed at a new market segment. This behaviour will lead to more than six variants being offered to the market – say, eight. The number of close substitutes is increased and the demand curve for each variant will shift inwards from $DH + F$ to $DH + F'$ in Figure 6.2, with the result that supernormal profits will be reduced to zero – i.e. P_2 and Q_2. If the production of the eight variants is distributed evenly between the two countries, intra-industry trade will result as producers supply consumers in both markets. It must be remembered, however, that the volume of this intra-industry trade will depend on the extent to which tastes overlap between the two countries. The smaller the overlap, the smaller will be the volume of intra-industry trade. A large number of factors influence consumers' tastes at the national level. Cultural factors, along with incomes, are most often suggested as the principal determinants of tastes. Thus, countries with similar cultural characteristics and incomes can be expected to experience intra-industry trade in horizontally differentiated products.

6.4.2 The 'love for variety' model

A complementary theory to that of the core property model has been developed based on the assumption that consumers love variety. Their aim is hypothesised to be the consumption of as many variants of a product as possible (Dixit and Stiglitz, 1977). If consumers maximise their utility by consuming as many variants as possible of, for example, beer, they will purchase variants not just from their own country but from other beer-producing nations.

Krugman (1979, 1980) and Dixit and Norman (1982) have utilised this approach to develop models of intra-industry trade. They assumed that there are two countries that are identical in terms of cost structures and consumption patterns and that all variants produced offer the same utility. The countries are, furthermore, assumed to be the same size. When trade is opened up between the countries consumers reduce their consumption of home-produced variants in order to purchase foreign variants. Under the strict assumptions outlined above, domestic demand for domestically produced varieties is reduced by half, but this is compensated for by an increase in foreign demand of an equal amount. The result is intra-industry trade. Even when the assumptions of identical country size and an equal number of variants are relaxed, the theory's qualitative results still hold.

6.5   Trade theories and vertically differentiated goods

The assumption that the demand for quality increases as income rises underpins the theoretical structure of trade in vertically differentiated products. Furthermore, it is assumed to be an increasing function. This approach parallels Linder's (1961) approach to inter-industry trade. Firms are also assumed to target their production primarily at the home market. As incomes in foreign markets grow niche markets are expected to develop for quality goods that can be supplied from factories in the home market. Those with low incomes in the high-income country, however, will not be able to afford the higher-priced goods of superior quality. A market will, therefore, exist for a lower-priced, lower-quality variant. In international trading terms, it is possible that the higher-income country producing the superior-quality good will supply goods to those who have high incomes in the lower average income country. That country, in turn, will send lower-priced, lower-quality goods to supply poorer consumers in the higher average income country. The result will be intra-industry trade in a particular product group. The volume of trade will, therefore, depend on the degree of income inequality.

Falvey (1981) has put forward a supply-side theory to explain intra-industry trade in vertically differentiated products. His analysis suggests that product differentiation in an industry is based on a country's factor endowments. By assuming perfect competition, constant returns to scale and identical production functions, his model approximates Heckscher–Ohlin.

The supply-side theory assumes that high-quality variants require relatively high capital inputs and, thus, that they are capital intensive. On the other hand, low-quality variants are assumed to be relatively more labour-intensive. As a result, capital-abundant countries will have a comparative advantage in the production and export of relatively high-quality products. The opposite will be the case for labour-abundant countries. Differences between countries' factor endowments will determine the nature and extent of intra-industry trade in vertically differentiated products.

Shaked and Sutton (1984) have also proposed a supply-side model but one that is not dependent on a 'many firms', constant returns to scale, identical demand patterns approach. They assumed that to vertically differentiate products firms have to carry out research and development. This is expensive and raises costs. The only way to lower average costs (if variable costs are constant) is to concentrate one's efforts on one variant and capture as large a market as possible. The increased output lowers average fixed costs and, hence, the average (total) cost declines. If firms are successful, the result will be an industry characterised by oligopoly. It is important to note that, in terms of market structure, vertically differentiated products can be produced by industries that are characterised by 'large numbers' of firms – akin to perfect competition – or by 'fewness' – i.e. oligopoly.

6.6 Institutional factors that encourage intra-industry trade

In addition to the demand and supply theories that have been outlined in the previous sections, institutional factors play a role in determining intra-industry trade. Some of these, such as transport costs, have already been alluded to, but others have not. For example, the existence of tariffs and quotas, trading arrangements such as free-trade areas, common markets, etc., the coexistence of multinational companies and foreign direct investment. How do these factors affect intra-industry trade? The existence of trade barriers, whether defined as transport or distance costs or as tariffs and quotas, have the effect of raising the prices of goods. As these barriers are reduced and prices fall the market for goods widens. Hence, as a result of technological change in transportation (Klein and Kerr, 1995) or negotiated reductions in trade barriers (Hobbs, 1996), previously prohibitively expensive foreign variants can now be purchased and intra-industry trade can ensue. Foreign direct investment and multinational activity act in a different way (Caves, 1981; Wickham and Thompson, 1989). Foreign direct investment could act as a substitute for intra-industry trade. Instead of a firm supplying a variety of a product to a foreign market from a domestic plant, it could set up a subsidiary to supply the foreign market from within. As a result, one would find an inverse relationship between intra-industry trade and foreign direct investment. The intra-industry effects of foreign investment may, however, be more complex. Firms may set up subsidiaries that specialise in the production of particular variants. These may then be shipped back to the home country, thus generating intra-industry trade. We will return to this point when the empirical work is discussed.

Having completed this brief overview of intra-industry trade theories, we now move on to discussing the empirical evidence.

6.7 The testing of intra-industry trade theories

There are two major types of empirical studies of intra-industry trade. The aim of the first is to establish the existence of the phenomenon of intra-industry trade (the so-called 'documentary studies'), while that of the second is to test the validity of intra-industry trade theories.

The first group has allowed economists to establish a number of 'stylistic facts' regarding intra-industry trade. For example, it appears that there is more intra-industry trade among developed countries than among developing or formerly centrally planned economies. Intra-industry trade is closely related to growing per capita income levels and is more extensive between countries that are members of a customs union or economic bloc. It is, moreover, concentrated in the trade of manufactured goods rather than non-manufactured goods.

As the primary interest in this book is the testing of trade theories, we concentrate here on the second type of empirical studies.

6.7.1 The measurement of intra-industry trade – the dependent variable

There are numerous measures of intra-industry trade. The first was developed by Balassa (1966). The Balassa index takes net trade in a particular commodity as a proportion of the total trade (that is, exports plus imports) in that commodity. More formally, we can write

$$A_j = \frac{\left| X_j - M_j \right|}{X_j + M_j} \tag{6.1}$$

where A_j is the index corresponding to a commodity and X and M represent exports and imports. A_j would vary between zero (when $X_j = M_j$) and one (where $M_j = 0$). When the index equals one it is tantamount to saying that all trade is inter-industry.

Most studies have not used the Balassa index. The preference among researchers is to use the Grubel and Lloyd index (Grubel and Lloyd 1975). This can be written as

$$B_j = \frac{\left(X_j + M_j \right) - \left| X_j - M_j \right|}{\left(X_j + M_j \right)} \tag{6.2}$$

where X_j and M_j have the same meanings as in (6.1).

This equation can be rewritten as

$$B_j = 1 - \frac{\left| X_j - M_j \right|}{\left(X_j + M_j \right)} \tag{6.3}$$

or

$$B_j = 1 - A_j \qquad\qquad (6.4)$$

The reason for researchers' preference for the Grubel and Lloyd index is that the values it takes are intuitively more appealing. For example, it takes a value of zero when there is no intra-industry trade and has a value of one where all trade is intra-industry. Hence, the Grubel and Lloyd index is positively related to the level of intra-industry trade, whereas the Balassa index is inversely related.

As with all measures, there are problems and caveats must be applied. For example, as the indexes are expressed relative to total trade, they can take on the same value for different absolute values of exports and imports. As total trade may not necessarily be related to domestic production or sales, the indexes may not reflect the importance of intra-industry trade to the economy or industrial sector under analysis.

More importantly, when using these indexes as the dependent variable in empirical work it is essential that they accurately reflect the extent of intra-industry trade in a product group, or sector, relative to the whole economy. The index will only be a true reflection of intra-industry trade if it is a weighted average of the indexes for each subgroup. The sign on the net trade balance in all subgroups must be the same for the index to be unbiased. Where opposite signs occur, it is likely that the overall index will be larger than the weighted average of the subgroup index. In other words, the index will overestimate the value of intra-industry trade. The extent to which this occurs will depend on the size of the net trade balances in question.

Grubel and Lloyd (1975) also pointed out that any measure of intra-industry trade at the aggregate level will be affected by the overall trade imbalance with one's trading partners. The greater the trade imbalance, the greater will be the share of net trade and the smaller the share of intra-industry trade. Grubel and Lloyd suggested that intra-industry trade should be adjusted to reflect the proportion of total trade minus the trade imbalance.

Aquino (1978) argued that, by adjusting the intra-industry trade index at the aggregate level, one was ignoring the effect of imbalances on individual sector trade flows. He therefore proposed that each individual index should be adjusted on the assumption that all sectors were affected proportionately by the balancing effect. Aquino's index, Q_j, therefore becomes

$$Q_j = 1 - \frac{\left| X_j - M_j \right|}{\left(X_j + M_j \right)} \qquad\qquad (6.5)$$

where

$$X_j = X_j \cdot \frac{1}{2} \left[\sum_{j=1}^{n} \frac{\left(X_j + M_j \right)}{\sum_{j=1}^{n} X_j} \right] \tag{6.6}$$

and

$$M_j = M_j \cdot \frac{1}{2} \left[\sum_{j=1}^{n} \frac{\left(X_j + M_j \right)}{\sum_{j=1}^{n} M_j} \right] \tag{6.7}$$

The signs of the industry or sector trade imbalances indicate the direction in which the B_j index should be adjusted.

Bergstrand (1983) suggested that a further adjustment is necessary, particularly when indexes are developed from bilateral data. Adjusting solely for the bilateral imbalance, he believed, was inappropriate because a bilateral imbalance might not be consistent with an overall balance. Like Aquino (1978), he proposed that the 'balancing' should be distributed across industries.

Greenaway and Milner (1981) questioned whether adjustments are appropriate. They argued that it is not known *a priori* whether a particular set of transactions will be balanced in equilibrium. Further, the nature or the effect of the balance of payments adjustments that are set in motion is not known. The theoretical justification of correcting for trade imbalances has also been questioned by Vona (1991), who suggested that they may lead to unreliable estimates. For these reasons, most empirical work on intra-industry trade uses the unadjusted Grubel and Lloyd (1975) index as the dependent variable.

6.7.2 Independent variables and their proxies

The various theories of intra-industry trade postulate that the following variables affect the level of intra-industry trade positively: taste overlap or similarity, economies of scale, market structure, the potential for vertical or technological differentiation, physical distance and the existence of trade barriers. A major problem when undertaking empirical work is finding real-world proxies that capture the true essence of the theoretical concepts under investigation.

Most economists have modelled taste overlap and similarity by using income per capita as their indicator. Is this appropriate? Although taste similarity gives rise to the possibility that more products will be supplied to satisfy consumer desires for variety, taste dissimilarity can also, in certain circumstances, give rise to intra-industry trade. The latter occurs when, for example, the distributions of tastes pertaining to quality attributes have different means in different countries and each country specialises in producing varieties that cater to its own mean tastes. The demand of consumers with tastes that reflect the extremities of the domestic distribution – but which are close to the mean in the other country – is satisfied by imports.

There are also problems with defining and measuring product differentiation. While it is obviously useful to distinguish between various classes of goods, it is not uncommon for goods to possess some aspects of more than one category. In attempting to test the various hypotheses, it would be useful if appropriate proxies for product differentiation could be found. In many of the studies that we refer to Hufbauer's (1970) index is used (see Chapter 5). This index is based on the variation in export unit values. If prices can be used as an indicator of product quality, Hufbauer's index can be used as a proxy for vertical product differentiation.

Hufbauer's index, however, suffers from a number of drawbacks. First, it can change drastically if the structure of trade is altered within the standard industrial trade classification categories that are often used to define industries. Second, although variation in export unit values can arise from product differentiation, it can also arise from firms practising price discrimination in markets in different countries. Separating these two influences is seldom possible. Transfer pricing within multinational firms can have similar effects. Third, the Hufbauer index may hide the fact that one country exports one variety of a good while it imports several varieties in return. Thus, it may not be wise to presume that trade in differentiated goods implies the exportation of different varieties to different markets.

Other studies resort to proxies for product differentiation based on advertising expenditures and census classification. Advertising intensity is usually associated with horizontal differentiation, with each producer expending resources to extol the characteristics of his goods – the hypothesis being that the more advertising there is, the greater the degree of product differentiation. Some studies use the proportion of advertising expenditure to total sales revenue as a proxy. Others use the ratio of workers employed in promotional activities to the total workforce. It could be the case, however, that producers operate in an interdependent environment and collusively limit the amount of advertising undertaken. In such situations the link between product differentiation and advertising would be broken.

Using the number of subgroup products in an industry as an indication of product differentiation is also beset with problems. The hypothesis is that subgroups are composed of similar but competing products. Given the way that industries are grouped, it is entirely possible that a subgroup constitutes a separate industry rather than a product variation. If this were the case, proxies of product differentiation based on the number or proportion of subgroups in an industry would be misleading.

There are also problems with the proxies that are used to reflect market structure. The most commonly used proxy is the crude concentration ratio for the industries in question. More sophisticated measures that temper the number of firms in the industry by their market share are also used. These measures of market structure and, hence, competitiveness suffer from several drawbacks. The principal deficiency is the way in which the concentration ratios are calculated. As they rely on domestic data, they do not take into account the competition posed by foreign imports. The extent to which potential competition is affected by entry barriers is also ignored.

Objections of a more methodological nature also arise from the use of market structure variables in empirical work. Here there are two issues. The first is whether a firm's behaviour can be inferred from the characteristics of the market in which it is operating. In other words, do firms in industries which exhibit high or low levels of concentration behave in particular ways? Could the causal chain work in the opposite direction? Could firm behaviour influence market characteristics rather than the other way round? A second concern is whether it is possible to infer anything about competitive behaviour from an examination of concentration ratios. Do firms in industries with low concentration ratios behave more competitively than firms in industries with high concentration ratios? It is possible to imagine situations where the reverse is the case.

There are, of course, no definitive answers to these questions, but it would be strange if market structure did not play some role in firm behaviour. Hence, in empirical work there are valid reasons for including variables that reflect market structure. So far, the proxies that are available have yielded ambiguous results.

The emphasis placed in the theoretical literature on economies of scale as a determinant of intra-industry trade ensures that a proxy is included in most empirical work. Several measures of such economies have been used. Some studies have used a static measure of minimum efficient scale. Dynamic proxies for economies of scale have been used by other authors. Each proxy attempts to capture a different aspect of the economies of scale concept. Even crude proxies such as GDP have been used as an indication of the potential to gain economies of scale and, hence, to produce differentiated goods.

Although the potential influence of economies of scale is not disputed, problems can arise in interpreting their influence when measures of minimum efficient scale are used as the proxy. It is assumed that if minimum efficient scale is associated with relatively high levels of output, a few firms would dominate the industry. Few varieties would be produced and the likelihood of intra-industry trade would therefore be greater. However, the converse could be true if high levels of minimum efficient scale led to the production of a standardised product by all the firms in an industry. In the case where low levels of minimum efficient scale exist, it is possible to envisage a situation in which each of the 'many' firms in operation produced their own variety. This large number of varieties can then be exchanged internationally. Hence, high levels of minimum efficient scale could lead to both more or less intra-industry trade. Low levels of intra-industry trade could also lead to greater variety and more intra-industry trade.

It has been argued (Bergstrand, 1983) that the measures of product differentiation and economies of scale are interrelated. The conditions under which economies of scale arise are also those which encourage producers to differentiate their products. To avoid multicollinearity, proxies for both these variables should not be included in the same study.

One would expect, on *a priori* grounds, that the physical distance between trading partners should influence the volume of intra-industry trade. Both the cost of acquiring information on markets and transportation costs fall the closer countries are. Countries with common borders should have higher levels of intra-industry trade than those that do not. Similarly, the greater the distance from a principal market, the smaller the volume of intra-industry trade. Proxies used for assessing the importance of distance have centred on transport costs, postage costs, physical distance (as a crude measure of both the former costs) and dummies that take into account the existence or otherwise of common borders. Once again, however, the issue of collinearity rears its head. The closer any two countries are, the more likely they are to share similar tastes. As a result, distance proxies and those used for measuring taste similarity and taste overlap will be related.

The adverse influence of tariff and non-tariff barriers has been modelled by utilising the average of nominal tariffs that apply to an industry in the case of the former and an index of non-tariff barriers in the latter case. The degree of a country's openness, i.e. the ratio of trade to GDP, has also been used as a proxy for its trade orientation.

Intra-industry trade can come about if a country exports a variety of a good manufactured using an 'old' technology while it imports a different variety from a country that utilises a 'new' technology. Difficulties in locating figures on the age of capital employed has led some authors to use alternative but less appropriate proxies. The proxies most frequently adopted include research and development expenditures, the ratio of technical personnel to total employment in an industry and the rate of product turnover.

As mentioned earlier, Caves (1981) hypothesised that foreign direct investment could act as a substitute for intra-industry trade. Instead of a firm supplying its variety of a product to a foreign market from its domestic establishments, it could, as an alternative, set up operations abroad. In this case one would expect to find an inverse relationship between intra-industry trade and foreign direct investment. By now the reader is probably aware that things are not as simple as they first appear. A plausible argument can be put forward for expecting an opposite result. A multinational corporation could set up a plant in a country to supply the domestic market and other foreign markets with one particular variety of the good. It could also supply the domestic market with other varieties from plants established in other countries. Thus, one might see the simultaneous production and exportation of one variety and the consumption and importation of other varieties. Proxies used to measure multinational activity include the extent of foreign investment and the level of trade between US multinationals and their foreign subsidiaries.

6.7.3 Aggregate empirical studies

What do empirical studies tell us about the causes of intra-industry trade? We concentrate our discussion on three types of studies. The first type examines the determinants of intra-industry trade for a single country or group of countries. The second concentrates on the causes of intra-industry trade found in a particular commodity/product group. Finally, the empirical work that applies to intra-industry trade in vertically differentiated products is discussed. There is a plethora of empirical work relating to intra-industry trade and it is impossible to cover all of it. We concentrate on those studies which we consider to be the most important.

The majority of studies have utilised cross-section or pooled data sets and have employed both linear and non-linear regression as well as logit analysis to carry out their tests. From the point of view of goodness of fit, one would not expect high R^2 results given the cross-sectional and/or pooled nature of the studies. Selected results from these studies are presented in Table 6.1. As can be seen from the table, R^2 values vary markedly. Authors have, therefore, placed more emphasis on the statistical significance of the variables under consideration. The empirical evidence shows, broadly, that the factors that are considered influential by theoreticians are statistically significant at either the 1, 5 or 10 per cent level. Taste overlap was found to be significant in all of the studies referenced in Table 6.1 except two – Bergstrand (1983) and Balassa (1986).

The proxies used to indicate product differentiation were shown to be significant in the studies by Pagoulatos and Sorensen (1975), Finger and De Rosa (1979), Caves (1981), Toh (1982), Greenaway and Milner (1984), Balassa and Bauwens (1987) and Lee (1989). In only five of the studies was the variable significant at the 1 per cent level. In the Greenaway and Milner study both the census classifications proxy of Grubel and Lloyd (1975) and that based on the ratio of advertising costs to sales revenue were significant at this level. The latter variable was also significant in Lee's work. The Hufbauer measure of product differentiation only achieves the 1 per cent level of significance in Toh's study, although it was significant at the 5 per cent level in some other studies.

Proxies for the product differentiation variable that possess the expected sign can be found in the work of Pagoulatos and Sorensen (1975) for the Hufbauer (1970) index, in Löertscher and Wolter (1980) for the census classification indicator and in the work of Tharakan (1984) and Balassa and Bauwens (1987) for the advertising costs to total sales revenue proxy.

Table 6.1   Summary of empirical studies of intra-industry trade (selected results)

Study	Trade overlap		Product differentiation				Scale economies		
	TO1	TO2	PD1	PD2	PD3	PD4	SE1	SE2	SE3
Pagoulatos and Sorensen (1975)	0.621 (3.76)***		0.229 (2.21)**	0.047 (0.272)					
Finger and De Rosa (1979)				+**					−
Löertscher and Wolter (1980)	0.296 (108.17)***		0.733 (0.45)				−0.3111 (91.23)***		
Caves (1981)			0.010 (2.01)**	7.778 (1.70)**	−0.109 (−0.20)	−0.286 (−0.56)	−0.437 (−1.02)		
Lundberg (1982)					−0.147 (0.109)*			0.012 (0.11)	
Toh (1982)	0.17 (1.35)*			5.85 (2.45)***				299.18 (2.61)***	
Bergstrand (1983)	0.003 0.098								0.538 (2.468)***
Greenaway and Milner (1984)	1.14 (6.63)***		0.15 (2.95)***			0.77 (2.47)***	0.37 (−1.75)**		
Tharakan (1984)	0.291 (7.66)***		−0.057 (−1.33)*			−0.043* (−0.14)			
Balassa (1986)	0.0548 (0.53)								
Balassa and Bauwens (1987)	0.691 (27.10)**	−1.038 (20.89)***	0.254 (12.03)***			3.628 (12.08)***	−2.248 (8.01)***		
Lee (1989)									
1970 data	−0.708 (5.09)***					0.23 (1.46)*			
	−0.726 (5.24)**		−0.049 (0.06)						
1980 data	−0.403 (4.11)**					0.038 (3.73)**			
	−0.412 (4.20)**		2.000 (343)**						
Lee and Lee (1993)	−2.647 (1.089)		−6.366 (4.804)***						
Stone and Lee (1995)	0.259 (5.205)***						0.081 (2.317)** (3)		

(*Table continues on next page*)

TO1, Per capita income similarity; TO2, Taste difference proxy.
PD1, Grubel and Lloyd (1975) index; PD2, Hufbauer (1970) index; PD3, Selling cost/Total cost; PD4, Advertising/Sales.
SE1, Average plant size/Ratio of value added per worker in small and large industries; SE2, Length of production run; SE3, Scale factor.
*Significant at 10%; **Significant at 5%; ***Significant at 1%.
(3), GDP.

Table 6.1 (*cont.*) Summary of empirical studies of intra-industry trade (selected results)

Study	Market structure			Technological factors			Foreign direct investment	
	MS1	MS2	MS3	TF1	TF2	TF3	FDI1	FDI2
Pagoulatos and Sorensen (1975)								
Finger and De Rosa (1979)						–		
Löertscher and Wolter (1980)								
Caves (1981)				1.073 (1.07)			−6.081 (−2.54)**	0.021 (2.70)**
Lundberg (1982)					0.088 (0.05)*			
Toh (1982)		−0.077 (4.16)***	−0.32 (1.81)**			0.0065 (2.16)**		
Bergstrand (1983)								
Greenaway and Milner (1984)	−0.18 (−1.76)**			0.98 (1.25)				
Tharakan (1984)								
Balassa (1986)								
Balassa and Bauwens (1987)	−2.085 (14.71)***						−0.395 (2.67)** (5)	−0.0121 (2.69)**
Lee (1989)								
1970 data				0.003 (0.24)			11.09 (4.05)** 11.123 (4.05)**	
1980 data				0.030 (3.43)** 0.016 (1.55)*			0.826 (2.13)** 0.833 (2.15)**	
Lee and Lee (1993)								
Stone and Lee (1995)								

(*Table continues on next page*)

MS1, Concentration ratio; MS2, Concentration ratio/Import share; MS3, Exports of country/Total world exports.
TF1, R&D/Sales; TF2, Technical personnel/Labour force; TF3, Average first trade date in the industry × number of patents.
FDI1, Foreign investment; FDI2, Trade with affiliated companies.
*Significant at 10%; **Significant at 5%; ***Significant at 1%.
(5), Inverse measure, so sign as predicted.

Trade theories and empirical evidence

Table 6.1 (*cont.*) Summary of empirical studies of intra-industry trade (selected results)

Study	Distance variables			Trade barriers		F-statistic	$\bar{R}^2$
	D1	D2	D3	TB1	TB2		
Pagoulatos and Sorensen (1975)		0.592 (2.85)***		−0.361 (2.66)***	−0.986 (1.20)	7.59	0.40
Finger and De Rosa (1979)						2.16	0.12
Löertscher and Wolter (1980)		−0.485 (44.52)***				39.72	0.072
Caves (1981)		1.497 (1.26)		1.145 (1.08)		3.237	0.274
Lundberg (1982)						4.69	0.207
Toh (1982)		−0.0101 (0.83)		0.206 (0.41)	−0.39 (0.41)	5.296	0.318
Bergstrand (1983)		−0.485 (3.565)***	−0.386 (1.85)*	−0.003 (0.094)		8.895	
Greenaway and Milner (1984)						10.58	0.50
Tharakan (1984)		−0.20 (−6.36)***				48.59	0.60
Balassa (1986)	−0.478 (9.64)***	0.40 (3.59)***					0.94
Balassa and Bauwens (1987)	−0.372 (49.15)***		0.302 (11.94)***	−2.753 (6.0)***			0.4430
Lee (1989)							
1970 data	−0.005 (1.41)*			−2.027 (2.07)***			0.566
	−0.005 (1.35)*			−1.899 (1.95)**			0.567
1980 data	−0.017 (6.36)**			−1.990 (1.77)**			0.538
	−0.017 (6.36)**			−2.321 (2.07)**			0.537
Lee and Lee (1993)	−1.219 (2.306)*** (1)	1.235 (1.040)		22.969 (2.404)*** (2)			0.3472
Stone and Lee (1995)	−0.813 (4.223)***			0.476 (3.964)*** (4)	−1.786 (6.581)***	130	0.8055

D1, Distance shared; D2, Inverse mean distance shipped in US; D3, Common border.
TB1, Tariff barriers; TB2, Now-tariff barriers.
*Significant at 10%; **Significant at 5%; ***Significant at 1%.
(1), Postage costs; (2), trade intensity; (4), openness.

Negative signs were obtained for the measure of product differentiation based on the proportion of sales personnel in the labour force in the Caves (1981) and Lundberg (1982) studies. The product differentiation variable, proxied by the census classification indicator, appear as negative and significant only in Tharakan's (1984) study.

What does the empirical work tell us about the product differentiation variable? It suggests that the evidence supports the theoretical hypotheses, but perhaps not quite as strongly as is the case with the taste overlap variables.

Positive and significant signs were found for economies of scale as proxied by the length of the production run, the proportion of the labour force employed in large plants and a scale factor proxying minimum efficient size by Lundberg (1982), Toh (1982), Bergstrand (1983) and Stone and Lee (1995). In contrast, the studies by Löertscher and Wolter (1980), Greenaway and Milner (1984) and Caves (1981) reported negative relationships. These latter results were, however, also taken as evidence supporting the economies of scale variable. How? Löertscher and Wolter (1980) suggested that, as their measure approximated the average firm size in each industry group, large size could be associated with standardised products. If to achieve economies of scale firms have to be large, it could be the case that a standardised product would be the result. Löertscher and Wolter cited the base metals industry as an example in support of their case.

Greenaway and Milner (1984) took a similar view, suggesting that a small minimum efficient scale would increase the number of firms in the industry and, hence, the number of varieties. The more the varieties that were produced, the greater would be the scope for intra-industry trade. Caves (1981) rationalised the negative sign of his economies of scale variable in a similar way.

Lee (1989) obtained an interesting and inconclusive result regarding economies of scale. He suggested that the Hufbauer (1970) index was a proxy for economies of scale. His coefficients had negative signs that were statistically insignificant in 1970 but significantly positive in 1980. This can be explained if it is assumed that, by 1980, there was an increase in intra-industry trade in industries with large economies of scale.

Proxies for market structure were used in only three of the studies mentioned (Caves, 1981; Toh, 1982; and Greenaway and Milner, 1984). The results suggest that, in general, these proxies conform to *a priori* expectations.

In the studies which attempted to assess the influence of technological factors on intra-industry trade the proxies used did not acquit themselves well. In only three studies are they both positive and significant – Lundberg (1982), Toh (1982) and Lee (1989). In the first two studies the variables are significant at only the 5 and 10 per cent levels. In the Lee study the results for this coefficient in 1970 indicate that there is a positive but insignificant relationship. By 1980, however, the variable is statistically significant. The empirical evidence suggests that intra-industry trade may not be greatly influenced by vertical differentiation. However, vertical differentiation may be becoming more important to intra-industry trade over time.

Caves (1981), Balassa and Bauwens (1987) and Lee (1989) attempted to determine the effect of FDI on intra-industry trade. On the whole the results are encouraging, the coefficients possessing the expected signs and being statistically significant. The hypothesis that intra-industry trade is encouraged by the existence and behaviour of multinational companies is supported.

The effects of physical or perceived distance on intra-industry trade – as modelled by mileage and postage costs, the existence of common borders or geographical location – were addressed in most of the studies. The physical distance variable appears to be an important influence. The coefficients possessing the expected signs were significant in all studies in which they were included.

The common-border variable used in the studies by Bergstrand (1983) and Balassa and Bauwens (1987) did not fare as well as physical distance. Only in the latter work are common borders perceived to have a positive effect on intra-industry trade. Bergstrand's results suggest that the opposite is the case. In the work of Lee and Lee (1993), however, geographical location appears to have a major influence on Korea's intra-industry trade.

When the reciprocal of the distance shipped in the US is used as a proxy the results are poor. Only Pagoulatos and Sorensen (1975) found a positive and significant effect on intra-industry trade. In the other studies the coefficient has a negative sign. In both Löertscher and Wolter's (1980) work and that of Tharakan (1984) it is both negative and significant.

Taken as a group, the effect of distance – especially when proxied by common borders or the reciprocal of distance shipped in the US – does not perform as strongly as other countries' specific variables. One of the reasons for this might be that multicollinearity exists between the independent variables. It is very likely that the distance variables are highly correlated with those which reflect taste overlap. Countries with similar per capita incomes are usually found to be in close geographical proximity. Similarly, cultural factors that affect tastes are more likely to be similar the nearer two countries are to one another. This cannot explain Caves' (1981) result. In his work the distance variable, measured by the inverse of distance shipped in the US, is negative. A taste overlap variable, however, was not included in Caves' work, and its omission may have affected the results obtained for the distance variable.

The evidence concerning the effect of trade barriers on intra-industry trade is very mixed. Where the average tariff level has been used as an indicator of the level of trade restrictions, only in the work of Pagoulatos and Sorensen (1975), Balassa and Bauwens (1987) and Lee (1989) are the coefficients both negative and significant. In Caves (1981) and Toh (1982) the proxy has a positive sign. One reason for the poor performance of this proxy could be that it is expected to capture too many influences on trade. Clearly, the effects of non-tariff barriers and voluntary export restraints are not adequately captured by the average tariff rate.

6.7.4 Disentangling vertically and horizontally differentiated products

The empirical work that has been discussed so far has treated intra-industry trade in differentiated products as being uniform. As we have seen from our overview of the theoretical work, this may be too restrictive an assumption. Intra-industry trade can be subdivided into horizontal and vertical categories. For empirical work this is an important distinction because different industries and, possibly, country characteristics may be associated with trade in these two product types. The conflicting results for the market/industrial structure variables in the aggregate empirical studies discussed in the previous section could be the consequence of not separating vertically and horizontally differentiated trade. The theoretical developments and empirical difficulties provided the impetus for work that has attempted to disaggregate the two types of intra-industry trade. We will examine one such study by Greenaway, Hine and Milner (1995).

The method suggested by these authors was to separate the two types of intra-industry trade to examine the relative price of exports and imports making use of unit values. The logic for using the price data was based on Stiglitz (1987). In situations where perfect information exists, a variety sold at a higher price must be of a higher quality than a product that sells at a lower price. Even in situations where information is imperfect, prices will tend to reflect quality.

To take into account the effects of imperfect information in empirical work, quality differences are measured as lying outside a specified range of the relative unit values. For their measure of quality difference, Greenaway, Hine and Milner chose the point where the ratio of export unit values (measured f.o.b.) to import unit values (measured c.i.f.) was outside a range of plus or minus 25 per cent of the mean value – a 'wide' range. Using both a 'narrow' (plus or minus 15 per cent) and 'wider' range allows some testing of the robustness of the model to variations in unit values.

6.7.5 Vertical and horizontal product differentiation – the empirical evidence

Greenaway, Hine and Milner (1995) tested two hypotheses in their study of the United Kingdom's vertical and horizontal intra-industry trade:

$$VB_j = a_0 + a_1 PD_j + a_2 SE_j + a_3 MS_j + a_4 MNE_j + e_j \qquad (6.7)$$

$$HB_j = a_0 + a_1 PD_j + a_2 SE_j + a_3 MS_j + a_4 MNE_j + e_j \qquad (6.8)$$

where VB_j and HB_j are vertical and horizontal intra-industry trade, respectively, PD_j is a proxy for product differentiation and SE_j is a proxy for economies of scale. The competitiveness of the industry is proxied by the market structure variables MS_j and MNE_j. The latter is a measure of the importance of multinational activity in industry j. The concentration ratio is used for MS_j.

Table 6.2 Intra-industry trade in vertically and horizontally differentiated goods

Independent variable	Dependent variable					
	Weighted least squares				Weighted Tobit	
	VB_j (±15%)	VB_j (±25%)	HB_j (±15%)	HB_j (±15%)	HB_j (±15%)	HB_j (±25%)
Constant	45.039 (12.12)***	36.282 (9.239)***	19.048 (4.665)***	27.791 (5.941)***	1.0817 (3.8184)***	1.4407 (4.9241)***
PD_j	−0.0848 (−3.264)***	−0.0439 (−1.597)*	0.0101 (0.3520)	−0.0310 (−0.9477)	0.0014 (0.7811)	−0.0016 (−0.8756)
SE_j	−0.1487 (−1.5087)*	0.0048 (0.0490)	−0.2045 (−1.987)**	−0.3578 (−3.3035)***	−0.00128 (−1.9399)**	−0.0198 (−2.1579)***
MS_j	0.0013 (4.231)***	0.0017 (5.230)***	−0.007 (−2.060)**	−0.0011 (−2.829)***	−0.0001 (−2.9929)***	−0.001 (−2.5930)***
MNE_j	0.0040 (0.0317)	−0.3315 (−2.483)***	0.1452 (1.046)	0.4727 (2.973)***	0.0092 (1.0265)	2.8407 (3.1253)***
N	77	77	77	77	77	77
R^2	0.287	0.339	0.059	0.22		
Standard error of estimate					17.339	18.173
Log likelihood function					−288.767	−322.125
Squared correlation between observed and expected value					0.084	0.277

*Significant at 10%; **significant at 5%; ***significant at 1%.
Source: Greenaway, Hine and Milner (1995).

A priori, one would expect VB_j to be positively associated with MNE_j and negatively associated with PD_j. It is difficult, however, to determine the expected values for SE_j and MS_j. If costs fall as output rises, SE_j could be positively related to VB_j. Contrary to this, however, would be the case where minimum economic size was small and, hence, allowed greater scope for firm entry and vertical product differentiation. Similarly, it is difficult to determine the sign for MS_j. If the production of vertically differentiated products is highly concentrated and dependent on fewness, a negative relationship would be implied (Shaked and Sutton, 1984). It could be the case, however, that many firms will not lead to vertical product differentiation if quality is based on factor inputs (Falvey, 1981). In this case the sign on MS_j would be positive.

With horizontal product differentiation, HB_j, it is easier to predict the signs of the relevant coefficients. It would be positively related to PD_j and MNE_j but negatively related to MS_j (measured by the concentration ratio) and SE_j (as represented by a minimum efficient size proxy).

The results of Greenaway, Hine and Milner (1995) are presented in Table 6.2. They suggest that VB_j is negatively related to PD_j whereas HB_j is positively related – although not significantly so. These results hold for both the plus or minus 15 per cent and the plus or minus 25 per cent criterion. Interestingly, a positive and significant relationship was found between VB_j and a proxy of vertical differentiation based on the proportion of non-manual labour to total labour employed in an industry. The assumption underlying this relationship is that product quality is systematically linked to skill intensity. The authors' findings suggest that some of the unexpected results for PD_j in the aggregate studies could be caused by not decomposing intra-industry trade into its component parts.

The results for the other explanatory variables are also interesting. The proxy VB_j was found to be directly related to the number of firms in the industry and thus supports the so-called 'large numbers' case – that more firms mean more products (Falvey, 1981). In other words, oligopolistic market structures are not necessary for this type of intra-industry trade to emerge. Support for this argument also comes from SE_j – lower minimum efficient size leads to more firms entering the market and supplying vertically differentiated products. A surprising result emerges when the MNE_j variable is examined: VB_j is negatively related to MNE_j, with a statistically significant coefficient, when one would have expected a positive and significant coefficient.

The regression and Tobit analysis carried out for HB_j also revealed some unexpected results. Although HB_j is positively related to PD_j and MNE_j, the relationship is only significant in the latter case when the range is extended to plus or minus 25 per cent. Scale economies, SE_j, has a negative sign that is significant at the 5 per cent level or better and, given the minimum efficient size proxy, in line with *a priori* expectations. The sign on the market structure coefficient, MS_j, however, is negative and significant, which conflicts with the previous result. This means that oligopolistic industries give rise to horizontal intra-industry trade. Greenaway, Hine and Milner (1995) suggested that this result goes against conventional wisdom since it implies that horizontal intra-industry trade is associated with monopolistic competition (many firms) while vertical intra-industry trade is related to oligopolistic competition (few firms). This would appear to confound the conventional theory.

6.8 Summary and conclusions

The growing importance of intra-industry trade led economists to develop theories that would account for the phenomenon. It was recognised early on that product differentiation was an important component in explaining intra-industry trade. Product differentiation could be divided into two types – horizontal and vertical. Two theoretical approaches to horizontal differentiation were proposed. One was based on the assumption that consumers try to purchase their 'favourite variety' (or at least the one that comes closest), which possesses the 'core properties' they deem essential to satisfying their needs. The second hypothesised a 'love for variety' on the part of consumers. Both theoretical explanations of horizontal product differentiation posited similar relationships for country characteristics. For instance, they accepted the importance of similarity in income levels and culture as explanations for intra-industry trade. They also both recognised industry-specific influences, such as the existence or potential for economies of scale. Where these models tended to differ was in terms of the expected effect of market structure. One approach assumed small minimum efficient size for firms and, hence, that a larger number of firms is associated with more varieties, while the other suggested that minimum efficient size is larger and, therefore, that variety is associated with few firms. These are, respectively, the so-called large and small numbers cases. The theoretical literature tends to support the large numbers situation as being a determinant of horizontal intra-industry trade.

Vertical product differentiation is defined by differences in quality between similar products. Again, country characteristics are expected to be important in generating trade in these goods. In this case, however, income and taste dissimilarity are the important determinants on the demand side – in contrast to the horizontally differentiated case. On the supply side the principal determinants are differences in countries' factor endowments. High-quality goods are produced by, for example, capital-abundant countries, whereas low-quality goods are produced by labour-abundant countries. Industry-specific factors may or may not have an important role in production. There is some suggestion that the production of vertically differentiated goods is compatible with both a small and a large number of producers. Unlike the horizontally differentiated trade situation, there is no *a priori* preference for either the large or small numbers case. Theoretical discussions also identify a wide range of institutional factors that influence the extent of intra-industry trade.

Most of the empirical work done on intra-industry trade does not distinguish between horizontal and vertical products. By and large, the aggregate empirical studies find fairly strong support for the so-called country characteristics and institutional explanations of intra-industry trade. The support for industry-specific factors, although less strong, is still fairly consistent with theoretical expectations. There are, however, some conflicting results that could be caused either by the use of inappropriate proxies or by the aggregate approach itself. The theoretical literature, after all, does suggest that horizontal and vertical intra-industry trade may have different determinants. More consistent results are obtained when intra-industry trade is subdivided into its component parts. Although this approach has been limited to one study, its results also suggest that – contrary to the commonly held beliefs – the large numbers case fits vertical intra-industry trade better than horizontal trade. These results suggest that further research is necessary before more definite conclusions can be drawn.

Although extremely important, the study of intra-industry trade represents a diversion from the main thrust of the interaction between trade theory and empirical evidence. We return to the central debate in Chapter 7.

References

Aquino, A. (1978), 'Intra-industry trade and intra-industry specialization as concurrent sources of international trade in manufactures', *Weltwirtschaftliches Archiv*, 114, pp. 275–96.

Balassa, B. (1965), *Economic Development and Integration*, Mexico City: Centro De Estudios Monetarios Latinoamericanos.

Balassa, B. (1966), 'Tariff reductions and trade in manufactures amongst industrial countries', *American Economic Review*, 56(3), pp. 466–73.

Balassa, B. (1986), 'Intra-industry trade among exporters of manufactured goods', in D. Greenaway and P. K. M. Tharakan (eds), *Imperfect Competition and International Trade*, Brighton: Wheatsheaf Books, pp. 108–28.

Balassa, B., and Bauwens, L. (1987), 'Intra-industry specialization in a multi-country and multi-industry framework', *Economic Journal*, 97, pp. 923–39.

Bergstrand, J. H. (1983), 'Measurement and determinants of intra-industry international trade', in P. K. M. Tharakan (ed.), *Intra-Industry Trade: Empirical and Methodological Aspects*, Amsterdam, North-Holland, pp. 201–53.

Brander, J. A. (1981), 'Intra-industry trade in identical commodities', *Journal of International Economics*, 11, pp. 1–14.

Brander, J., and Krugman, P. (1983), 'A reciprocal dumping model of international trade', *Journal of International Economics*, 15, pp. 313–21.

Caves, R. E. (1981), 'Intra-industry trade and market structure in the industrial countries', *Oxford Economic Papers*, 33(2), pp. 203–23.

Dixit, A., and Norman, V. (1980), *Theory of International Trade*, Cambridge: Cambridge University Press.

Dixit, A. and Stiglitz, J. (1977), 'Monopolistic competition and optimum product diversity', *American Economic Review*, 67(3), pp. 297–308.

Falvey, R. E. (1981), 'Commercial policy and intra-industry trade', *Journal of International Economics*, 11, pp: 495–511.

Finger, J. M., and De Rosa, D. A. (1979), 'Trade overlap, comparative advantage and protection', in H. Giersch (ed.), *On the Economics of Intra-Industry Trade*, Tübingen: JCB Mohr, pp. 113–41.

Gray, H. P. (1973), 'Two-way international trade in manufactures: a theoretical underpinning', *Weltwirtschaftliches Archiv*, 109, pp. 19–39.

Greenaway, D., Hine, R., and Milner, C. (1995), 'Vertical and horizontal intra-industry trade: a cross industry analysis for the United Kingdom', *Economic Journal*, 105, pp. 1505–18.

Greenaway, D., and Milner, C. (1981), 'Trade imbalance effects in the measurement of intra-industry trade', *Weltwirtschaftliches Archiv*, 117, pp. 756–62.

Greenaway, D., and Milner, C. (1984), 'A cross section analysis of intra-industry trade in the UK', *European Economic Review*, 25(3), pp. 319–44.

Greenaway, D., and Milner, C. (1986), *The Economics of Intra-Industry Trade*, Oxford: Blackwell.

Grubel, H. G., and Lloyd, P. J. (1975), *Intra-Industry Trade: The Theory and Measurement of International Trade in Differentiated Products*, New York: John Wiley and Sons.

Helpman, E. (1981), 'International trade in the presence of product differentiation, economies of scale and monopolistic competition', *Journal of International Economics*, 11, pp. 305–40.

Hesse, H. (1974), 'Hypothesis for the explanation of trade between industrial countries, 1953–1970', in H. Giersch (ed.), *The International Division of Labour: Problems and Perspectives*, Tubingen: JCB Mohr, pp. 39–59.

Hobbs, J. E. (1996), 'Evolving marketing channels for beef and lamb in the United Kingdom – a transaction cost approach', *Journal of International Food and Agribusiness Marketing*, 7(4), pp. 15–39.

Hufbauer, G. C. (1970), 'The impact of national characteristics and technology on the commodity composition of trade in manufactured goods', in R. Vernon (ed.), *The Technology Factor in International Trade*, New York: National Bureau of Economic Research, pp. 145–231.

Klein, K. K., and Kerr, W. A. (1995), 'The globalization of agriculture: a view from the farm gate', *Canada's Journal of Agricultural Economics*, 43(4), pp. 551–63.

Krugman, P. R. (1979), 'Increasing returns, monopolistic competition and international trade', *Journal of International Economics*, 9, pp. 469–79.

Krugman, P. R. (1980), 'Scale economies, product differentiation and the pattern of trade', *American Economic Review*, 70(5), pp. 950–9.

Lancaster, K. (1979), *Variety, Equity and Efficiency*, New York: Columbia University Press.

Lancaster, K. (1980), 'Intra-industry trade under perfect monopolistic competition', *Journal of International Economics*, 10, pp. 151–75.

Lee, Y. S. (1989), 'A study of the determinants of intra-industry trade among Pacific Basin countries', *Weltwirtschaftliches Archiv*, 125, pp. 346–58.

Lee, H., and Lee, Y. (1993), 'Intra-industry trade in manufactures: the case of Korea', *Weltwirtschaftliches Archiv*, 129, pp. 159–71.

Linder, S. B. (1961), *An Essay on Trade and Transformation*, New York: John Wiley and Sons.

Löertscher, R., and Wolter, F. (1980), 'Determinants of intra-industry trade: among countries and across industries', *Weltwirtschaftliches Archiv*, 116, pp. 280–93.

Lundberg, L. (1982), 'Intra-industry trade: the case of Sweden', *Weltwirtschaftliches Archiv*, 131, pp. 67–85.

Ohlin, B. G. (1933), *Interregional and International Trade*, Harvard Economic Studies no. 39, Cambridge, Mass.: Harvard University Press.

Pagoulatos, E., and Sorensen, R. (1975), 'Two-way international trade: an econometric analysis', *Weltwirtschaftliches Archiv*, 111, pp. 454–65.

Shaked, A., and Sutton, J. (1984), 'Natural oligopolies and international trade', in H. Kierzkowski (ed.), *Monopolistic Competition and International Trade*, Oxford: Oxford University Press, pp. 34–50.

Stiglitz, J. E. (1987), 'The causes and consequences of the dependence of quality on price', *Journal of Economic Literature*, 25, pp. 1–48.

Stone, J. A., and Lee, H. (1995), 'Determinants of intra-industry trade in manufactures: a longitudinal, cross-country analysis', *Weltwirtschaftliches Archiv*, 131, pp. 67–85.

Tharakan, P. K. M. (1984), 'Intra-industry trade between the industrial countries and the developing world', *European Economic Review*, 26(1–2), pp. 213–27.

Toh, K. (1982), 'A cross section analysis of intra-industry trade in US manufacturing industries', *Weltwirtschaftliches Archiv*, 118, pp. 281–301.

Varian, H. (1990), *Intermediate Microeconomics, 2nd Edition*, New York: W.W. Norton and Co.

Verdoorn, P. J. (1960), 'The intra-block trade of Benelux', in E. A. G. Robinson (ed.), *Economic Consequences of the Size of Nations*, London: Macmillan, pp. 291–329.

Vona, S. (1991), 'On the measurement of intra-industry trade: some further thoughts', *Weltwirtschaftliches Archiv*, 127, pp. 678–700.

Wickham, E., and Thompson, H. (1989), 'An empirical analysis of intra-industry trade and multinational firms', in P. M. K. Tharakan and J. Kol (eds), *Intra-Industry Trade: Theory, Evidence and Extensions*, Basingstoke: Macmillan, pp. 37–51.

CHAPTER 7

Comparative tests of trade models and attempts at theoretical reconciliation

7.1 Introduction

Although individual alternative trade theories had been tested (see Chapter 5), Hufbauer (1970) was the first to carry out an empirical analysis that pitted the Heckscher–Ohlin model and alternative models against one another on a common set of commodities and countries. The comparative testing approach has led either to the selection of one theory as the appropriate explanation of trade patterns or to attempts to develop an amalgamation of the individual theories into a general theory of international trade. It should be noted that for the first time in this book it is those economists doing the empirical testing who are providing the direct stimulus for those working on theoretical developments. In part, this reflects the increased prominence given to empirical training in the education of economists. It also, however, reflects the changing expectation within the profession that theories should be subject to empirical validation.

The first part of this chapter is devoted to the developments in empirical testing, beginning with Hufbauer's (1970) seminal paper and the principal studies that came after it. We also examine studies which use a more eclectic approach to explaining international trade patterns. The eclectic approach recognised the strengths of each of the theories – both Heckscher–Ohlin and the alternatives – and allowed different models to explain the trade patterns of a subset of goods. The second part of the chapter outlines the response of trade theorists to the empirical evidence provided by the comparative tests – particularly attempts at reconciling or amalgamating Heckscher–Ohlin with some of its rivals. The final section of the chapter will attempt to provide an explanation for why the Heckscher–Ohlin theory has persisted as the general model of international trade when the empirical evidence suggests a more agnostic approach to the study and teaching of international trade.

7.2 Testing the rival theories

7.2.1 Multi-country, multi-commodity studies

Hufbauer (1970) viewed the various trade theories as being the offspring 'of an economic marriage between product characteristics and national attributes' (p. 146). Trade acts as a compensating mechanism for international structural differences. For example, the product characteristic might be *standardised commodities* and the related national attribute *industrial sophistication*. Country I could be a country that did not possess a highly skilled labour force but was well endowed with labour and capital suitable for producing relatively unsophis-ticated standardised goods. Thus, it would have a comparative advantage in producing such products. If country II had a slightly more sophisticated industrial endowment with more advanced capital equipment and a better-skilled labour force, its comparative advantage would lie in the production of goods that were more sophisticated and less standardised than those produced by country I. A third nation (country III), endowed with even more sophisticated capital and labour, would have a comparative advantage in specialised products such as single-order capital goods or combat aircraft.

To test whether trade flows reflected economic structure, Hufbauer (1970) used data from twenty-four non-communist bloc countries which accounted for 90 per cent of world exports in manufactures in 1965. Besides the centrally planned command economies, countries specialising in manufactured exports requiring non-transportable natural resources and nations with small manufac-turing export sectors were excluded from Hufbauer's examination. As a result, the tests undertaken were biased in favour of giving support to the economic structure hypothesis from the outset as the tests did not include all goods and all nations. Given the limitations of the data available, however, one should not place too great an emphasis on this deficiency.

Commodities were classified according to the twenty-eight two-digit divisions and the 102 three-digit categories identified in sections 5, 6, 7 and 8 of the Standard International Trade Classification (SITC). By restricting the goods to be examined to those in these SITC categories, manufactured products with a high content of non-transportable natural resources were excluded as well as direct trade in raw materials.

The various characteristics attributed to goods in each SITC category were developed from US data. Hufbauer was aware that the available data had limitations. The characteristics could only be improperly measured, and using US data to ascribe characteristics to non-US exports denied any variation in commodity characteristics among countries. Furthermore, characteristics were derived from industry data rather than commodity data, and although manufactured goods embody characteristics acquired from inputs drawn from ancillary industries, his analysis was carried out in terms of direct inputs and characteristics.

Hufbauer used both simple and Spearman weighted rank correlations to discern the relationship between national attributes and the characteristics embodied in the exports and imports of the countries that were used in his study. Weighting the data according to a country's contribution to the total exports of the sample countries is essential as the Spearman rank correlation technique cannot directly compensate for the importance of international trade to different countries.

National attributes were: (1) fixed capital per manufacturing employee, calculated by summing the outlays on gross investment between 1953 and 1964 and dividing the total by manufacturing employment in the latter year; (2) skilled employees as a percentage of the economically active population; (3) total manufacturing output; and (4) GDP per capita. Fixed capital per manufacturing employee was used to test the Heckscher–Ohlin factor proportions explanation for trade patterns. The skilled employment ratio was used to test the human skills theory; manufacturing output to assess the effect of economies of scale; and GDP per capita to examine the importance of both technological gap and product cycle theories.

Product characteristics included: (1) capital per employee; (2) the ratio of skilled to unskilled labour; (3) wages per employee; (4) an economies of scale proxy based on value added; and (5) plant size, as shown by the number of people employed in the commodity's production. Other characteristics were: first trade date (the date at which the product first appeared in the trade statistics); and product differentiation, as proxied by the product's coefficient of variation in US export unit values to different countries in 1965.

The results of the simple and weighted rank correlations between commodity characteristics and national attributes are presented in Table 7.1 and the simple correlation coefficients are given in Table 7.2. To limit the effects of outlier observations, the country most at odds with the predictions of each theory was dropped from the calculations of the rank correlation procedures. Thus, each theory was tested against favourable data and allowed to look its 'best' statistically. Note, in the case of the consumer goods ratio, that a negative correlation indicates a relationship in agreement with the hypothesis for exports; the reverse is true in the case of imports.

Testing the Heckscher–Ohlin hypothesis by correlating fixed capital per man and capital embodied in national exports appeared to give the theory considerable support. The Spearman rank and weighted rank correlation results in Table 7.1 are 0.704 and 0.736, respectively, while the simple correlation in Table 7.2 is 0.625. When Mexico was excluded on the grounds that non-ferrous metal capital-intensive goods accounted for 35 per cent of its exports, the Spearman correlation coefficient rose to 0.814. On the imports side, the results in Table 7.2 show that the relationship was negative and that it was not strong or significant. Although the aggregate results lent support to the Heckscher–Ohlin theory, findings for some individual countries – such as the US, Japan, Germany,

Israel and Taiwan – did not. Hufbauer, nevertheless, concluded that the factor proportions theory was an appropriate framework within which to analyse international trade flows.

The correlations in Tables 7.1 and 7.2 also lent support to the human skills/capital hypothesis whether the skill ratio or wages per employee was used as a proxy. The Spearman rank correlation between the skill ratio and exports is 0.695 while the weighted correlation is 0.822. The corresponding figures for

Table 7.1 Rank correlations between commodity characteristics and national attributes (24 countries)

Commodity characteristics of exports	National attributes			
	Fixed capital	Skilled employees	Manufacturing output	GDP per capita
Capital per employee				
Rank correlation	0.704[a]			
Weighted rank corr.	0.736			
Skill ratio				
Rank correlation		0.695[b]		
Weighted rank corr.		0.822		
Wages per employee				
Rank correlation		0.784[c]		
Weighted rank corr.		0.960		
Scale economies				
Rank correlation			0.627[d]	
Weighted rank corr.			0.778	
Consumer goods ratio				
Rank correlation				−0.818[e]
Weighted rank corr.				−0.801
First trade date				
Rank correlation				0.698[f]
Weighted rank corr.				0.864
Product differentiation				
Rank correlation				0.724[g]
Weighted rank corr.				0.763

a 0.814 with Mexico excluded.
b 0.796 with Israel excluded.
c 0.912 with Israel excluded.
d 0.710 with India excluded.
e −0.864 with Mexico excluded.
f 0.764 with Taiwan excluded.
g 0.788 with Canada excluded.
Source: Hufbauer (1970).

wage rates are 0.784 and 0.960, respectively. Dropping Israel from the sample of countries increased the rank correlations to 0.796 for skills in trade and 0.912 for wages in trade.

In attempting to analyse the effect of economies of scale on exports, Hufbauer (1970) took a simpler view than that of Drèze (1960). Drèze suggested that the length of production runs rather than the absolute size of plants was the appropriate proxy, but data limitations led Hufbauer to employ the statistical relationship between value added per worker and plant size as a proxy. Relating this proxy to manufacturing output gave a Spearman rank correlation (Table 7.1) of 0.627, which rose to 0.710 when India was eliminated – the weighted correlation is 0.778. The simple correlation coefficient, however, was much lower at 0.457 and not significantly different from zero (Table 7.2). Relating scale

Table 7.2 Simple correlations between commodity characteristics and national attributes (24 countries)

Commodity characteristics	National attributes			
	Fixed capital	Skilled employees	Manufacturing output	GDP per capita
Capital per employee				
Exports	0.625	0.396*	0.067*	0.500*
Imports	−0.353*	−0.429*	0.232*	−0.257
Skill ratio				
Exports	0.696	0.714	0.437*	0.777
Imports	−0.409*	−0.604	−0.476*	−0.552
Wages per employee				
Exports	0.789	0.700	0.345*	0.799
Imports	−0.171*	−0.375*	−0.193*	−0.283*
Scale economies				
Exports	0.739	0.760	0.457*	0.809
Imports	−0.383*	−0.463*	−0.374	−0.516
Consumer goods ratio				
Exports	−0.748	−0.736	−0.192*	−0.727
Imports	0.414*	0.535	0.274*	0.505
First trade date				
Exports	0.657	0.735	0.480*	0.765
Imports	0.166*	0.139	−0.229*	0.054*
Product differentiation				
Exports	0.633	0.717	0.392*	0.749
Imports	−0.321*	−0.438*	−0.428*	−0.458*

*Not significant at the 1% level.
Source: Hufbauer (1970).

Table 7.3 Spearman and weighted rank correlations between commodity characteristics

Spearman rank correlations

	Capital per employee	Skill ratio	Wages per employee	Scale economies	Consumer goods	First trade	Product differentiation
Capital per employee	1.000						
Skill ratio	0.590	1.000					
Wages per employee	0.695	0.642	1.000				
Scale economies	−0.058*	0.165*	0.094*	1.000			
Consumer goods ratio	0.479	0.204*	0.418	−1.50*	1.000		
First trade date	0.105*	0.236*	0.220*	0.157*	0.123*	1.000	
Product differentiation	−0.119*	0.547	0.199*	0.061*	0.039*	0.169*	1.000

Weighted rank correlations

	Capital per employee	Skill ratio	Wages per employee	Scale economies	Consumer goods	First trade	Product differentiation
Capital per employee	1.000						
Skill ratio	0.547	1.000					
Wages per employee	0.655	0.579	1.000				
Scale economies	0.298	0.501	0.374	1.000			
Consumer goods ratio	0.505	0.234*	0.513	0.191*	1.000		
First trade date	0.111*	0.377*	0.349	0.366	0.086	1.000	
Product differentiation	−0.173*	0.686	0.018*	0.077*	0.054*	0.011*	1.000

*Not significantly different from zero at the 1% level.
Source: Hufbauer (1970).

economies to GDP per capita, however, gave a higher coefficient of 0.809 – which was significant. Hufbauer suggested that this difference in results might have arisen because the benefits of economies of scale accrued not just to size but also to economic sophistication. Small European countries that had access to large markets could, therefore, export products benefiting from economies of scale, whereas poorer but larger economies might not be able to export effectively because their products lacked the sophistication to appeal to foreign consumers.

Hufbauer took first trade dates as his proxy for the existence of technological gaps and related these to his proxy for industrial sophistication – GDP per capita. The Spearman rank correlation was 0.698, while the weighted version was higher at 0.864 (Table 7.1). Excluding Taiwan from the sample – because it had a younger set of exports than its level of GDP would indicate – increased the Spearman rank correlation to 0.764. The simple correlation coefficient was also high and significant with a value of 0.765 (Table 7.2).

Vernon's (1966) product cycle was tested by relating the coefficient of variation in unit export values to GDP per capita, with the latter again acting as a proxy for economic sophistication. The reasoning underlying this approach was that the more complex its economic structure, the more a country would specialise in and export differentiated goods. The results given in Table 7.1 indicate a strong relationship, with a Spearman rank coefficient of 0.724 and a weighted coefficient of 0.763. Excluding Canada, because it had highly standardised exports despite being a rich country, raised the Spearman rank correlation to 0.788. The simple correlation coefficient in Table 7.2 was 0.749 and significant.

These empirical results suggested that each alternative theory as well as the traditional Heckscher–Ohlin hypothesis have a role in explaining trade patterns. This led Hufbauer (1970) to conclude that as no single theory could be said to have a monopoly of explanatory power, an amalgam might be more appropriate as a general theory. However, he wondered whether the good performance of one proxy could actually be due to its positive correlation to the good performance of another proxy. For instance, if a capital-intensive good also used a high proportion of skilled manpower in its production, then both the Heckscher–Ohlin theory and the human capital hypothesis could be used to explain international exchange in the good. This possibility was investigated by examining the intercorrelations between commodity characteristics. Again, both Spearman and weighted rank correlations were calculated, and they are presented in Table 7.3.

The results indicate that there are significant interrelationships between the commodity characteristics. For example, the capital–labour ratio can be seen to be closely correlated with both the skill ratio and wage rates. Of course, the skill ratio and wage rate are also correlated. Thus, it seemed that goods that were capital-intensive were also skill-intensive. The product cycle proxy – product differentiation – was also found to be related to the skill ratio but not to the capital–labour ratio, wage rates, scale economies or the first trade date. Economies of scale were not significantly correlated with the capital–labour ratio, skill ratio or wages in the Spearman rank correlations, although a somewhat stronger relationship appears in the weighted rank correlations. The intercorrelations among the commodity characteristics led Hufbauer (1970) to the conclusion that trading patterns that either confirmed or denied the Heckscher–Ohlin theory also supported or undermined the human skills thesis. Furthermore, as differentiated commodities (i.e. those associated with the product cycle) also required skilled labour, the human capital and product cycle hypotheses were linked.

Significant simple and Spearman correlations were also found between national attributes. These results are given in Table 7.4. All the attributes except manufacturing output were closely related. Hufbauer concluded that a composite attribute might perform just as well or as poorly in explaining different export characteristics, as was the case when the individual proxies were used.

In summing up his findings, Hufbauer suggested that export patterns exhibited 'an intriguing kind of selectivity' in that goods were favoured which contained characteristics that matched a country's economic structure. Complex trading patterns could, therefore, be explained by a number of theories, but his preference was for a neo-factor proportions model that incorporated human capital. The neo-technology theories were not dismissed, but Hufbauer considered them to be inferior. This conclusion was reached largely as a result of the

Table 7.4 Spearman and simple correlations between national attributes

Spearman rank correlations

	Fixed capital per employee	Skilled employees	Total manufacturing output	Gross GDP per capita
Fixed capital per employee	1.000			
Skilled employees	0.889	1.000		
Total manufacturing output	0.545	0.469*	1.000	
GDP per capita	0.947	0.892	0.579	1.000

Simple correlations

	Fixed capital per employee	Skilled employees	Total manufacturing output	Gross GDP per capita
Fixed capital per employee	1.000			
Skilled employees	0.848	1.000		
Total manufacturing output	0.480*	0.334*	1.000	
GDP per capita	0.914	0.879	0.579	1.000

*Not significantly different from zero at the 1% level.
Source: Hufbauer (1970).

difficulties involved in measuring the largely intangible concepts of technological lead, the newness of products, product differentiation and economies of scale. The modified Heckscher–Ohlin approach based on the more tangible explanatory variables of physical capital and labour of different types and qualities did not suffer from similar constraints on their use.

Hufbauer's (1970) was a path-breaking study because it incorporated not only the US's but also other manufacturing nations' exports and because it matched exports with both national attributes and commodity characteristics. The study did, however, have two major drawbacks. It applied US product characteristics to the goods produced by all countries and only one year's data (1965) were used in the calculations.

A series of studies by Hirsch (1974a; 1974b; 1975) and one by Aquino (1981) tried to overcome the criticisms of the Hufbauer (1970) study and further test the modified Heckscher–Ohlin model. The modified model allowed for different labour skill levels and non-homogeneous capital. This neo-factor proportions theory was tested against the technology models. Leamer (1974) used an alternative statistical approach to examine the relative explanatory power of the different trade theories. Hirsch, Aquino and Leamer came to different conclusions than those of the Hufbauer (1970) study. We will now proceed to summarise Hirsch's studies before going on to examine Aquino's and Leamer's work.

Although Hirsch (1974a) adopted Hufbauer's (1970) basic approach, his study differed in one major aspect. In Hufbauer's work comparative advantage was implicit rather than explicit. He believed that the validity of a trade model was proved by demonstrating a reasonable statistical relationship between a country's attributes and the characteristics of the goods it exported. Hirsch, however, made the relationship explicit by attempting to show that the matchings between country and industry attributes yielded a comparative advantage.

Hirsch (1974a) proposed that comparative advantage arose from the interactive outcome between factor endowment – which is a country variable – and factor intensity – a commodity characteristic. For expository purposes he ascribed only two values, high or low, to endowments, intensity and comparative advantage. Thus, a country would have a high comparative advantage in a good when high factor intensity was combined with high factor endowment or when low factor intensity was combined with low factor endowment. Conversely, comparative advantage was low when high factor intensity was combined with low factor endowment or low factor intensity was combined with high factor endowment.

To link comparative advantage with both factor intensity and factor endowment, Hirsch's (1974a) methodology involved calculating an export performance index for each industry in every sample country and correlating this index with a measure of the country's capital and skill endowments. These simple correlation coefficients were then ranked in descending order of magnitude. In the next step five additional sets of rankings were calculated from industry characteristics: research and development, the proportion of skilled labour and average wages – which were used as proxies for neo-technology variables. Physical and overall capital intensity were used as characteristics that would be important for the Heckscher–Ohlin orthodoxy. The rankings of characteristics were then correlated with the industry rankings obtained earlier. Hence, Hirsch was able to connect a country's factor endowment with its industries' factor intensities and the comparative advantage of its exports.

Hirsch (1974a) applied this methodology to twenty-nine developed countries and eighteen manufacturing industries for which comparative data were available for 1970. Lack of data led to the exclusion of many developing countries as well as some notable advanced industrialised economies, such as France, the Netherlands and Switzerland.

The countries' index of comparative advantage was calculated by using Balassa's (1965) formulation, which can be summarised by the equation

$$EP_{ij} = \left(\frac{E_{ij}}{E_i} \right) \bigg/ \left(\frac{E_j}{W} \right)$$

where EP_{ij} is the export performance of good i in country j, E_{ij} is the export of good i by country j, E_i is world imports of good i, E_j is total exports of country j, and W is total world imports of manufactured goods.

The term E_{ij}/E_i is the share of country j's export of the total sample's trade in good i, while E_j/W shows country j's total exports as a proportion of world trade. Thus, industry i's performance was related to the total performance of country j's industries.

Factor endowments and factor intensities were also estimated by Hirsch (1974a). Given the existence of multicollinearity between research and development, value added, wages, the proportion of skilled employees in the labour force and income per capita, he decided to use only one measure as the proxy to represent a country's endowments of capital and technology. The weighted average value added per employee in the non-agricultural sector of the economy was selected because it possessed two qualities. First, it represented the contribution of both capital and skills (human capital) to production, and, second, it was the non-agricultural sector's equivalent to GDP per capita.

Factor intensities were also estimated. Capital intensity was measured in two ways. The first, K_i, used the non-wage element of value added per employee. As value added was composed of employment costs plus the share of capital, K_i was considered a suitable measure. One drawback of this measure was that the profit element in K_i could have been abnormally high or low in a particular year and/or it could have been influenced by monopoly prices in the industries under investigation.

As a result of the limitations of K_i, Hirsch decided to use an alternative proxy – total value added per employee, VA_i, in each industry. By including wage costs, which can act as a proxy for skill differentials, VA_i was expected to capture the human capital approach to factor intensity.

The neo-technology indicators of factor intensity were represented by research and development expenditure as a percentage of net sales, $R\&D_i$, and wages per employee, W_i, which reflected the skills of the labour force. The higher a worker's level of skill, the higher the wage he could command. Hirsch's final technological proxy was the more conventional percentage of skilled employees in the labour force, S_i. In common with other studies, all the proxies for factor intensities were based on data for US industries.

Hirsch's (1974a) results from correlating VA_j with EP_{ij} are presented in Table 7.5, where they are ranked and subdivided according to their values into three types of industries. Industries whose comparative advantage was positively correlated to per capita value added and equal to or greater than 0.48 were classified as 'H' industries. Those with large negative correlations were called 'L' industries, while the 'N' classification consisted of those whose comparative advantage was neither positively nor negatively correlated with value added. In addition, a number of industries were classified as resource based ('R-B'). Due to their special features they were excluded from the remainder of the analysis.

Table 7.6 shows the ranking of industries based on the correlations reported in Table 7.5 against the rankings of both the neo-technology variables ($R\&D$, S and W) and the neo-factor proportion variables (K, VA). The corresponding Spearman rank correlations are also reported. The rank correlations show that in the eighteen-industry sample the highest correlations were achieved by the neo-technology proxies $R\&D$, S and W followed by the neo-factor proportions variables VA and K, with the latter not significant at the 5 per cent level. The factor intensity rankings were widely and consistently out of line with the ranking of the correlation coefficients for drugs and non-metallic minerals, and these industries were dropped. The correlations were recalculated on a sub-sample of sixteen industries. The magnitude of all the Spearman rank

Table 7.5 Correlation between value added per employee and export performance

H goods $r \geq 0.48$		N goods $-0.07 \leq r \leq 0.17$		L goods $r \leq -0.21$		R-B goods	
0.76	Motor vehicles	0.17	Metal goods	−0.21	Clothing	−0.23	Beverages
0.72	Non-electrical machinery	0.13	Plastics	−0.24	Non-metallic minerals	−0.06	Tobacco
		0.07	Shipbuilding			−0.03	Wood
0.55	Electrical machinery	0.01	Iron and steel	−0.25	Footwear	0.22	Paper
		0.00	Drugs	−0.47	Textiles	−0.17	Fertiliser
0.55	Instruments	−0.03	Furniture	−0.50	Leather	−0.02	Basic chemicals
0.48	Synthetics	−0.03	Rubber				
		−0.07	Printing and publishing			−0.20	Non-ferrous metals

Source: Hirsch (1994a).

correlations improved and the correlation for K became significant. The neo-technology variables, particularly $R\&D$, were still more highly correlated with the industry ranking than the neo-factor proportion proxies. These results led Hirsch (1974a) to propose that industries whose export performances were positively associated with large capital endowments were more likely to be $R\&D$- than capital-intensive. This can be seen clearly from Table 7.6, where five out of the six top-ranking industries in terms of $R\&D$ belong to the 'H' group, whose comparative advantage index is positively correlated with per capita value added.

Table 7.6 Ranked H, N and L industries and rankings of neo-technology and neo-factor proportions proxies

| Industries ranked by correlation between EP_{ij} and VA_j | Proxies | | | | |
| | Neo-technology | | | Neo-factor proportions | |
	R&D	S	W	K	VA
1. Motor vehicles (H)	6	6	3	4	3
2. Non-electrical (H) machinery	4	8	4	7	6
3. Electrical machinery (H)	1	4	9	11	11
4. Instruments (H)	3	3	6	3	4
5. Synthetics (H)	5	2	5	2	2
6. Metal goods (N)	9	7	11	9	10
7. Plastics (N)	13	14	13	10	12
8. Shipbuilding (N)	11	11	7	18	13
9. Iron and steel (N)	10	13	2	12	8
10. Drugs (N)	2	1	1	1	1
11. Furniture (N)	14	12	14	15	14
12. Rubber (N)	7	10	8	5	5
13. Printing and publishing (N)	12	5	10	8	9
14. Clothing (L)	16	16	18	17	18
15. Non-metallic minerals (L)	8	9	12	6	7
16. Footwear (L)	18	18	17	16	17
17. Textiles (L)	17	17	16	14	16
18. Leather (L)	15	15	15	13	15
Spearman rank correlations					
Eighteen industries	0.76*	0.65*	0.70*	0.46	0.53*
Sixteen industries (excluding 10 and 15)	0.84*	0.74*	0.74*	0.62*	0.72*

*Significantly different from zero at the 5% level.
H, N, L are industry groupings – see Table 7.5.
Source: Hirsch (1974a).

An additional test of the relative performance of the two models provided further evidence to confirm the relative importance of the technology variables. The export/output ratios of the sampled industries by country were regressed against skill intensity, capital intensity, a scale variable and a dummy variable denoting resource-based industries. The regressions yielded some interesting results. The skill variable performed as expected, with positive and significant coefficients for a group of high-income countries – exceptions being Denmark, Finland and Austria. Results for the capital variable showed that the coefficients were negative in all high-income countries except one and, therefore, the relationship was contrary to expectations. The scale variable, represented by average value added per establishment, was positive in all the high-income countries save one but was significant in only three. The dummy variable proxying resource-based industries exhibited a significant positive relationship with exports in all countries that possessed a high ratio of land area to population.

At the other end of the spectrum, the exports of countries with low incomes per head also provided interesting results. As one would expect to find an association between low per capita incomes and low skill levels, countries' exports would not be expected to be positively related to skills. Hirsch's (1974a) results appear to confirm this hypothesis, with the skill variables being negative in seven of the nine low-income group countries. This group of low-income countries also had negative capital intensity coefficients, although they were higher than those for the high-income group of countries.

For the two intermediate groups of countries, comprising those with medium to high and medium to low GNPs per capita, Hirsch (1974a) found that on the whole exports were negatively related to both capital and skill intensity.

Both the rank correlations and multiple regressions indicated that the proposition that human capital endowments and the export performance of human capital-intensive industries were positively related was upheld. The evidence did not, however, support the Heckscher–Ohlin view that material capital endowments were correlated with the exports of capital-intensive industries. To Hirsch (1974a), it was clear that when capital was disaggregated into material and human elements the neo-technology model explained trade patterns better than the Heckscher–Ohlin model.

In another paper Hirsch (1975) came to similar conclusions, although in this case the tests carried out were specifically designed to compare the product cycle theory with Heckscher–Ohlin. Hirsch examined eight industries in twenty-eight countries, dividing them into four sub-groups. These were high (Hl) and low labour skill (Ll) industries and those with high and low capital intensity (Hk and Lk, respectively). Data from 1969 were used.

Consistent with his (1974a) paper, Hirsch (1975) maintained that the export performance of an industry (as measured by an index of comparative advantage) should be related to national attributes. For example, countries with an abundance of physical capital should have a comparative advantage in capital-intensive industries. Accepting the empirical evidence that capital and skills are related via GNP (i.e. countries with high GNP per capita are highly endowed with both skills and physical capital), Hirsch found it useful to substitute GNP per capita for physical capital and skills. Thus, when testing the Heckscher–Ohlin theory, where capital and labour are the two factors in question, one would expect to find a positive relationship between the export performance of capital-intensive industries and GNP per capita. As long as high-skill industries are also capital-intensive, they too would have a positive relationship with GNP per capita. If they were labour-intensive, however, one would expect the opposite result. The reasons for these expectations relate to Hirsch's interpretation of Heckscher–Ohlin. In his strict interpretation of factor proportions, skills had no role to play in the determination of trade flows.

A different set of results was expected for the product cycle model. Here a positive relationship was expected between the export performance of high-skill industries and GNP per capita. The latter was used as a surrogate for skill abundance. This positive relationship would be expected whether the high-skill industries were capital- or labour-intensive. The predictions for low-skill industries were in line with those of Heckscher–Ohlin – namely, negative correlations between export performance and GNP per capita.

This still left predictions made in respect of capital-intensive industries to be dealt with. Hirsch (1975) suggested that expectations regarding these industries were ambiguous and depended on whether one took a more or less extreme version of the product cycle as a reflection of reality. For example, if skills alone determined comparative advantage, then high capital requirements for a given industry need not adversely affect the comparative advantage of low-income countries in these industries. Adopting a less extreme version of the product cycle – which included capital intensity in determining comparative advantage over the phases of the product cycle – led to the conclusion that per capita GNP was positively related to the export performance of low-skill, capital-intensive industries. Table 7.7 presents the expected signs for the relationship between export performance and per capita output by industry as predicted by the two trade models under consideration.

Table 7.7 Predicted relationship between exports and GDP per capita for industry groupings

Trade model	High-skill industries		Low-skill industries	
	Hk	Hl	Lk	Ll
Heckscher–Ohlin	+	−	+	−
Product cycle – extreme version	+	+	−	−
Product cycle – mild version	+	+	+	−

Source: Hirsch (1975).

Assuming that export performance and factor endowments were linearly related, Hirsch (1975) estimated

$$E_j = a_j + b_j Y$$

where E is export performance, j denotes the four industry sub-groups Hl, Hk, Ll and Lk, Y is GNP per capita, and a and b are constants.

The results of these regressions – presented in the upper part of Table 7.8 – are consistent with the expectations of the product cycle model. Industries classified Hl were predicted to have a negative relationship between export performance and GNP per capita in the Heckscher–Ohlin theory but a positive relationship in the product cycle approach. Furthermore, the weaker product cycle hypothesis gained credibility given its assumption of a positive relationship between export performance and GNP per capita in industries classified as Lk.

Hirsch (1975) suggested that there were two possible biases that might have affected the results. The first related to the selection of industry groups and the range of countries in the sample. For instance, the low-income countries' exports were highly skewed towards natural resource-intensive industries. With

Table 7.8 Regressing exports on GNP per capita

Industry group	a	b	r^2
Independent variable: Exports by industry/Total exports (based on 28 countries)			
High skill – capital intensive (Hk)	1.823	0.00239 (3.199)	0.29
High skill – labour intensive (Hl)	3.743	0.00654 (3.954)	0.38
Low skill – capital intensive (Lk)	2.131	0.00387 (2.68)	0.22
Low skill – labour intensive (Ll)	18.678	−0.00498 (−2.378)	0.18
Independent variable: Exports by industry/Exports of four groups of industries (based on 28 countries)			
High skill – capital intensive (Hk)	14.527	0.0017 (0.802)	0.03
High skill – labour intensive (Hl)	11.920	0.0123 (5.647)	0.55
Low skill – capital intensive (Lk)	12.523	0.0047 (1.563)	0.09
Low skill – labour intensive (Ll)	60.998	−0.0188 (−6.983)	0.66
Independent variable: Exports by industry/Total exports (based on 18 countries*)			
High skill – capital intensive (Hk)	2.93	0.0023 (2.116)	0.22
High skill – labour intensive (Hl)	10.52	0.0051 (2.994)	0.35
Low skill – capital intensive (Lk)	5.13	0.0034 (1.823)	0.16
Low skill – labour intensive (Ll)	31.86	−0.0097 (−4.823)	0.59

*Selected on the basis that the export share of the four industry groups exceeded 30% of total exports.
t-values in parenthesis.
Source: Hirsch (1975).

the export of industrial goods thus reduced as a percentage of total exports, low industrial export performance would have been related to low GNP per capita rather than to export endowment. Hence, the correlation coefficient between export performance and GNP per capita would have been systematically biased.

By relating each industry's exports to those of its group rather than to total exports, Hirsch (1975) hoped to eliminate much of the bias that would arise in the more general regressions. The results obtained by using this alternative export performance variable are given in the middle part of Table 7.8. The coefficients have the same signs as those in previous regressions, although the relationships are not as strong. The results appear to support the more extreme version of the product cycle model and suggested to Hirsch that skills, and not capital endowments, are the main determinants of comparative advantage.

A second source of bias could have arisen from the inclusion of countries with low GNP per capita and low industrial exports. The potential bias was expected to be reduced by including only the eighteen countries whose industrial exports were equal to or exceeded 30 per cent of total exports. The results, which appear in the lower part of Table 7.8, differ little from those in the upper panel.

The two studies by Hirsch (1974a, 1975) appear to confirm that technology – and the factors that contribute to the product cycle theory in particular – are the major determinants of comparative advantage and, therefore, trade patterns. This conclusion depends crucially on Hirsch's assumption that skill intensity has no influence in the Heckscher–Ohlin model. While this may be true in the strict version of Heckscher–Ohlin where only physical capital and labour are considered factors of production, it could not be said to be the case for the later and modified variants of the theory, which included skilled labour as separate factor categories.

Aquino (1981) attempted to resolve the appropriate model question by using a time-series, cross-section approach. His study was intended to take account of the extent, pace and timing of changes in the pattern of comparative advantage in manufactured goods. Aquino postulated that technologically rich countries had a comparative advantage in the production of new goods, which were, by their nature, technology-intensive. As these products matured, however, their production would move to countries that were relatively well endowed with factors other than skilled labour and technical know-how. For Aquino, the decreasing technological intensity of goods over time set the product cycle model of trade apart from the revised Heckscher–Ohlin theory that allowed for differences in human capital.

Aquino proceeded to assess the importance of technological endowments by testing two models and comparing the signs of the parameters. His reading of the trade theory literature led him to adopt two specific models for testing. In the first, a trade pattern – once again shown by Balassa's (1965) index of revealed comparative advantage – was tested against a technology variable and a proxy for scale economies – the size of the domestic market. The second model included a measure of capital endowments as an additional independent variable.

More formally, these relationships were specified as

$$S_{ijt} = a_{it} T_{jt}^{e_{it}^T} M_{jt}^{e_{it}^M} \tag{7.1}$$

$$S_{ijt} = a_{it} T_{jt}^{e_{it}^T} C_{jt}^{e_{it}^C} M_{jt}^{e_{it}^M} \tag{7.2}$$

where S_{ijt} is the Balassa index for country j and product i in year t. T_{jt}, C_{jt} and M_{jt} measure country j's endowments of technology, capital and home market size, respectively.

Aquino used a composite measure of technology. For fifteen of the twenty-six countries in his sample he took as his proxies: weighted past expenditures on R&D up to 1955; the number of innovations per capita between 1945–68 and the per capita receipts for patents and licences in 1963–64; and the total wage cost per working hour. For the remaining eleven countries GDP per capita was taken as a proxy for technology endowments. Aquino conceded that his composite measure had many flaws, but he found that it performed just as well as the proxy based solely on GDP per capita.

The physical capital endowment proxy used was cumulative gross fixed capital investment per capita. Where possible, it was weighted to allow for depreciation over the period under analysis. Whether Aquino's linear system of weights was appropriate is open to question. Alternative weightings that increasingly discounted older equipment might have been more realistic.

In line with previous studies, Aquino took total GDP as his proxy for domestic market size. He did make some adjustments, however, to reduce the possible overvaluation of the per capita incomes of richer countries that could arise from conversion to US dollars.

Aquino himself was aware that his measures were open to criticism, and his results should be viewed as tentative in nature. He emphasised this point by drawing attention to the problems associated with the use of standard published sources. For example, product classifications should, ideally, refer to homogeneous goods, but in practice they are a somewhat heterogeneous mix of products.

Aquino's (1981) empirical work showed that, of the twenty-five manufacturing industries analysed, fifteen exhibited clear shifts of comparative advantage. Only seven shifts in comparative advantage could be detected if estimating equation (7.1) was used to arrive at the technology elasticity and only four if specification (7.2) was used. Over time, four shifts were detected by both models, but in three cases the type of shift differed substantially between the two specifications of the estimating equations.

Aquino suggested that multicollinearity between technology endowments and capital endowments could account for the disappearance of the shifts found in (7.1) when (7.2) was used. For the four cases where both models showed shifts in the technology coefficient, Aquino's preferred model was (7.2) because the $\bar{R}^2$ value increased substantially.

Scale elasticity was significant and positive over the period 1962–74 in the cases of passenger motor cars, motor vehicle parts, organic chemicals and aircraft. For 1966–71 this was also true for office machines. For six industries, scale elasticity was nearly positive and increased in statistical significance over the period of analysis, becoming significantly different from zero towards the end of the period. It was negative and significant in one industry over the whole period and negative and significant over part of the study period for three other industries. It was negative and not significant for the remaining industries.

What are the theoretical implications of Aquino's (1981) results? While admitting the problems of data and multicollinearity among the independent variables, he felt that his work confirmed the previous findings that a model incorporating inter-industry differences in skills or technological intensity explained international specialisation in manufactures at any given moment of time. Aquino felt that his results showed that the product cycle model satisfactorily explained changes in the trade patterns of manufactured goods over time.

Using a different methodology and statistical technique, Leamer (1974) also attempted to 'filter the empirically relevant from the empirically irrelevant theories' (p. 350). He classified trade-determining variables into three groups: first, those that indicated a country's state of development, such as GDP and population; second, resistance variables, such as tariffs and distance from markets; and, third, resource variables covering capital intensity, R&D, education levels and electricity use. Electricity use was chosen as a proxy for industrial sophistication. These three groups of independent variables were then used to explain a dependent variable that was defined as the share of imports (expressed as a proportion of the GNP). A sample of twelve countries and twenty-eight two-digit group industries selected from the SITC categories 51 and above were used.

Formally, Leamer's (1974) model was

$$\log M_{ik} = \alpha_k + \beta_{1k} \log Y_i + \beta_{2k} \log Y_{j(i)} +$$

$$+ \beta_{3k} \log N_i + \beta_{4k} \log N_{j(i)} +$$

$$+ \left(\gamma_{1k} + \gamma_{2k} Y_i\right) \log\left(1 + t_{ik}\right) + \gamma_{3k} \log\left(1 + t_i\right) +$$

$$+ \gamma_{4k} \log\left(1 + t_{j(i)}\right) + \delta_k \log D_i +$$

$$+ \sum_l \in_{lk} \log\left(\frac{E_{il}}{E_{j(i)l}}\right)$$

where M is imports, Y is GNP, N is population, t is tariff level, D is distance to the market, and E is resource endowments. The subscripts are as follows: i denotes countries, k refers to commodities and $j(i)$ are i's trading partners; l represents resource endowment subscripts – i.e. capital, R&D, education and electricity, all relative to population.

This equation was then estimated by conducting a Bayesian analysis of the data that began with 'guesstimates' of all the parameters, the data being used to suggest improvements to the guesstimates. This is in contrast to regression analysis, which uses the data to determine the values of the parameters directly.

The guesstimates were revised in the following way. Sample information for a parameter β involved an estimate, $\hat{\beta}$, and a variance, $V(\hat{\beta})$. In addition to providing an original guesstimate of β called g_1, which Leamer associated with a variance $V(g_1)$, he indicated that β was likely to be in the interval $g_1 \pm 2\sqrt{V(g_1)}$ at the 0.95 probability level. The data-improved guesstimate, g_2, was then a weighted average of $\hat{\beta}$ and g_1, with weights inversely proportional to $V(\hat{\beta})$ or $V(g_1)$, respectively.

Thus

$$g_2 = (V^{-1}(\hat{\beta}) + V^{-1}(g_1))^{-1} (V^{-1}(\hat{\beta})\hat{\beta} + V^{-1}(g_1)g_1)$$

The variance of g_2 was also calculated:

$$V(g_2) = (V^{-1}(\hat{\beta}) + V^{-1}(g_1))^{-1}$$

Leamer (1974) called the guesstimates 'prior means', while the data-improved guesstimates were referred to as 'posterior means'. Information on prior means for GNP, population and distance elasticities was obtained from published studies. Data on income, tariff and resource elasticities were chosen on an ad hoc – best-guess – basis.

Having estimated an equation for each commodity class, Leamer tried to propose a 'best' commodity-specific theory from his results. Although he believed that the best theory was necessarily a composite, he nevertheless felt that it was possible to develop a theory sufficiently general to cover the majority of commodities traded.

How was the best theory selected? Leamer used the method of irreducible expected squared error loss. In other words, when variables or groups of variables were dropped, what penalty was paid in terms of a model's predictive powers? Examining his equations in this way, Leamer came to the conclusion that the development variables – GNP and population – best explained trade, followed by the resistance group and with the resource group a poor third. As it could have been argued that the significance of the development variables was the result of the separate treatment of GNP and population, the exercise was rerun using GNP per capita. With GNP per capita varying less across the sample than the separate variables, Leamer expected that the development group would suffer. This was not the case. The development group continued to perform better than the other variables, but admittedly only marginally better than the resistance group. Within the resource group the R&D variable performed best, but only when coupled with either capital intensity or education. The importance of this finding should, however, be put in context – i.e. remembering that the resource group as a whole was not significant. Overall, the results suggested to Leamer that the economies of scale-cum-Linder hypothesis was in operation, with perhaps some influence from the product cycle. He tentatively suggested that the poor performance of the resource variables could be ascribed to the inherent difficulties involved in their measurement.

Replacing the dependent variable with the ratio of imports to exports and rerunning the model excluding some insignificant variables but including the balance of payments, Leamer obtained some contradictory results. In this case the resource group proved superior both to the resistance and development groups. Among the resource group, R&D was the best performer.

Leamer suggested some reasons for the difference in the results. For instance, dividing imports by exports netted out some of the influence of the development and resistance variables but enhanced the effect of the resource variables. The increased availability of production capital arising from policies that encouraged the export of capital-intensive goods but discouraged their importation had a double effect on the ratio. The scale effect of GNP, however, affected both imports and exports in an identical way.

Leamer (1974) found the superiority of the R&D variable in the resource group a little more difficult to explain – recalling, however, that it had pre-dominated in the studies conducted by Hirsch (1974a, 1975). A suggested, but somewhat inconsistent, possibility was that exports were determined by neo-technology factors while imports were not. To Leamer, this new set of results suggested that the neo-technology model was important in determining the trade patterns under consideration.

Setting the methodological and statistical arguments to one side, the empirical studies that have been examined point to a rejection of a simple Heckscher–Ohlin model as a general theory of international trade. Hufbauer (1970) proposed a neo-factor proportions approach – essentially, Heckscher–Ohlin incorporating human capital. Hirsch (1974a, 1975) suggested a neo-technology theory with the product cycle predominating. Aquino (1981) placed greater weight on skills and technological intensity, with the product cycle apparently being confirmed when data were examined over time. Leamer's (1974) study also cast doubt on the general validity of the simple Heckscher–Ohlin model. His results, when imports were used as the dependent variable, supported the Linder hypothesis and economies of scale approaches. In so far as GNP and R&D were positively linked, they also indicated support for a neo-technology model. In contrast, when the ratio of imports to exports was taken as the dependent variable, the resource group – and in particular R&D – were found to be significant determinants of trade patterns.

Although these studies suggested that the simple Heckscher–Ohlin model may not be a valid general theory, no other single hypothesis appeared as a distinct alternative. As Leamer (1974) suggested, a composite model was probably the best, but its exact form was not yet clear. In response to the evidence that had been presented a divergent view began to emerge. Given the wide range of goods traded and their different input requirements, it might make more sense to abandon attempts to establish a general theory of trade and, rather, accept that individual trade models might be appropriate in different circumstances.

The genesis of this line of reasoning was Hufbauer's (1970) seminal paper, but it was more fully developed and tested by Hirsch (1974b). Hirsch began with the premise that it was possible to divide goods into a relatively small number of classifications to which the existing trade models applied. Three categories were proposed – Ricardo goods, Heckscher–Ohlin goods and product cycle goods.

Ricardo goods covered minerals, agricultural products and goods containing a high proportion of domestically available natural resources. In other words, those where a country's comparative advantage was determined largely by climate and natural resource endowments. Hirsch expected that the bulk of these goods would be exported from developing to developed countries.

The Heckscher–Ohlin category embraced goods whose technologies were fairly stable and easily available to those who wished to enter an industry. Product specifications would be simple and universally accepted. Goods such as textiles, metals, building materials and even simple electronics components were included in this grouping. As advanced industrialised countries were relatively well endowed with capital and less advanced or developing countries were abundant in labour, it followed that capital-intensive goods with these characteristics would be exported from the former to the latter group of countries. The opposite would be the case for labour-intensive goods.

The product cycle category captured those goods whose technology was evolving rapidly and was not available to all potential producers. In other words, those which required a great deal of research and development effort not only to refine the goods' specification but also to stabilise the production function. In their initial phases of economic growth developing countries would, for the most part, be the recipients of these types of good. Over time, as production technologies became standardised, this trade flow might be reversed. For example, if the technology required relatively high capital inputs, production and exports would continue to be concentrated in the developed countries. If labour intensity was required, they would be located in developing countries with a relative abundance of labour. Nevertheless, developed countries – with their higher and growing per capita incomes giving rise to demand for new goods and their abundant supply of skilled manpower – would be the natural home of product cycle goods in their pre-standardisation period. Of course, some goods would be continuously evolving.

To summarise, the trade flows of developing countries would be dominated by Ricardo goods and labour-intensive mature goods. Mature capital-

Table 7.9 Trade balance and share of developing countries in the trade of industrial countries, 1968–71

Area	Export/import ratio		Percentage share of developing countries	
	Total	With developing countries	Exports	Imports
Ricardo goods				
North America	1.11	0.46	21	50
Japan	0.09	0.08	52	57
EEC	0.47	0.10	9	39
EFTA	0.43	0.13	10	33
Capital-intensive mature goods (iron and steel)				
North America	0.49	5.09	32	3
Japan	12.24	22.76	38	20
EEC	1.47	10.37	11	2
EFTA	0.99	27.00	14	1
Capital-intensive mature goods (road motor vehicles)				
North America	0.80	93.25	14	<0.5
Japan	26.50	∞	29	<0.5
EEC	2.02	∞	13	<0.5
EFTA	1.21	227	22	<0.5
Labour-intensive mature goods (textiles and clothing)				
North America	0.32	0.29	35	38
Japan	8.23	9.11	50	45
EEC	1.27	1.56	9	8
EFTA	0.85	0.73	13	15
New product cycle goods (chemicals)				
North America	1.95	6.62	31	9
Japan	1.30	13.94	49	5
EEC	1.46	10.56	18	2
EFTA	1.01	4.65	22	5
New product cycle goods (engineering)				
North America	1.54	8.14	28	5
Japan	3.51	49.17	36	3
EEC	1.53	41.45	18	1
EFTA	1.24	17.79	20	1

Source: Hirsch (1974b).

intensive goods and new goods would play a very small role. For developed countries one would see the opposite pattern, with new goods and mature capital-intensive goods – depending on incomes – making up the lion's share of exports.

Precluded by data constraints from rigorously testing the trade flows of developing countries, Hirsch (1974b) was forced to concentrate on developed countries. The trade patterns of the European Economic Community (EEC), the European Free Trade Association (EFTA), Japan and North America were examined. The study encompassed six groups of goods, with primary products taken as one group while manufacturers were split into five groups: iron and steel; road motor vehicles; textiles and clothing; chemicals; and engineering products. Manufactures were allocated among capital intensive–mature, labour intensive–mature and new–product cycle goods.

The allocation of manufactures to their classifications was carried out using two criteria: capital per employee and the skill ratio. Industries were classed as being of high or low capital intensity depending on whether capital per employee was above or below $10,000. Industries were classed as 'new' if the percentage of professional, technical and scientific personnel exceeded 9 per cent of its labour force.

Once the industries were allocated to their respective categories, Hirsch examined the export/import ratios and the percentage share of the developing countries in the exports and imports of North America, Japan, the EEC and EFTA. Table 7.9 reports his results. In the labour-intensive–mature category, consisting of textiles and clothing, the industrialised countries are either net importers from, or have small surpluses with, the developing countries. This result largely conforms with the expectation that relatively labour-abundant countries lacking in skills would export labour-intensive–mature products. The major exception, Japan, being a relative newcomer to industrialisation, had not yet lost its comparative advantage in labour-intensive textile and clothing production.

In the capital-intensive and new product-cycle industries, *a priori* expectations were confirmed. Trade between the developed and developing countries was highly skewed in favour of the developed countries. Looking at mature capital-intensive goods – iron and steel and road and motor vehicles – North America had a substantial trade deficit, the EEC and Japan a surplus (the latter substantially so), while EFTA's trade was roughly in balance. Chemicals and engineering, regarded as new product cycle industries, exhibited a different pattern. Here, North America was in surplus with the developing countries, as were the EEC, EFTA and Japan. Both the EEC and EFTA had, furthermore, higher export/import ratios in this class of goods than in the mature capital-intensive group.

The lack of data on developing countries led Hirsch to examine the trade patterns of Ricardo-type goods at a more aggregated level. Examining these goods as a group, apart from North America, all the remaining export/import ratios were less than one, signifying a trade deficit with the developing countries. Again, *a priori* expectations were largely confirmed.

If one accepts that it is possible to allocate goods to specific classes, Hirsch's (1974b) study shows that it may be fruitful to think of each of the main trade theories as describing the trade patterns of particular commodity groups. This approach might be preferable to attempting to use one theory as an all-encompassing explanation of trade patterns. Hirsch's study, however, was carried out at a high level of aggregation and covered only a limited group of commodities. One cannot, therefore, conclude that his approach is any better than those which tried to establish a common set of trade determinants. Although an important study for establishing this approach, it did not prevent trade theorists, including Hirsch himself (as we have seen), from attempting to synthesise the neo-factor proportions and neo-technology theories.

Clearly, the issue of *whether there is one best model or whether the best model is actually an amalgamation of existing theories* had not been settled empirically by the early 1980s. This is still the case. After the considerable effort to resolve the issues reported here, multi-country, multi-commodity studies were to a large extent abandoned. Given the importance of the question and the absence of a clear resolution, why there ceased to be an interest in the question is a mystery. Certainly, tests of the individual models continued apace, but not comparative studies. In part, the energies of trade economists were captured by the questions posed by the new theoretical developments in intra-industry trade and the implications of imperfect competition. Attempts to arrive at a generic synthesis no longer appear to have been part of the empirical agenda. According to Bensel and Elmslie (1992, p. 254):

> Since 1980, three distinct research agendas within the field of neo-classical trade theory have developed. First are those theorists who have continued the attempt to empirically validate a strict version of the Heckscher–Ohlin–Samuelson (H-O-S) theorem. Second are those who are willing to explore issues related to industrial organisation and trade, but only when it can be incorporated into a generalised H-O-S framework. Finally, there are those willing to abandon H-O-S altogether.

Although broad-based empirical tests failed to resolve the question of the 'best' model, considerable additional insights can be gleaned from studies of narrower scope. It is to this work that we now turn.

7.2.2 Country studies

Although individual country studies in themselves are not as satisfactory for testing the general applicability of a single trade theory or group of trade theories as multi-country studies, they do have their uses. In statistical tests, country studies allow the incorporation of variables for which data are not widely available. For example, country studies allow variables that measure industrial structure, such as concentration ratios, to be used. They also facilitate the inclusion of a variety of measures that can reflect more accurately R&D activity and the skills of the labour force. In this way they contribute in a positive, albeit piecemeal, fashion to our understanding of the determinants of trade patterns.

Some of the studies discussed in this section have already been alluded to in Chapter 5. There we concentrated on the support they gave the technology gap/product cycle theories, whereas here we will examine their contribution to the 'best theory' debate.

The country studies covered in this section look at the trade of the US, the UK, West Germany and Sweden. In some country studies overall trade was examined on a bilateral basis whereby trade with important trading partners – or groups of trading partners such as the European Economic Community – provide the focus. In other studies trading partners were classified according to their level of economic development – i.e. less-developed countries, middle income countries and so forth. Any attempts at generalising the results of the country studies is hampered because all differ in terms of sample size, dates at (or over) which they were carried out, and in their coverage of products. They also differ in their use of dependent as well as independent variables. Even when the same independent variable appears to have been used, it sometimes differed in its exact definition. As a result, direct comparisons cannot be made, and conclusions should be regarded as tentative rather than definitive statements.

In the work by Baldwin (1971) and Morrall (1972), and in some of the econometric modelling by Smith *et al.* (1983), the dependent variable was defined as the net trade balance, i.e. exports minus imports. One drawback of this measure is that it does not take into account the size of home demand – a factor that is likely to affect net exports. Carlsson and Ohlsson (1976) attempted to correct for this deficiency, as did Smith *et al.* (1983), in some model specifications by using net exports as a proportion of apparent consumption. Apparent consumption was defined as output minus exports plus imports. This adjusted proxy has the further advantage that it corresponds more closely with what is usually understood by specialisation. To the extent that comparative advantage is better reflected by exports, this measure also has the advantage of weighting successful industries more heavily than the less successful. The measure does have drawbacks, however, in that it is non-symmetrical between imports and exports and is bounded from below but not above.

In his study of Germany, Wolter (1977) used a variant of Balassa's (1965) measure of revealed comparative advantage to overcome the aforementioned problems. Wolter's index was formulated as follows:

$$100 \ln \left(\frac{x_{ijt}}{m_{ijt}} \right) \Big/ \left(\frac{X_{jt}}{M_{jt}} \right)$$

where i is industry, j is region, t is a time index, x is industry exports, m is industry imports, X is total manufacturing exports, and M is total manufacturing imports.

In all the studies the independent variables fell into two categories: those reflecting the countries' factor endowments and those reflecting industrial structures or the social factors that were expected to influence trade performance. Hence, the former broadly measured capital–labour ratios, the proportion of skilled and unskilled labour in industry, average wages and earnings, and raw material intensities. The latter encompassed concentration ratios, scale variables based on employees per plant and the degree of unionisation, R&D expenditure, output accounted for by foreign affiliates, the percentage of employees engaged in firms that were not part of industrial disputes, and wages and value added per employee.

In the most general of the country studies examined the trade of the nation in question is with all other trading partners. For the United States, Baldwin (1971) found that there was a positive and significant relationship between the percentage of engineers and scientists, craftsmen and farmers and net export surplus. When length of education was substituted for other indicators of skills, the proportion of the labour force with more than thirteen years education (i.e. university, college or technical college courses) was positively and significantly related to exports. In so far as engineers and scientists are major inputs to R&D, Baldwin found that R&D played a major role in US trade performance. On the other hand, the capital–labour ratio, measures of economies and diseconomies of scale and industrial concentration were not significant determinants of US trade patterns.

Morrall's (1972) work lent support to neo-technology and neo-factor proportions variables. His preferred equation contained the skilled labour index and the ratio of labour to capital (a proxy for capital intensity).

Carlsson and Ohlsson's (1976) analysis of Sweden's foreign trade suggested that the main determinants of trade patterns were the availability of forest products, capital intensity and inputs embodying technical know-how. When both direct and indirect inputs (the integrated processor) were taken into account, natural resources in the form of forest products and iron ore plus the supply of technical personnel provided significant explanations for trade patterns. The authors suggested that the poor performance of the capital-intensity variable was probably due to collinearity between it and the natural resource variables. Choosing between regression equations on the basis of the size of their R^2 values led them to select as preferred those models with the full range of independent variables. This specification implies that an amalgam of factor proportions, neo-technology and natural resource endowments is the best determinant of trade patterns.

The cross-section estimates carried out for West Germany by Wolter (1977) gave equal support to the neo-factor proportion and neo-technology approaches. The values of R^2 for each of Wolter's model specifications were, however, too similar in size to warrant a clear choice between the equations on that criterion.

Smith *et al.*'s (1983) study of the United Kingdom's trade with all trading partners indicated that proxies for human capital and skills outperformed the other variables. As with Baldwin's (1971) study of the US, the capital–labour ratio, although significant in most of the models estimated, possessed the wrong sign. Smith *et al.* used two human capital proxies: the percentage of professional and technical workers and average earnings by industry. They considered the former a superior proxy as it was always both positive and significant. The usefulness of average earnings was viewed as suspect as a proxy for human capital because it can be influenced by factors other than skills owing to distortions in the labour market. Average earnings was not statistically significant and had an incorrect sign when included in the estimating equation. Other variables that were insignificant and/or had the wrong sign included the R&D proxy, the level of concentration and the percentage of managerial workers employed. Poor industrial relations, measured by the number of days lost through strikes or by the percentage of industry employment in plants unaffected by industrial disputes, were statistically significant influences on trade.

The trade of individual countries with their major trading partners – as opposed to the rest of the world – was also examined by a number of authors. Baldwin (1971) found that the trade of the US with its major partners was influenced by scientists and engineers and the proportion of farmers and farm labourers. The capital–labour ratio was statistically significant in multiple regressions on Western European and Japanese trading partners but had the wrong sign. The economies of scale proxy exhibited the same behaviour. The large export surplus in agricultural products was suggested as a possible explanation for the unexpected performance of these variables.

The more general measures of skill and human capital encompassed by average cost, years of education and average earnings were found by Baldwin to be statistically significant only in the case of US trade with Japan. The percentage of employees with thirteen or more years of education, however, was significantly and positively related to US trade performance in the Western European and Japanese markets.

Trade with Canada could not be explained by any of the independent variables used in Baldwin's (1971) work. Only the capital–labour ratio and the percentage of non-farm labour were significant, but they had the wrong signs.

For West Germany's trade with the developed market economies, Wolter (1977) found that the neo-factor proportions models competed with the neo-technology model for dominance in explanatory power (as measured by the size of R^2). In his specifications designed to test the simple and extended Heckscher–Ohlin theories, the capital intensity variables had the wrong sign. Labour intensity, measured by the capitalised difference between the average hourly wage and that of unskilled workers, however, both had the correct sign and was significant. The R&D and the scale economies variable possessed correct signs and were significant statistically, and, hence, the neo-technology hypothesis appeared to explain West Germany's trade with developed market economies. In his conclusions, however, Wolter adopted an eclectic view which allowed some role for natural resource endowments in explaining trade patterns.

Smith *et al.* (1983), in their analysis of UK–EEC trade, found four variables that showed a tendency to be significant in determining trade. These were the number professional and technical workers, industrial relations, foreign ownership and the earnings of manual labourers.

The most consistently positive and significant variable – professional and technical workers – suggest that Britain's export performance in its trade with the EEC is dominated by technology-intensive goods. The results for the manual earnings variable and those for the skill variable – being negative and only occasionally significant – are surprising given the behaviour of the previous variable. One interpretation of this could be that UK exports to the EEC, although technology-intensive, are not intensive in high-quality manual skills. Foreign ownership also appeared to be a positive and significant influence on Britain's trade with the EEC, suggesting perhaps that multinational companies are effective organisers of international exchange and specialisation.

The industrial relations variable was consistent with *a priori* expectations in the equation where exports/total sales was the dependant variable, but it had an unexpected sign when net exports as a fraction of apparent consumption was used as the dependent variable. Thus, some doubts were created for Smith *et al.* (1983) concerning the usefulness of the industrial relations variable.

Baldwin (1971), Wolter (1977) and Smith *et al.* (1983) also examined the determinants of their studied country's trade with developing countries.

Of Baldwin's (1971) three significant variables, the capital–labour ratio had the wrong sign, but the human skills variables measuring the proportion of craftsmen and foremen and farmers and farm labourers behaved as expected. Although one would expect that developing countries would have a comparative advantage in agricultural products, it should not be forgotten that the US was a substantial net exporter of agricultural products to these areas either as a result of its greater efficiency, its protection of agriculture through trade restriction or, at that time, its large food-aid programmes.

In Wolter's (1977) results, the positive and significant influences on West Germany's trade with developing countries were the labour-intensity variables and the scale economies proxy in an equation that was specified to test the neo-technology hypothesis. Although the raw materials intensity variable was significant, it possessed a negative sign.

The regression results for UK–developing country trade (Smith *et al.*, 1983) appear to confirm the expectation that differences in factor endowments are important influences on export performance. The human capital proxies were significant determinants of trade patterns – in particular the proportion of professional and technical personnel and the average weekly manual worker's earnings. The former rose in significance when the latter was excluded from the analysis. The capital-intensity variable was negative and significant, suggesting a bias in favour of capital intensity in developing country production.

A contrary conclusion was put forward in a paper by Hufbauer and Chilas (1974). Likening inter-regional trade to international trade but with artificial trade barriers removed, they attempted to explain the specialisation seen in the trade patterns between the four principal regions of the US. Regional consumption was assumed to be proportional to regional income, and the difference between production and consumption gave an estimate of regional net exports. If the same factors that determined US international trade also determined US regional trade, then the ratio of international trade to regional trade in any particular commodity would equal one.

Interestingly, the ratios revealed that regional trade was determined more by factor endowments than by any other proxies. This result was in direct contrast to those for the US international trade. According to Hufbauer and Chilas, the difference in in the results arose because of the existence of trade barriers. They maintained that in the US these were highest against Heckscher–Ohlin type goods and lowest against Ricardian goods and product cycle goods, which required specific factors for their production. In the case of Ricardian goods the specific factors were natural resources. For product cycle goods they were know-how. Trade barriers were lower for Ricardian and product cycle goods because vested interests with an incentive to lobby for protection are less likely to develop in these goods. If specialised resources or knowledge do not exist in a country, there is no one seeking protection for them. If trade barriers did not exist, specialisation would take place along Heckscher–Ohlin lines and the alternative trade theories would lose their explanatory power.

What do the studies of individual advanced countries tell us about trade theories? What they suggest is that the simple Heckscher–Ohlin model of trade does not capture the fundamental determinants of advanced countries' trade patterns. At best, the model has to be extended to including measures of raw material endowments or human capital. However, the common finding of negative capital–labour ratios creates doubts over extensions to the Heckscher–Ohlin model. It would appear, on the other hand, that as far as the advanced countries are concerned neo-technology factors have a more important role to play in explaining trade patterns. Interestingly, the negative influence of capital–labour ratios indicates that developing countries' exports to advanced countries are more capital-intensive than one would expect on *a priori* grounds. Taken as a whole, the empirical evidence of the period suggested that an amalgam of trade theories might provide a truer reflection of the major determinants of trade.

As the efforts of empirical trade economists could not provide a consensus on the form of a general trade model that would incorporate elements of all the major contending trade models, the ball was put directly back into the court of the trade theorists. Spurred on by the damning empirical evidence on Heckscher–Ohlin and the eclectic evidence regarding the other trade models, some trade theorists began to investigate the possibility of reconciling the various approaches.

7.3 Theoretical developments

The discrepancy between the theoretical literature – which centred on individual alternative models of trade – and the empirical evidence – which was pointing in the direction of a composite theory of international trade – led to a number of formal developments. Much of this effort was aimed at reconciling the neo-factor proportions model with both the Linder hypothesis and the neo-techno-logy model. Another area of theoretical endeavour attempted to reconcile the simultaneous occurrence of inter-industry and intra-industry trade. Both these avenues of theoretical inquiry are examined in the rest of this chapter.

7.3.1 Amalgamating Linder and Heckscher–Ohlin

At first glance it might seem unlikely that the Linder hypothesis and the Heckscher–Ohlin model could be reconciled. Linder (1961) suggested that the intensity of trade between a pair of countries is positively related to similarity in their per capita incomes. Heckscher–Ohlin predicts that, in so far as divergent factor endowments reflect different per capita incomes, dissimilarity of per capita incomes creates trade. By relaxing the assumption that transfer costs are zero, however, Arad and Hirsch (1981) were able to achieve what might have seemed an impossible reconciliation.

Arad and Hirsch began their analysis by examining the relationship between price ratios and factor endowments in the Heckscher–Ohlin model. In a two-country (i and j) model with two products x and z, with the former being labour-intensive relative to the latter, relative costs are defined by $C_{ji} = P_j/P_i$, where $P_j = (P_x/P_z)_j$ and $P_i = (P_x/P_z)_i$, where P denotes prices.

The relationship between C_{ji} and factor endowments is illustrated diagram-matically in Figure 7.1. The vertical axis shows the ratio of the production costs, P_j/P_i, of a reference country j, while the horizontal axis depicts factor endowments. $\bar{Y}_j$ and $\bar{Y}_i$ are the relative endowments of capital to labour in countries j and i, respectively – i.e. $\bar{Y}_i = K_i/L_i$, where K_i is capital endowment in i and L_i is labour endowment in i.

Where $\bar{Y}_j > \bar{Y}_i$ it follows that $P_i < P_j$, and when $\bar{Y}_j < \bar{Y}_i$, $P_i > P_j$. The cost ratio, C_{ji}, is unity when the relative endowments of the two countries are equal, i.e. $\bar{Y}_i = \bar{Y}_j$.

Thus, x is imported by i when $\bar{Y}_i > \bar{Y}_j$ and, hence, $P_i > P_j$. When it is imported into j, it follows that $\bar{Y}_i < \bar{Y}_j$ and $P_j > P_i$.

Next, Arad and Hirsch considered Linder's hypothesis. Goods, they suggested, encompass a series of characteristics conforming to specific tastes that vary from market to market. Goods which were initially produced for the home market could also be exported, but only after they had been modified to take into account foreign tastes. Hence, firms incur *adjustment costs*. As the variation in tastes between countries was a function of the difference between their per capita incomes, adjustment costs would be lower the closer these incomes were. In other words, the strong assumption was made that countries with the same

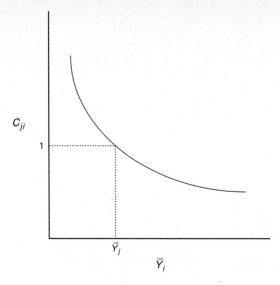

Figure 7.1 Relationship between price ratios and endowments – Heckscher–Ohlin. (*Source:* Arad and Hirsch, 1981)

per capita income also share the same tastes. Countries with similar per capita incomes would trade more intensively with one another because their adjustment costs would be lower. As high capital endowments are positively correlated with high incomes, they are in turn also positively correlated with per capita incomes.

The concept of adjustment costs is depicted in Figure 7.2. The adjustment cost, m_{ji}, incurred by reference country j when attempting to export a good to country i is on the vertical axis. The closer country i's per capita income – depicted by the factor endowment $\bar{Y}_i$ – approaches our reference country's (j's) per capita income, denoted by the factor endowment measure $\bar{Y}_j$, the smaller the adjustment costs. The adjustment costs are minimised when $\bar{Y}_i = \bar{Y}_j$.

Thus, both the expected trade patterns arise from this model. In the Heckscher–Ohlin world differences in endowments and, hence, per capita incomes lead to trade, while the opposite is the case in the Linder hypothesis. Arad and Hirsch reconciled the two models by explicitly including adjustment costs within the Heckscher–Ohlin framework.

Arad and Hirsch (1981) suggested that both production and adjustment costs vary between countries and that a good's tradability depends on the sum of these two costs. They termed this new relative total cost C_{ji}^{*}. More formally, we can say that

$$ C_{ji}^{*} = \left(1 + m_{ji}\right) \frac{\left(P_x / P_z\right)_j}{\left(P_x / P_z\right)_i} = \left(1 + m_{ji}\right) C_{ji} $$

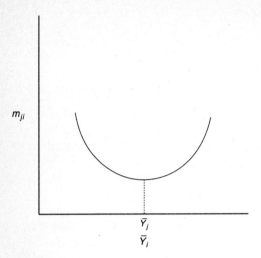

Figure 7.2 Adjustment costs and per capita incomes. (*Source:* Arad and Hirsch, 1981)

Exports would take place if, at the minimum point, C_{ji}^* had a value less than unity. Figure 7.3 shows two possible relationships between total cost, C_{ji}^*, and $\bar{Y}_i$. If C_{ji}^* is decreasing everywhere as $\bar{Y}_i$ increases (Figure 7.3(a)), the good would be classed as Heckscher–Ohlin in type. If C_{ji}^* falls and then rises after having dipped below unity (Figure 7.3(b)), the good in question is a Linder-type good.

In this combined model, factor endowments still determine trade patterns. Capital-rich countries export capital-intensive goods to capital-poor countries and import labour-intensive goods from them. Adjustment costs, however, being correlated with the difference in per capita incomes, limit the range of countries with which it is possible to trade. Thus, Heckscher–Ohlin goods are traded with all countries whose endowments and, hence, per capita incomes differ from the reference country. Linder goods, by contrast, are exported to countries with a more limited range of endowments.

It also follows that the difference between the per capita income of the reference country and that of the nearest supplier of Linder-type goods will be larger than the difference between its per capital income and that of the nearest supplier of Heckscher–Ohlin goods. Why should this be so? In Figure 7.3, $\bar{Y}_k$ is the GNP of the country whose C_{ji}^* equals unity. For Linder-type goods to be exported, manufacturers must enjoy substantial cost advantages to overcome the adjustment costs involved. This, however, is not necessary with Heckscher–Ohlin goods as a small manufacturing cost advantage will lead to a flow of exports. If one ranks import sources by their per capita incomes and compares the per capita income of the reference country with the 'nearest' supplier of Linder and Heckscher–Ohlin goods in terms of per capita incomes, there is a larger difference in the case of the Linder goods.

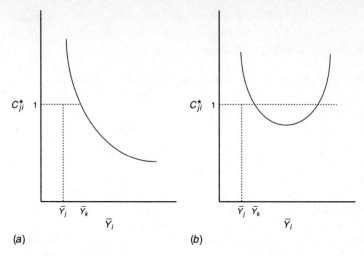

Figure 7.3 Relationship between sum of production and adjustment costs and per capita income. (*Source:* Arad and Hirsch, 1981)

Arad and Hirsch (1981) supported their reconciliation hypothesis with empirical evidence. They compared the inter-country distribution of trade in a representative sample of Linder and Heckscher–Ohlin goods. These were distinguished from one another on the basis of Hufbauer's (1970) product differentiation index (see section 7.2.1). A high index value denotes a Linder good, while a low index value, or similarity, characterises a Heckscher–Ohlin good.

To test that trade in Linder-type goods is more narrowly distributed, in terms of per capita income, between trading partners than is trade in Heckscher–Ohlin goods, a distribution function of import sources by GNP per capita was computed and examined for a number of countries and country groupings. Arad and Hirsch found that for all countries and groups of countries, except Ireland, the dispersion of GNP per capita of import sources was narrower in Linder-type goods than in Heckscher–Ohlin goods. Hence, their hypothesis appeared to be confirmed.

They also found that the difference between the per capita incomes of the country where trade starts and the reference country was *not smaller* in Linder-type goods than in Heckscher–Ohlin goods (although it should be noted that this is a weaker statistical test than trying to prove that the differences were greater).

Both sets of results appeared to support Arad and Hirsch's (1981) theoretical amalgamation of the Linder hypothesis with the Heckscher–Ohlin theory. However, two words of caution are required. First, as we saw in Chapter 5, it is not clear whether Linder's hypothesis is a valid theory. As the empirical evidence does not give a clear indication, its amalgamation with the Heckscher–Ohlin model may be unwise. Second, even if we accept the amalgamation, the division of goods into Linder and Heckscher–Ohlin types is fraught with difficulties. For example, Gray and Martin (1980) have outlined several major shortcomings of the Hufbauer index of product differentiation. Thus, although the theoretical reconciliation of the Linder hypothesis and Heckscher–Ohlin theory shows promise, it awaits further empirical validation.

7.3.2 *Technological gap theories and the Heckscher–Ohlin model*

The question whether the technological gap theory is actually different from the human skills-augmented Heckscher–Ohlin model was investigated by Katrak (1988). The basic question he asked was whether the two theories predict similar or different trade patterns. He suggested that this was a valid question in view of the number of empirical studies that had treated the two theories as emphasising different sets of underlying forces.

Katrak (1988) discussed two other related issues. First, he examined the reasons for inter-country differences in the level of R&D activity – the economic force driving the technological gap theory. Second, he dealt with the role of exogenous technology. In the human skills-augmented Heckscher–Ohlin model technology was assumed to be freely available. In the technology gap theories, the level of technology available to any one country was a function of its own R&D effort and was not costless. If, however, some technology was free, the interesting question posed by Katrak was: how will the technological gap model be affected? As these two issues have important implications for the techno-logical gap hypothesis as a trade theory, they will be discussed first.

An important feature of Katrak's (1988) model was that R&D requires the input of skilled labour, which, in turn, can also be used in the production process. Thus, a company's physical output will be a function of material inputs, unskilled labour and skilled labour. The quality of the product, however, depends on either free technology or skilled labour input via the R&D process. For a profit-maximising firm that is experiencing diminishing returns in all factors, the optimum allocation of skilled personnel between production and R&D will be determined by bringing the marginal revenue to be gained from switching labour from one function to another into equality. In other words, Katrak argued, the decrease in profits brought about by reducing output because of the shift in personnel is equal to the increase in profits brought about by the increased quality that results from increased R&D. The more productive skilled labour is in raising quality compared to raising output, the more it will be allocated to R&D. This activity will be expanded until diminishing returns in R&D cease to make its expansion worthwhile. Quality, however, is also a function of the level of free technology. The more free technology available, the smaller will be the influence of any given amount of R&D and the lower the optimal level of skilled personnel in R&D.

If a country experiences an autonomous increase in skilled labour and this is distributed equally between the productive and R&D activities, assuming that skilled labour's productivity is higher in the latter activity, the marginal revenue product of labour in the former sector will fall. In order to maintain the equality of the marginal revenue product of labour in both activities, profit-maximising firms will transfer skilled labour from production to R&D.

Analogously, it follows that a country that has more skilled labour than a rival will commit more labour to R&D. If both countries have the same access to free technology, the country that has more skilled labour in the R&D sector will also make products of higher quality. This will confer on it a comparative advantage in technologically intensive, high-quality goods. It is important to note that absolute levels of factor endowments have important effects on the level of R&D activity and, hence, comparative advantage.

Katrak (1988) realised that the difference in the quantity of skilled labour between countries was not the only variable that could affect comparative advantage. Other influences included the comparative efficiency of the skilled labour working in the two countries' R&D sectors. If one country's R&D efficiency increased relative to the other country's, the marginal revenue product of its R&D skilled labour would rise relative to skilled workers in production. To maintain equality between the marginal revenue product of both types of skilled labour, workers would be transferred from the production sector to the R&D sector. Again, the country that enjoyed greater efficiency would commit more resources to R&D and acquire an advantage over its rival in the production of higher-quality goods.

Another influence on the level of R&D activity was expected to be the demand conditions prevailing in the countries. For example, in a pre-trade situation – where domestic demand conditions are the only ones that matter – the level of R&D will be higher the greater is the elasticity of price with respect to quality and the more elastic the price is with respect to quantity changes. When trade is opened up foreign demand conditions must be catered for, and they will affect the level of R&D. In an empirical study Hughes (1986) found that the opening up of trade increased the level of R&D, although he was unable to provide a theoretical explanation for this statistical relationship. Katrak (1988) showed that such a relationship would be predicted if foreign conditions were more price-sensitive than home demand. That is, as the demand for exports rises resources are transferred to R&D. Goods therefore increase in quality and demand for them is further increased. As a result, additional resources will be devoted to R&D.

By examining how countries distributed skilled labour between production and R&D, as well as the role of free technology, Katrak (1988) was able to deduce the following. Countries with large physical endowments of skilled labour are able to allocate more of this resource to R&D activities. Since this enhances the quality of the products they produce, they are able to obtain a comparative advantage over their rivals in goods requiring R&D as an input. Greater efficiency in the use of skilled labour applied to R&D and/or favourable domestic and foreign demand conditions can enhance this process. The effectiveness of skilled resources employed in the R&D process will, however, be affected by the level of free technology. When free technology is plentiful, quality will not be greatly enhanced by committing extra resources to it. The opposite will be true when the level of free technology is low because the marginal product of skilled labour will be higher and, therefore, more of this type of labour will be committed to R&D.

What implication does Katrak's (1988) work have for trade theory? First, it showed that factor endowments were fundamental in the underlying logic of the technological gap theories. The level of skilled labour determined R&D activity. Second, the existence of free technology also affected the value of R&D. Third, Katrak differentiated between the human skill-augmented Heckscher–Ohlin theory and the technology gap theory. For example, the former would predict that the existence of skilled labour leads to the production of technological or advanced goods. Exports of these, however, would depend on the abundance of skilled labour relative to unskilled labour, with skill-rich countries exporting to skill-poor countries. In Katrak's analysis, comparative advantage does not depend on the ratio of skilled to unskilled labour but on the absolute size of the skilled labour force. Countries with a plentiful supply of skilled labour would have a comparative advantage in advanced goods and would export them to other countries that possessed skilled labour. In contrast, the strict form of the Heckscher–Ohlin model predicts that there would be no trade between countries that had similar relative endowments.

Although Katrak (1988) did not formally test his hypothesis, he did point to some indirect evidence to support his case. For example, in his comparative study based on the US and the UK (Katrak, 1973), he found that absolute inter-industry differences in the total numbers of skilled labour employed were positively associated with a higher proportion of skilled labour engaged in R&D activity. In addition, he cited the work of Hughes (1986) as evidence of the two-way relationship between trade and R&D.

As with the reconciliation of Heckscher–Ohlin and Linder discussed in the previous section, Katrak's (1988) hypothesis also appears to be awaiting critical empirical investigation. As a result, these major issues in trade theory remain confined to the theoretical realm.

7.3.3 Explaining the existence of and differences in the volume of intra- and inter-industry trade

Although intra-industry trade became a major focus for the work of trade economists in the 1980s and 1990s (see Chapter 6), little effort was made to integrate explanations of intra-industry trade with theories of inter-industry trade. An attempt was made by Markusen (1986) to explain both the volume and direction of trade between developed countries and patterns of trade between developed and developing countries. In particular, he tried to explain why the volume of trade between developed countries is greater than that between developed and developing countries. He used a theoretical framework which combined Linder's hypothesis with the Heckscher–Ohlin model and included non-homogeneous tastes, scale economies and product differentiation. In an earlier paper, Helpman (1981) had predicted a larger volume of trade between developed countries than that between developed and developing countries. This result depended on: the developed countries having larger GNPs than developing countries; and differentiated manufactured goods constituting a large share of world GNP. Markusen felt that Helpman was implying that the second condition was a consequence of the relative wealth of developed countries. He did not consider this to be an adequate explanation as it placed all goods produced in either the increasing returns/differentiated or constant returns categories.

Markusen's (1986) approach involving dividing the world into a capital-abundant 'North' (developed countries) and a labour-abundant group of developing countries, which he called 'South'. The North was further subdivided into two identical regions called 'East' and 'West'. One production sector produced differentiated capital-intensive manufactured goods with increasing returns to scale, while the other produced homogeneous labour-intensive food goods with constant returns to scale.

On the demand side, per capita incomes differed between North and South because the former had more capital per worker. The assumption was that income was spread evenly over all workers in the North so that no separate class of capitalists existed whose savings activities would add an unnecessary complication. It was also assumed that income elasticities of demand differed for the two goods produced. For manufactures, the income elasticity was considered to be greater than unity, while that for food was less than one. Consumers were expected to demand variety in their manufactured goods as their incomes grew. Manufacturers, it was hypothesised, would respond to this by supplying a greater variety of goods as demand expanded. Given the differences in per capita income, Markusen also assumed that demand was biased towards manufactured goods in the North and towards food products in the South.

What implications did these assumptions have for trade direction and volumes? Under the Heckscher–Ohlin hypothesis the North would concentrate its production effort on, and export, capital-intensive goods, while the South would do the same in labour-intensive goods. Trade between the eastern and western halves of the North would be intra-industry trade. As incomes rose in both the North and South demand for both goods would rise, but the increase in demand would be greater for manufactured goods with their higher income elasticity. Trade volume, both North–South and East–West, however, would increase in line with the increase in demand. The assumption of biased tastes – arising from differences in income – changed this conclusion because it diverted consumption away from food produced in the South. Analogously, those in the South biased their consumption towards food. Consumers in the North required greater variety. Manufacturers in the East and West supplied this demand; then, given that the income elasticity of manufactures was assumed to be greater than unity, it followed that the volume of East–West trade would increase relative to that between North and South.

Thus, Markusen's (1986) model explained one of the empirical *stylised facts* – that trade volumes between the developed countries increased faster than those between developed and developing countries. As non-homotheticity of demand was fundamental to his conclusions, a legitimate question to ask was how reasonable an assumption was it to make? Some of Markusen's own collaborative work (Hunter and Markusen, 1988) provided considerable empirical support for the non-homotheticity assumption. A linear expenditure system was estimated for thirty-four countries covering eleven commodities. The estimated deviations from homotheticity were highly statistically and economically significant. Demand for food provided particularly strong support, having a low elasticity of demand and absorbing a very high proportion of consumption expenditure in low-income countries. As a proportion of total personal consumption expenditure, food ranged from over 60 per cent in the lowest per capita income country to 13 per cent in the highest per capita income country. For homotheticity to be confirmed, a constant share for food consumption would have to be observed.

Markusen's (1986) analysis also depended on there being a connection between capital intensity and high income-elasticity of demand in consumption. Although no formal study was done to confirm this relationship, he suggested that the data set used in Hunter and Markusen (1988) provided some corroborative evidence. For example, there appeared to be a correlation between specialisation in production and consumption for both the top and bottom third of the countries examined. In the absence of subsequent empirical evaluations, Markusen's thesis has neither been confirmed nor denied.

7.4 Summary

This chapter has pursued two themes. First, it examined the simultaneous testing of the traditional and alternative trade theories at both the multi-country, multi-commodity level and the individual country level. The results of these empirical studies led to no discernably superior model. New directions for theoretical inquires were, however, indicated. Hence, the second theme of the chapter was the ensuing attempts at theoretical reconciliation of the Heckscher–Ohlin model and some of the alternative approaches to explaining trade patterns.

The empirical evidence, whether it is from Hufbauer (1970) and his simple correlation methods or the more sophisticated analyses of Hirsch (1975), Aquino (1981) and Leamer (1974), suggests that a number of factors combine to determine trade patterns. The empirical studies all stress the importance of technological factors in explaining trade patterns to a greater or lesser degree. Given the methodological difficulties inherent in the empirical studies, one cannot be more precise. Even the country studies, with their more consistent and disaggregated data sets, do not lead us to definite conclusions. The country studies did, nevertheless, show that technological factors cannot be ignored in producing a general theory of international trade. The theoretical attempts at producing a synthesis of neoclassical and alternative theories conceded this point. Similarly, the reconciliation of traditional inter-industry and intra-industry trade theories is reflective of the strong empirical evidence that both types of trade are found in the real world.

Why the Heckscher–Ohlin or neoclassical theory has survived for so long as the principal trade model when the evidence suggests that it requires, at the least, some modification is the subject of the final chapter.

References

Aquino, A. (1981), 'Changes over time in the pattern of comparative advantage in manufactured goods', *European Economic Review*, 15(1), pp. 41–62.

Arad, R. W., and Hirsch, S. (1981), 'Determination of trade flows and the choice of trade partners: reconciling the Heckscher–Ohlin and the Burenstam Linder models of international trade', *Weltwirtschaftliches Archiv*, 117, pp. 276–97.

Balassa, B. (1965), 'Trade liberalization and revealed comparative advantage', *The Manchester School of Economic and Social Studies*, 33(2), pp. 99–123.

Baldwin, R. E. (1971), 'Determinants of the commodity structure of U.S. trade', *American Economic Review*, 61(1), pp. 126–46.

Bensel, T., and Elmslie, B. T. (1992), 'Rethinking international trade theory: a methodological appraisal', *Weltwirtschaftliches Archiv*, 128, pp. 249–65.

Carlsson, B., and Ohlsson, L. (1976), 'Structural determinants of Swedish foreign trade: a test of conventional wisdom', *European Economic Review*, 7(2), pp. 165–74.

Drèze, J. (1960), 'Quelques réflexions sereines sur l'adaptation de l'industrie Belge au Marché Commun', *Comptes Rendus des Travaux de la Société Royale d'Economie Politique de Belgique*, no. 275, pp. 47–62.

Gray, H. P., and Martin, J. P. (1980), 'The meaning and measurement of product differentiation in international trade', *Weltwirtschaftliches Archiv*, 116, pp. 322–9.

Helpman, E. (1981), 'International trade in the presence of product differentiation, economies of scale and monopolistic competition', *Journal of International Economics*, 11, pp. 305–40.

Hirsch, S. (1974a), 'Capital or technology? Confronting the neo-factor proportions and neo-technology accounts of international trade', *Weltwirtschaftliches Archiv*, 110, pp. 535–63.

Hirsch, S. (1974b), 'Hypotheses regarding trade between developing and industrial countries', in H. Giersch (ed.), *The International Division of Labour: Problems and Perspectives*, Tübingen: J.C.B. Mohr, pp. 65–82.

Hirsch, S. (1975), 'The product cycle model of international trade – a multi-country cross-section analysis', *Oxford Bulletin of Economics and Statistics*, 37(3), pp. 305–17.

Hufbauer, G. C. (1970), 'The impact of national characteristics and technology on the commodity composition of trade in manufactured goods', in R. Vernon (ed.)*The Technology Factor in International Trade*, New York: Columbia University Press, pp. 145–231.

Hufbauer, G. C., and Chilas, J. G. (1974), 'Specialization by industrial countries: extent and consequences', in H. Giersch (ed.), *The International Division of Labour: Problems and Perspectives*, Tübingen: J.C.B. Mohr, pp. 3–38.

Hughes, K. S. (1986), 'Exports and innovation: a simultaneous equation model', *European Economic Review*, 30(2), pp. 383–99.

Hunter, L., and Markusen, J. (1988), 'Per capita income as a determinant of trade', in J. Feenstra (ed.), *Empirical Methods for International Trade*, Cambridge, Mass.: MIT Press, pp. 89–109.

Katrak, H. (1973), 'Human skills, R and D and scale economies in the exports of the United Kingdom and the United States', *Oxford Economic Papers*, 25(3), pp. 337–60.

Katrak, H. (1988), 'R&D, international production and trade: the technological gap theory in a factor endowment model', *The Manchester School of Economic and Social Studies*, 56(3), pp. 205–22.

Leamer, E. E. (1974), 'The commodity composition of international trade in manufactures: an empirical analysis', *Oxford Economic Papers*, 26(3), pp. 350–74.

Linder, S. B. (1961), *An Essay on Trade and Transformation*, New York: John Wiley and Sons.

Markusen, J. R. (1986), 'Explaining the volume of trade: an eclectic approach', *American Economic Review*, 76(5), pp. 1002–11.

Morrall, J. F. (1972), *Human Capital, Technology and the Role of the United States in International Trade*, Gainsville: University of Florida Press.

Smith, S. R., White, G. M., Owen, N. C., and Hill, M. R. (1983), 'UK trade in manufacturing: the pattern of specialization during the 1970s', Government Economic Service working paper no. 56, London: HMSO.

Vernon, R. (1966), 'International investment and international trade in the product cycle', *Quarterly Journal of Economics*, 80(2), pp. 190–207.

Wolter, F. (1977), 'Factor proportions, technology and West German industry's international trade patterns', *Weltwirtschaftliches Archiv*, 113, pp. 250–67.

CHAPTER 8

Disequilibrium or disarray?

8.1 Introduction

This book has traced major developments in international trade theory and the principal empirical evidence surrounding them. Although many texts provide discussion of the various trade theories, their empirical validation receives scant attention. In particular, the important role which the absence of strong empirical evidence in support of any of the major theories has played in stimulating new theoretical explorations is overlooked. We have tried to provide some insights into the interaction between theory and empirical testing. This interplay furnishes an intriguing case study of how progress in economics – and, for that matter, in all of social science – takes place. It is a slow process. It is not a linear progression. False roads are difficult to discard and true paths even more difficult to confirm. Currently, there is no single theory of trade but, rather, a polyglot of theories. Each has its advocates and detractors. Old theories continue in popularity alongside new, 'hot' areas of academic inquiry. Empirical testing remains at the heart of the debate. Of course, new debates will continue to arise; that is the nature of scholarly activity. It is, however, important to reflect on what has gone on before.

We have attempted to provide a discussion of the major empirical works in the literature on international trade. Having access to this compilation, in one place, should be of use to prospective trade economists whether their inclinations are empirical or theoretical. Our discussion of the empirical studies should help to identify the major issues addressed by the studies and demonstrate how individual works have added to our understanding of international trade patterns. It is also hoped that the convenient grouping of empirical studies will prove useful to those charged with the guidance of prospective economists.

To make the task manageable a number of topics have been excluded. Principally, these are Marxist ideas on international trade and distance- or spatially based 'gravity' models. Despite these omissions, we feel that the material included captures the essential elements of the main theoretical debates that have arisen in the literature.

8.2   Covering the ground again with perspective

8.2.1   The ruling paradigm

The rise and subsequent decline in popularity of the classical model and its eclipse by the neoclassical model based on Heckscher–Ohlin (Ohlin, 1933) provided the jump-off point for this book. The discussion of the classical model traced its development from a normative theory concentrating on the benefits of trade to a more positive theory predicting the direction and patterns of trade. The abandonment of the constant opportunity costs assumption in favour of increasing opportunity costs was chronicled. The latter innovation gave rise to the concave production possibility curve, which is common to a range of international trade models. Once Harbeler's (1936) opportunity cost approach was accepted, the proposed motivation for countries engaging in international trade became differences in relative prices. Further, specialisation would be partial rather than the complete specialisation predicted by the constant opportunity cost version of the classical model. Demand factors were also introduced into the classical model. However, although they affected the terms of trade, they had little effect on the basic predictions of the theory.

The Heckscher–Ohlin approach largely supplanted the Ricardian-based classical theory because, in addition to predicting trade patterns, it provided an explanation as to why production possibility curves differed between countries. In the Heckscher–Ohlin model countries are assumed to use the same production technology. Hence, as long as factor endowments differ between countries, and these differences are reflected in their relative price, capital-abundant countries will specialise in and export capital-intensive goods. Labour-abundant countries will specialise in and export labour-intensive goods. Thus, Heckscher–Ohlin could explain the pattern of trade and the source of comparative advantage. The general equilibrium approach in which this neoclassical-based theory was anchored enabled it to act as a vehicle for analyses of changes in tariff rates, the effects of technological change and variations in factor prices.

The conclusions of the Heckscher–Ohlin approach are, however, heavily dependent on the assumptions that underlie the model. Some of the assumptions for which the model is often criticised were not as crucial as others. The model is often criticised by those outside the academic community because of its two-good, two-country and two-factor (two-by-two-by-two) assumptions. The real world has many goods, countries and factors. However, these particular assumptions are imposed primarily to simplify exposition. The model can be generalised from its two-by-two-by-two structure without affecting its conclusions when demand factors are introduced. Although the two-goods and two-countries simplifications have not proved overly restrictive, the two-factor assumption may have been fundamental to the difficulties encountered in empirically validating the model's predictions. Consequently, altering this assumption in a systematic way – in particular, allowing for labour with different skill levels – has been a major line of research.

Adding transport costs and tariffs to the neoclassical model reduced the volume of trade but did not alter the model's qualitative conclusions. By converting production to a per capita basis, theoretically consistent patterns of trade could also be predicted when countries of unequal size traded with one another.

The assumptions of the neoclassical model that relate to factor immobility, production conditions and production functions are central to its predictions. For example, if factors were costlessly mobile between countries, trade in goods would not take place; instead, there would be trade in factors. Similarly, the model's predictions would not hold if the same technology were not used in the two countries or if the good produced could not be classified as either capital- or labour-intensive. Furthermore, if production did not take place under conditions of constant returns to scale, a labour-abundant country could find itself exporting capital-intensive goods. If increasing returns did occur, then prices would not reflect marginal costs. This would also be the case if imperfect competition was the dominant market structure rather than perfect competition. When any of these fundamental assumptions is relaxed the actual trade pattern could differ from that predicted by Heckscher–Ohlin.

The early empirical work of Leontief (1954) and others failed to find support for the predictions of the neoclassical Heckscher–Ohlin model and led to a full-scale reappraisal of the approach. Some theorists sought rehabilitation of Heckscher–Ohlin through expansion of the number of factors of production by the inclusion of natural resource endowments or subdividing capital and labour into their human capital components. At the same time, an alternative research programme was pursued by another group of trade theorists. This line of enquiry began by taking all that Heckscher–Ohlin had assumed as given and turning it on its head. Production functions were allowed to vary among countries and the existence of economies of scale and imperfect competition was recognised. Demand conditions were also allowed a more positive role. In the case of developing economies, the assumption that countries operate on their production possibility frontiers was dropped.

8.2.2 Technology and trade

The availability theory proposed by Kravis (1956) was a milestone on the road to incorporating the influence of technology on trade patterns. By making trade dependent on the relative as well as the absolute availability of factors, he showed that access to superior technology could endow a country with a comparative advantage. This advantage might only be temporary, however, as other nations learned of and adopted the technology. Later work by Posner (1961) and Hufbauer (1966) formalised and further developed this line of inquiry.

Posner's (1961) approach was to assume equal factor proportions between trading countries and then introduce technological changes in some industries. The conceptual problems of assuming equality of relative factor endowments when inputs are non-homogeneous, as well as the assumption that production functions vary between countries in the same industry, were difficult to deal with effectively. Posner proposed two solutions to these theoretical difficulties: either assume that factor price equalisation has occurred, or assume that inter-country valuations of capital stock are equal. Another dilemma remained, however. As a country undertook capital investment or accumulated know-how it would increase its capital stock relative to other countries. This violated the assumption of equality in inter-country capital endowments. Posner resolved the dilemma by limiting his discussion to a specific or narrow group of industries – meaning, effectively, that overall equality among countries could be assumed.

Posner's (1961) stylised model can be summarised in the following way: a firm in one country either adopts a new cost-cutting method of production or produces a new product. To avoid bankruptcy, other firms in the industry may copy the innovation, but with a lag. This lag has two components. First, there is the time firms take to adjust to the new competitive situation – the 'reaction lag' – and, second, there is the time required to assimilate the new product or process – the 'learning period'. These two delays taken together give the 'domestic imitation lag'. If the innovation is first adopted abroad, the lag increases, giving rise to the 'foreign reaction lag'. The foreign reaction lag will be longer because firms are less aware of foreign developments. In the interim period, before a country's firms can react to foreign innovativeness, exports come in from abroad. These trade flows need not take place in only one direction as no one country has a monopoly on innovation. By further assuming that innovations occur over a period of time and in a variety of industries, Posner's model could predict a constant flow of trade between countries.

Dynamic economies of scale are central to the operation of Posner's model. The length of production runs gives innovating firms and the countries in which they are located an advantage over their rivals.

Hufbauer's (1966) approach was similar to Posner's (1961). Hufbauer, however, suggested that the learning process is based on experience. Longer production runs rather than the volume of production are the key ingredient in experience. As with Posner's hypothesis, any advantage gained will be short-lived owing to imitation – unless new innovations are developed. One result of Hufbauer's approach was the conclusion that small countries could, through trade, establish and maintain – at least for a period – an advantage over larger countries, which were ostensibly more likely to benefit from economies of scale.

A major departure from Posner's (1961) approach was Hufbauer's (1966) relaxation of the assumptions of equal proportions in factor endowments and factor price equalisation. The existence of high- and low-wage countries gave his model a different focus. Technological improvement and, hence, exports were likely to be concentrated exclusively in high-wage economies. Over time, however, firms in low-wage countries would produce domestic substitutes for imports. Their lower wage costs would eventually confer a comparative advantage in production and the flow of trade in the particular commodity would be reversed. As there was a technology gap between countries, Hufbauer predicted that the exports of rich (i.e. high-wage) countries would be dominated by new products. The empirical evidence appeared to confirm this hypothesis. Why the production of new goods should be located in high-wage rather than low-wage countries was left to Vernon (1966) and Hirsch (1967) to explain.

Vernon (1966) argued that economies with high average per capita incomes and high wages were the most likely to generate demand for new products and labour-saving processes. During a new product's or process's initial phase, uncertainties surrounding its specifications and application required ease of communication between producer and consumer. This made it advantageous to locate production close to the market. When foreign demand for the product or process first arose it was met by exports from the innovating country. Further increases in demand would subsequently be met by shifting production overseas in order to be nearer new and expanding markets. By locating abroad firms would also be able to avail themselves of lower labour costs. As the product/process matured further and reached a phase of advanced standardisation, competitive pressures made low-wage countries even more attractive as centres of production. Eventually, the flow of exports was reversed and the advanced high-wage economy would find itself an importer of the very goods it used to export.

While broadly accepting Vernon's view of the product cycle, Hirsch (1967) placed greater emphasis on the skilled labour required in the early phase of a product's development and production. The flexibility of skilled labour is the principal reason for the location of new industries in advanced countries. In the early phases of production before a product or process is standardised, frequent changes are needed that require the use of highly skilled labour. As large quantities of skilled labour are found only in advanced countries, Hirsch concluded that the production of new goods and the adoption of new processes would be concentrated in these countries. As a product or process was refined, its production would follow the usual pattern and gravitate to low-wage countries over time. Trade patterns would reflect this evolutionary cycle in the location of production.

Refinements were subsequently made to the theory of the product cycle. Rapp (1975) provided a more workable definition of newness; Magee (1977) formalised the nature of technological transfer; and Finger (1975a) suggested that product development could form part of a competitive strategy.

In the technological gap theories, including the product cycle models, high incomes were considered to be the spur to the development of new products or labour-saving processes. Previously, Linder (1961) had advanced the view that similarity of income determined the trade in manufactured goods between countries. Linder hypothesised that a country's manufactured exports would be to others with similar tastes and, hence, demands. As the characteristics of consumer demand are a function of income, exports would be greatest to countries with similar incomes. Criticisms of Linder's model, principally that by Johnson (1964), focused on the determinants of comparative advantage. Both the need for strong domestic markets and the presumed difficulties faced by entrepreneurs in obtaining information about foreign markets were called into question. As a result, Linder's approach was not accepted to the same degree as the technological alternatives to Heckscher–Ohlin. The same fate befell the economies of scale approach proposed by Drèze (1960) because it could not explain why a country had achieved economies of scale while its rivals had not. The Linder hypothesis and economies of scale did, however, play a significant role in the development of intra-industry trade models.

How should the technological models be assessed relative to the neo-classical factor proportion explanations of trade patterns? The technology theories, unlike the Heckscher–Ohlin model, were essentially dynamic in that they suggested continuously evolving patterns of trade. The introduction of the time element added a dash of realism to the study of international commodity movements as trade patterns do change over time. Although, at first sight, the two approaches to modelling trade seem irreconcilable, this is not necessarily the case. For example, if goods are recast into their component characteristics, the conflict disappears. Thus, high-income countries would export new consumer goods that pander to the diverse tastes that arise from high incomes as well as capital equipment that was labour-saving. These types of products require large inputs of skilled labour to carry out the necessary R&D. Advanced countries are abundant in these factors. Hence, advanced countries export the goods that make use of their abundant factor. Developing countries, on the other hand, have a comparative advantage in producing highly standardised products that can make do with unskilled labour – which developing countries tend to have in abundance. Between the first and last phase of the product cycle factor intensity reversal occurs, but at any given moment in time entrepreneurs are not presented with the option of changing their capital–labour ratios. In this way, Heckscher–Ohlin and the technology models can be reconciled if the former is not strictly interpreted in relation to the definition of what constitutes factors – in other words, if factors are no longer defined solely as homogeneous capital and labour.

There are other criticisms of technology-based models. First, they depend on real income growth to generate innovations. Hence, trading patterns could change dramatically if growth slowed. Second, the product cycle approach ignored the possibility of multinationals transferring production technology rapidly to overseas subsidiaries. This criticism was forcefully expressed by Giddy (1978) and partially accepted by Vernon (1979). Last, the technology models are partial equilibrium models of trade and do not give a clear guide to the nature of causality. The assertion is that it runs from high income growth to the development of new technologies and products. It could be equally valid to suggest that technological improvements lead to high incomes.

In defence of the technological theories, they do bring technological progress to the forefront of the trade debate and also explain why innovations in technology and new products come about. The Heckscher–Ohlin approach can-not explain why firms should undertake innovative activity. This is particularly important when markets are assumed to be perfectly competitive. Of course,

Heckscher–Ohlin assumes perfect competition as the dominant market structure. Furthermore, as Vernon (1979) suggested, the existence of multinationals may shorten the transfer time in the product cycle, but it does not necessarily remove it altogether. Although it is true that the technological gap models adopt a partial rather than a general equilibrium analysis, this alone should not disqualify them from consideration. While they may not be as mathematically elegant as the Heckscher–Ohlin model, they do highlight important influences, such as newness, quality, and technological leadership, in determining trade patterns. The static nature of the neoclassical approach is simply not amenable to these dynamic influences on trade relationships.

8.2.3 Competing theories and empirical tests – steps forward or steps back?

It is probably not surprising that empirical evidence was called upon to provide a resolution to controversies arising from the differing theoretical approaches. Empirical validation has become an increasingly recognised theme of research in the social sciences. Difficulties, however, were encountered over the empirical methodology to adopt, the appropriate statistical techniques to use and the suitability of some of the proxies that were devised to model theoretical ideas.

Deardorff (1984) neatly summarised the problems associated with testing trade theories. He saw trade theories as trying to answer the question: What goods do countries trade and why? Trade volumes and the choice of trading partners were also important questions. The principal models of international trade explain the pattern of trade in terms of comparative advantage. That is, countries export those goods which have the lowest relative cost and, thus, prices under autarky. One difficulty for empirical testing is deriving autarkic prices when countries have been trading for a very long period of time. The method used by empirical economists to circumvent this difficulty is indirect testing that links comparative advantage to observable characteristics.

A further empirical problem is that trade patterns may not be linearly related to autarkic prices. As we saw in Chapter 2 for the Ricardian model, the direction of trade depends on the difference between autarkic and world prices but the quantity traded does not. The quantity of a good traded depends on world demand and a country's capacity to produce the good. The same is true in the neoclassical model except that there is an added complication that when the number of goods does not match the number of factors, the direction of trade may become indeterminate. If observable characteristics do not proxy autarkic prices, if the postulated relationships are non-linear and if the theoretical models do not reflect real-world commodity composition, the determinacy of trade flows is called into question. One should, then, be sceptical of statistical and other results that rest on contrary assumptions. In particular, doubts arise as to the appropriateness of regression analysis in testing trade theories. Similar difficulties attend the use of logit and probit analyses, which, unlike regression analysis, attempt to predict only the direction of trade and not its quantity.

As an alternative to finding suitable arrangements to overcome the difficulties created by the absence of autarkic prices, one can examine the relationship between trade and prices by utilising Leontief's (1954) input–output matrix. In this approach trade is related to factor abundance through factor intensity in production. Again, however, there are problems of a methodological nature. The difficulty of obtaining trading partners' input–output coefficients led analysts to base their tests of the Heckscher–Ohlin model on the assumption that similar production functions prevailed in different countries. This strong abstraction from the true state of technical capability internationally was made solely so that the only input–output coefficients available – those of the US – could be used for all other countries.

Furthermore, a debate surrounds the correct form of the Heckscher–Ohlin model to test using Leontief's techniques. It is not clear whether the *commodity* version or the *factor content* version of the model is the correct version to test.

One procedure whereby a direct and deterministic relationship between prices and trade could be assumed was developed by Balassa (1963). He made use of indices of export performance to reveal a country's comparative advantage. These indices were calculated by dividing a country's share of exports in a particular commodity category by its share in total world (or the sub-sample of countries under consideration) exports of the commodity. The indices produced for each country could then be ranked in descending order of magnitude. Low numbers would indicate that a country had a comparative advantage in that particular good.

The advantage of Balassa's (1963) approach was that it avoided the trap of assuming that because a country exported a good, it must have a comparative advantage in its production. There are, however, problems associated with his measure. The first is that in time-series tests improvements in rankings may not necessarily indicate improvements in comparative advantage. Second, data based on broad commodity groups could be unreliable. For example, a country may have a large market share in a subsector but a small share of the overall commodity group. Calculations based on the group would indicate incorrectly that the country had a low comparative advantage in the sector. By using a system of weights and reclassifying commodity groups more narrowly, these problems can be overcome. An additional difficulty arises, however, when inter-country comparisons are made. For example, if a particular commodity group heads the index in, say, country A but is fifth in country B, one cannot say that country B is absolutely less efficient than A in its production. Recalculating the indices in absolute terms can overcome the problem of comparing rankings, but it complicates the analysis and the validity of the results may be questioned.

Although the empirical analyses that have been carried out are flawed, they should not be discarded altogether because they have provided many insights into the causes of trade patterns. The deficiencies outlined above, however, mean that disagreements will continue to arise among trade economists.

A major difficulty for the evaluation of the constant opportunity cost version of the Ricardian model was how to test a theory that predicted complete specialisation when the observable facts so blatantly contradicted this prediction. Furthermore, even if complete specialisation did exist, it would be impossible to attribute trade to differences in relative labour costs because the relevant industries in the importing country would not exist!

The complete specialisation problem was overcome by accepting Hufbauer's (1966) modification of Ricardian theory whereby increasing opportunity cost replaced constant opportunity cost as a key assumption. Specialisation is no longer complete and relative labour costs are observable. The question then arises, however, as to how international comparisons should be made. Given the low volume of trade between rivals in a particular commodity, the approach adopted by most researchers was to relate countries' export performance in third markets to the ratio of their costs. Using variants of this methodology, MacDougall (1951, 1952), Stern (1962) and Balassa (1963) found support for the Ricardian proposition.

Bhagwati (1964), however, argued that the Ricardian approach did not necessarily mean that a country with a comparative advantage would export more to third markets than its rivals. Thus, tests based on third markets were invalid. Moreover, his own work did not find a relationship between relative labour costs and export prices. There were two responses to these criticisms. First, Ricardian theory suggested something stronger: that the country with the comparative advantage would be the only exporter to third markets. Second, export prices were not a test of the Ricardian theory, which attributed trade to relative costs. Observed export prices could have been influenced by the trade process and not the other way round. Further, prices might not reflect costs in industries that did not approach perfect competition.

The testing of the Heckscher–Ohlin theorem comprised two approaches: Leontief's input–output technique; and regression analysis, along with its variants such as probit and logit analysis. Input–output analysis was mainly applied to test the factor content version of Heckscher–Ohlin, while the other techniques were used to test the commodity version.

Leontief's (1954) analysis of the trade position of the US, as well as those studies carried out on other countries, came to the same (so-called) paradoxical conclusions. The empirical evidence indicated trade patterns which were direct opposites to the predictions of Heckscher–Ohlin. By and large, the paradox could be resolved if other factors were included rather than just labour and capital. Allowing for human capital also provided a promising alternative specification. Even this innovation, however, could not explain the empirical observation that in a relatively capital-rich country, such as the United States, exports were more labour-intensive than imports.

Leamer (1980) responded by insisting that one compare the factor ratios embodied in production and consumption rather than exports and imports because the trade data could be affected by trade imbalances. A capital-abundant country could, when trade was imbalanced, be found to export goods that were not intensive in its abundant factor. Leamer found that the capital–labour ratio in US production was higher than that embodied in consumption. Stern and Maskus's (1981) results, however – using data from different years than Leamer had considered – cast doubt on the validity of Leamer's work as they indicated a lower capital–labour ratio in production than consumption.

The regression, probit and logit results were also unkind to the strict Heckscher–Ohlin model, which allows only capital and labour as factor inputs. Baldwin (1971) found that US trade was negatively related to capital–labour ratios but positively associated with the level of educational attainment and the skill intensity of the labour force.

Harkness and Kyle's (1975) use of logit analysis upheld the Heckscher–Ohlin theorem by ascribing a positive role to capital. The work by Branson and Monoyios (1977), using cross-section and time-series data and probit analysis, failed to confirm Harkness and Kyle's results and conformed to the Leontief paradox.

The testing of the technology-based theories was carried out both at the country and cross-country/commodity level. The case studies on individual or groups of industries and the cross-country/commodity investigations provided support for the various hypotheses. As with the tests of the Heckscher–Ohlin model, these studies increased in technical sophistication and coverage. Thus, the simple correlation analysis of Keesing (1966) gave way to the regression analysis of Gruber and Vernon (1970), Baldwin (1971), Goodman and Ceyhun (1976) and Soete (1981) and the comparative studies of Katrak (1982), Smith *et al.* (1983) and Hughes (1983).

All of these authors used slightly different measures of technological sophistication. Keesing (1966) based his measure of skill on eight labour categories. Gruber and Vernon (1970) looked at the proportion of scientists and engineers employed in industry but also used expenditure on R&D as a proxy for skill levels. Goodman and Ceyhun (1976), though restricting their analysis to the US, divided their sample into old and new industries and used principal components analysis to overcome the problem of collinearity among the independent variables. Like Gruber and Vernon, they included proxies for non-technological factors of production in their work. This also was true of Baldwin (1971), who developed a variety of measures of labour skills. Using the skill variables defined in this way, he was unable to determine whether labour skills were simply an additional input in the non-strict version of Heckscher–Ohlin or a true technology variable. Soete (1981) studied the influence of technology by making use of an output measure of R&D activity based on patents awarded rather than what he considered a poor input-based proxy – the expenditure on R&D, which had been used in previous studies. He believed that his output measure allowed one to distinguish between the modified Heckscher–Ohlin factor proportions approach to trade and the technological gap theories. Again, the results proved to be favourable to the technological theories, especially in *newer* industries.

His findings were also in line with Goodman and Ceyhun's (1976) results for the US.

Other studies (Katrak, 1982; Smith *et al.*, 1983; and Hughes, 1983) tried to unravel the dual influence of R&D as a factor endowment and a measure of a country's innovativeness. The skill factor showed a positive influence on exports in all these studies, but R&D was significant only in the study by Hughes.

As incomes in the United States have historically been high relative to other countries and because innovators were thought of as being influenced primarily by local markets, most tests of the product cycle have concentrated on the US. Case studies by Hirsch (1972), Wells (1972) and Poh (1987) supported the idea that the trade of advanced countries was associated with new industries, newness being variously defined in terms of of rapid growth rates in high value-added industries, export growth rates or the difference between current product use and potential product use – the saturation gap. Notwithstanding some criticism, they all lent support to the product cycle theory.

Morrall's (1972) study of twenty-two US industries confirmed the findings of the case studies. He tested four distinctive product cycle proxies – the percentage of scientists and engineers employed, the growth of value added, an index of efficiency growth and an index encompassing the marketing, communications, consultancy and legal costs associated with new products. The coefficients, for the most part, possessed the expected signs and were statistically significant. These results strongly implied that the product cycle model was a valid explanation of trade. Tsurumi (1977), using Japanese data, found that exports from that country were also closely associated with new products and processes.

Although ad hoc empirical specifications of the product cycle provided support for the model, problems with the assumptions underlying the cycle cast theoretical doubts on its continued validity as a theory. Mansfield, Romeo and Wagner (1979) and Dunning and Buckley (1977) found that innovations in products and production processes could be transferred quickly to foreign subsidiaries. Thus, the degree of influence of the product cycle on trade patterns was likely to be considerably reduced and the possibility was raised that, as a theory, it had reached its mature phase.

Empirical tests of the Linder (1961) hypothesis – that trade is concentrated among countries with similar income levels – focused on its implication that the quality of products demanded is influenced by the level of per capita income. Linder's own tests supported his hypothesis, but they lacked empirical sophistication. Later investigators used more advanced statistical techniques that incorporated time-series and cross-sectional data. The evidence provided by these additional studies suggested that many countries do indeed trade disproportionately with countries that have similar per capita incomes.

One major problem faced by all empirical studies of the Linder (1961) hypothesis was that countries with similar per capita incomes are in close proximity to one another. Other factors, such as political, cultural and social ties, were also felt to have an influence on the pattern of trade. Thus, although

Fortune (1971), Sailors, Qureshi and Cross (1973), Ahmad and Simos (1979) and Shelburne (1987) found in favour of Linder's hypothesis, Hoftyzer (1975), Greytak and McHugh (1977) and Kennedy and McHugh (1983) did not. Greytak and McHugh's methodology of using domestic regional data in the US to test international trade theories weakened their case. Kennedy and McHugh based their test on changes in per capita incomes and trade over time, thereby neutralising the distance factor, but failed to find support for Linder's hypothesis. Shelburne, using a gravity model, did find evidence to support the hypothesis – although it was very weak. Stronger, more positive, evidence was forthcoming when the data were disaggregated by commodity. New and human capital-intensive goods in the disaggregated model had highly correlated trade and income coefficients.

The evidence supporting economies of scale as a determinant of trade is indirect in that it was found in studies undertaken to test other theories. It is also contradictory: Baldwin (1971) found no evidence that economies of scale determined US trade patterns, whereas Katrak's (1982) study indicated a positive influence in the case of the UK.

Both income similarity and economies of scale had more relevance in testing the hypotheses concerning intra-industry trade. Even there a major difficulty in testing the influence of economies of scale was the lack of agreement on a suitable proxy.

Once the technology-based theories and the modified Heckscher–Ohlin model had achieved a degree of empirical support, a number of researchers attempted to test the models simultaneously. Hufbauer (1970) tested the Heckscher–Ohlin model and the alternative technology gap and economies of scale models. Using simple statistical techniques and a data set drawn from the leading industrial countries, he concluded that all the theories had a role in explaining trade patterns. He found that export characteristics were strongly correlated with national attributes. Although no one theory could be said to monopolise the explanation of export patterns, he did feel that the high rank correlation between relative capital endowments and capital–labour ratios embodied in exports lent strong support to the Heckscher–Ohlin model. Nevertheless, his preferred and more general model was a modified Heckscher–Ohlin model constructed by augmenting the capital–labour ratio with labour skills. Two weaknesses of Hufbauer's study should be noted. First, his statistical techniques were rudimentary. Second, he used US data to define commodity characteristics for other countries.

While accepting Hufbauer's (1970) basic approach, Hirsch (1974) attempted to make the relationship between country/industry attributes and comparative advantage more explicit. His work covered the trade data of twenty-five industries in twenty-nine countries. Using Balassa's (1965) measure of revealed comparative advantage, he calculated export performance indicators for every industry in each country. He then calculated and ranked the simple correlation coefficients between an industry's export performance in each country and the country's value added per employee. His next step was to rank the industry characteristics that reflected the various theories – producing five sets of data, which were then correlated with the initial industry rankings. His results gave positive support to the technological variables but only limited confirmation for those reflecting the Heckscher–Ohlin theory. Complementary tests for each country, which involved regressing skill, capital, scale and resource variables against its industries' export ratio, again provided support for the technological theories. The skill variables conformed with *a priori* expectations, but the capital variable did not. On the basis of both sets of empirical evidence and since capital is internationally highly mobile, Hirsch concluded that the technology-based theories were superior in explaining trade patterns.

In a subsequent study, Hirsch (1975) undertook a series of regressions for eight industries of twenty-eight countries. His procedure involved regressing an industry's share of a country's exports on per capita income. Industries were divided into two groups – high export share or low export share. These groupings were further subdivided into labour-intensive or capital-intensive sectors. Hirsch again found that the Heckscher–Ohlin variables did not perform as well as the variables that had been chosen to reflect the product cycle models. An important reservation concerning his results was that he tested only the strict form of the Heckscher–Ohlin model with two factor inputs – capital and labour.

Aquino's (1981) approach made use of time-series and cross-sectional data to identify changes in the pattern of comparative advantage in manufactured goods over time. Two models were tested; both included a technology and an economies of scale variable but only one incorporated a measure of capital endowments. Aquino's findings strongly suggested that the technological variables were the best determinants of international trade patterns at any given moment of time, whereas changing trade patterns were best explained by the variables reflecting the product cycle hypothesis.

Leamer (1974) divided trade-determining variables into three groups reflecting an economy's level of development, the existing hindrances to trade and available resources. These were then used in a Bayesian statistical analysis to account for the country's share of imports as a proportion of its GDP. The same variables were also applied to imports as a proportion of exports. Trying to generalise his results by the use of the irreducible expected squared-loss measure, Leamer found that the resource group did not perform very well. Within the group of resource variables, however, the R&D proxy performed best – but only when combined with capital intensity or education levels. When imports as a proportion of exports were taken as the measure of trade success, the resource group – in particular the R&D variable – appeared to be the most important determinant of trade patterns.

In the individual country studies in which the models where put in competition with one another, a similar pattern of support for technology-based theories and/or the modified Heckscher–Ohlin model emerged. Using a variety of measures of export performance, Baldwin (1971) and Morrall (1972) for the US, Carlsson and Ohlsson (1976) for Sweden, and Smith *et al.* (1983) for the UK all found that the major determinants of each country's trade in the world economy were skilled labour/human capital inputs of one type or another. In the case of West Germany, however, Wolter (1977) concluded that it was difficult to differentiate clearly between neo-factor proportions variables and neo-technology variables.

Minor variations were apparent in the influence of the various measures of skills and technology from country to country, but the overall results suggested that the simple Heckscher–Ohlin model was not appropriate for describing the trade of advanced countries. These country-specific results have, in general, confirmed that some theoretical amalgam might best explain trade or, alternatively, that one should use each theory to account for the trade in particular types of goods (Hirsch, 1974).

Why, if there is so much empirical evidence against it, does the Heckscher–Ohlin theorem still survive as the dominant research model for economists who specialise in international trade and as the major pedagogical tool in both undergraduate and postgraduate education? It survives for several reasons. First, the alternative models also suffer from methodological difficulties such that, in their present form, none provides an entirely satisfactory alternative. Second, these methodological deficiencies cannot be satisfactorily controlled for in empirical tests. As a result, the empirical tests remain ad hoc and, hence, less than conclusive. Third, in its modified form (i.e. allowing human capital to be an input), there appears to be considerable empirical support for Heckscher–Ohlin – sufficient support to satisfy many economists. A fourth, more philosophical, reason has been proffered by DeMarchi (1976). He suggested that the Heckscher–Ohlin theorem is part of a widespread research programme within economics as a whole. This programme focuses on studying how resources are allocated efficiently. Its framework is, moreover, based on the idea of free markets. DeMarchi argued that trade theory has been greatly influenced by the prevailing value judgement that free markets are good. The neoclassical model, through its durability, tends to justify the existence and continuation of free markets – including international markets – rather than acting as a theory that asks questions about the composition of capital and the appropriateness of perfect competition as an assumption in a world where international firms with considerable market power clearly exist.

The alternative models of trade, on the other hand, do not necessarily defend free trade per se. Borkakoti (1975), in his paper on the welfare implications of Posner's (1961) model, has shown that in order to maximise its welfare a country can legitimately adopt protectionist measures. Krugman (1979) has also shown that a case can be made for government intervention. His analysis began by accepting that comparative advantage may well explain trade but in addition, he suggested, countries may find it beneficial to specialise. Thus, countries which have identical endowments can produce different sets of goods. The benefits that flow from this type of specialisation are, according to this analysis, based on increasing returns to scale.

The traditional justification for free trade was that markets left to themselves would allocate resources efficiently unless distortions, rigidities or externalities existed. If any of the latter conditions prevailed, theory suggested that government intervention was allowed – via subsidies – to encourage a return to the efficient allocation of resources. In the neoclassical view, resources would move into a particular sector until high returns were competed away. In Krugman's (1979) view, many goods are traded in markets where competition cannot be relied on to eliminate high returns. In an industry characterised by increasing returns, a few firms or a country that gains a head start in that industry may acquire a persistent advantage. By encouraging the growth of a sector that enjoys increasing returns, a government can raise the welfare of its citizens at the expense of foreigners. When dynamic aspects of technology drive trade, governments should intervene to pick winners to be fostered. Alternatively, governments should be responsible for providing conditions that are conducive to innovation. If human skills are important, then government – through its responsibility for education – may have a role in creating comparative advantage. Only when endowments of factors are the sole determinants of trade is there no role for government.

If De Marchi's conjectures on the propensity of economists to defend free markets are correct, it is hard to understand why the great theoretical and empirical diversion into intra-industry trade and trade under conditions of imperfect competition should have taken place in the last quarter of the twentieth century. What is still more difficult to explain, however, is why interest in resolving the anomalies thrown up by the conflicting theories of international trade almost disappeared in the late 1980s. Part of the answer is related to the efforts put into the study of intra-industry trade and imperfect competition. Given the rather rudimentary nature of the models that were tested into the 1980s and the advances in econometric techniques that have occurred since then, much fertile ground remains to be ploughed.

8.2.4 Diverted energies – intra-industry trade and trade under imperfect competition

The appearance and growing importance of intra-industry trade in the 1950s and 1960s led economists eventually to turn their energies to explaining the phenomenon. In parallel with theoretical developments, issues surrounding the existence of the phenomenon and its measurement were also studied. Finger's (1975b) contention that the factor content of goods varied more within industries than between them cast doubt on whether intra-industry trade existed at all. However, improvements in measurement techniques and the finer disaggregation of trade data provided continued evidence that the volume of intra-industry trade was large.

Although earlier studies had made reference to intra-industry trade, it was not until Grubel and Lloyd's (1975) work that serious theoretical efforts to explain intra-industry trade began. Intra-industry trade takes place in both homogeneous and non-homogeneous goods. In the case of the former most trade flows could be accounted for by market distortions, such as subsidies, transport costs and seasonality. Observed entrepôt trade could be explained within the Heckscher–Ohlin framework or a more controversial duopolistic Cournot framework. It was intra-industry trade in non-homogeneous goods where the major theoretical effort was required. Models explaining the existence of such trade are of two types – informal and formal. The latter are divided into those that explain trade between identical economies and those which examine intra-industry trade between non-identical economies.

An example of the informal approach was that presented in Grubel and Lloyd's (1975) study, which emphasised differences in style and quality between countries with similar incomes coupled with both static and dynamic economies of scale as explanatory factors. Later studies explored economies of scale more fully as well as the influence of prices on intra-industry trade.

Formal modelling was more rigorous and drew on theoretical developments in the literature concerning consumer behaviour and economies of scale. An industrial structure dominated by monopolistic competition and economies of scale as well as consumers' desire for variety were invoked as possible explanations.

Altering the assumption of consumers' behaviour so that they maximised utility by purchasing a preferred variety explained intra-industry trade as long as the preferred product varied from individual to individual. Which varieties were produced in which country could not be predicted. It was suggested that the location of production was influenced by random historical or cultural factors.

Oligopolistic models have also been adapted to explain intra-industry trade in both vertically and horizontally differentiated goods. Shaked and Sutton's (1984) model assumed that improvements in quality imposed higher costs on firms. Consumers had identical tastes, but inequality of income prevented all of them from buying the highest-quality goods. In this way price became part of the budget constraint. When trade was opened up between countries the competitive process ensured that the firms with the lowest costs supplied the individual market that was created as a result of income inequality. Shaked and Sutton's analysis also implied that, as a result of trade, prices would fall and the quality of goods would rise. As long as it was assumed that incomes differed between countries, it was possible to determine which varieties would be produced by which country. For example, high-income countries would produce high-quality varieties of products, while the opposite would be true of low-income countries.

Eaton and Kierkowski's (1986) approach adopted Lancaster's (1969) assumptions regarding consumers' attitudes to variety but accepted that they might trade off their ideal against price. The entry of firms was not controlled by cost factors but by the demands of consumers for variety. Thus, in a simple two-country world with one firm in each country producing its own variety of a good, intra-industry trade could take place as long as tastes in each country were clustered around its domestically produced variety. If they were spread out along a spectrum, a third firm could set up and supply the market with an intermediate variety. An essential assumption for the existence of two-way trade was that the economies were of roughly equal size. Otherwise, the larger country's firms would benefit from economies of scale, capture the total market and supply both countries.

Attempts were also made to account for intra-industry trade between dissimilar economies. Falvey and Kierkowski (1984) put forward the hypothesis that as the quality of goods changed, so did their factor inputs. In other words, as quality increases a good could evolve from being labour-intensive to being capital- intensive. Countries would concentrate on producing the qualities that used their abundant factors most intensively – a prediction that is in line with the Heckscher–Ohlin hypothesis. Intra-industry trade would occur as long as demand existed for both high- and low-quality goods in each country.

In the empirical studies of intra-industry trade, one of the first problems to be encountered was whether variables could be found that reflected the theoretical concepts embodied in the various models. When proxies could be found, there were a number of alternatives for the representation of taste overlap, economies of scale, product differentiation, technology and barriers to trade. Furthermore, in the case of economies of scale there was even some doubt about the expected sign of the coefficient. Despite these difficulties, most of the studies did, nevertheless, find that the variables tested conformed to the *a priori* expectation of the models. The non-specific nature of the intra-industry trade theories, however, made it impossible to identify either a superior model or the way to a *new* general model of trade. As with the previous explorations of alternative inter-industry trade models, the diversion of effort into the study of intra-industry trade has left more questions unanswered than it answered. A consensus on an appropriate general trade model remains elusive.

8.3 Whither trade theories and empirical evidence?

In conclusion, what can we say about trade theories and the related empirical evidence? Principally, there is not at present a general theory of international trade. The existence of both inter- and intra-industry trade has complicated theoretical inquiry and the large number of factors that have been found to influence trade has rendered an empirical reconciliation impossible up to the present. Whether trade theorists should continue to attempt to formulate a new general theory is a moot point. Certainly, there are economists who cannot see the need for such a development, but this apathy has to be balanced against some relatively successful attempts at reconciliation. Examples of the latter include Arad and Hirsch's (1981) work on combining Linder's hypothesis with the Heckscher–Ohlin theorem and Katrak's (1988) on the influence of factor endowments on R&D activity. Markusen's (1986) explanation for the existence of both inter- and intra-industry trade is also an important example of an attempt to develop an integrated theory of trade. As we have seen throughout this book, what appear to be advances beget only further questions. Both the alternative theories to Heckscher–Ohlin and some of the intra-industry models still have difficulty explaining why countries choose to produce and trade a particular set of goods. Dynamic economies of scale have been suggested as an answer, but the questions then arises as to why some countries are more dynamic.

The posing of ever more questions is the essence of the ongoing interplay between empirical investigation of the hypotheses of trade theorists and the generation of new hypotheses. After reading this book one could easily conclude that nothing has been resolved. This conclusion would be correct – but there are now a lot more questions. Since the computer revolution, which has for the first time allowed economists to attempt to validate the propositions of trade theorists empirically, far more questions have been raised about trade theory than had been raised since the mercantile debates of the early part of the nineteenth century. The classical and, subsequently, Heckscher–Ohlin theories of trade were allowed long periods of refinement because no substantive empirical evaluation could be undertaken. The result is the elegant, logically consistent, pedagogically appealing and, for many, intellectually satisfying trade model that still dominates both academic journals and today's textbooks. Neoclassical trade theory is an intellectual thing of beauty that might be worth learning simply for the discipline it imparts to logical thinking even if it did not explain international trade at all. In reality, of course, it provides a great deal of insight into matters of trade.

The theories which have been advanced as alternatives to the neoclassical trade model since the earth-shattering quandary created by the empirical evidence that has become known as the Leontief paradox have not had the luxury of decades of refinement. They simply do not have the pedigree that comes from decades of close intellectual scrutiny. As a result, they tend to be ad hoc, prone to logical inconsistency, ideas in formation and/or justifications for a set of empirical evidence. In this unrefined state they are easy targets for criticism by those whose skills in logic have been honed in the neoclassical orthodoxy. This criticism is not a bad thing. It is the same process that led to the refinement of the propositions of international trade first put forward by Smith and Ricardo so long ago.

Now, however, the new theories also face almost immediate empirical evaluation. As empirical methods have become a standard part of an economist's training, those who propose new theories also perform the first empirical tests. Other empirical tests typically follow quickly. As the account we have presented clearly illustrates, no theory has received consistent validation. The evidence has always been mixed. The questions that are raised by the empirical evidence, however, have led to new directions for research. New theoretical explanations for trade patterns are devised – and tested.

The study of international trade has been invigorated by this process. What may be disconcerting to some readers is that these new avenues in the study of international trade may not have a clearly defined destination. We have outlined some of the efforts to devise a reconciliation of newer theories with the propositions of Heckscher–Ohlin or to develop a new general theory of international trade, but these are only two threads among many. It is possible that no new general theory of international trade will arise to replace the ordered world of neoclassical trade theory. One thing is certain, however: if there *is* a new general theory of international trade waiting in the wings, not only will it have to stand up to close intellectual scrutiny, it will also have to undergo rigorous empirical evaluation. All new theories of international trade will be subject to empirical investigation.

This book was written largely as a prompt for those at the start of their careers as economists. There is a great deal of fertile ground for empirical investigation in the field of international trade. Statistical methods – and, in particular, econometrics – have advanced theoretically and in computing power since the first attempts at empirical investigation of trade theories. Many of the tests upon which the great controversies in trade theory are based appear naive by the standards of today's empirical testing. This suggests that one place to start might be to reformulate the original tests using today's methods. We suspect that this approach would yield a plethora of new questions and, as in the past, few definitive answers. Questions, as we have seen, lead to new ideas. Of course, problems with data will remain a bane of empirical investigation. Data are, however, available for a wider range of countries than ever before. Ironically, fewer data may be available for some key developed countries owing to the impact of governments' fiscal difficulties on statistical services. Data may also be more expensive than in the past as government statistical services begin to sell their information to generate revenue. On the other hand, the electronic communications revolution has made it much easier to share data. Collaboration can be instantaneous. If trade theory tells us anything, it is that as the barriers to trade in information and collaboration come down, economists should become more efficient. The pace at which progress in the study of international trade is made should increase.

Is trade theory in disarray? Given the logical progression arising from the interaction of the devisors of theory and the devisors of empirical tests, we think not. Trade theory is, however, clearly in disequilibrium. The question is whether it is converging to a new equilibrium – and if it is, will it be a stable equilibrium? At this point the answers to those questions cannot be discerned. The simple conclusion is that a lot more work needs to be done. With little concluded, the opportunities for fruitful inquiry appear almost unlimited.

References

Ahmad, A., and Simos, E. O. (1979), 'Preference similarity and trade in manufactures: an alternative test of Linder's hypothesis', *Rivista Internazionale di Scienze Economiche e Commerciali*, 26(8), pp. 721–40.
Aquino, A. (1981), 'Changes over time in the pattern of comparative advantage in manufactured goods', *European Economic Review*, 15(1), pp. 41–62.

Arad, R. W., and Hirsch, S. (1981), 'Determination of trade flows and choice of trade partners: reconciling the Heckscher–Ohlin and the Barenstam Linder models of international trade', *Weltwirtschaftliches Archiv*, 117, pp. 276–97.

Balassa, B. (1963), 'An empirical demonstration of classical comparative cost theory', *The Review of Economics and Statistics*, 45(3), pp. 231–8.

Balassa, B. (1965), 'Trade liberalization and revealed comparative advantage', *The Manchester School of Economic and Social Studies*, 33(2), pp. 99–123.

Baldwin, R. E. (1971), 'Determinants of the commodity structure of U.S. trade', *American Economic Review*, 61(1), pp. 126–46.

Bhagwati, J. N. (1964), 'The pure theory of international trade: a survey', *Economic Journal*, 74, pp. 1–84.

Borkakoti, J. (1975), 'Some welfare implications of the neo-technology hypothesis of the trade pattern of international trade', *Oxford Economic Papers*, 27(3), pp. 383–99.

Branson, W. H., and Monoyios, N. (1977), 'Factor inputs in US trade', *Journal of International Economics*, 7, pp. 111–31.

Carlsson, B., and Ohlsson, L. 'Structural determinants of Swedish foreign trade: a test of the conventional wisdom', *European Economic Review*, 7(2), pp. 165–74.

Deardorff, A. V. (1984), 'Testing trade theories and predicting trade flows', in R. W. Jones and P. B. Kenen (eds), *Handbook of International Economics*, vol. I, Amsterdam: North-Holland, pp. 467–517.

DeMarchi, N. (1976), 'Anomaly and the development of economics', in S. J. Latsis (ed.), *Method and Appraisal in Economics*, Cambridge: Cambridge University Press, pp. 109–27.

Drèze, S. J. (1960), 'Quelques réflexions sereines sur l'adaptation de l'industrie Belge au Marché Commun', *Comptes Rendus des Travaux de la Société Royale d'Economie Politique de Belgique*, no. 275, pp. 47–62.

Dunning, J. H., and Buckley, P. J. (1977), 'International production and alternative models of trade', *The Manchester School of Economic and Social Studies*, 45(4), pp. 392–403.

Eaton, J., and Kierkowski, H. (1984), 'Oligopolistic competition, product variety and international trade', in H. Kierkowski (ed.), *Monopolistic Competition and International Trade*, Oxford: Oxford University Press, pp. 49–60.

Falvey, R., and Kierkowski, H. (1984), 'Product quality, intra-industry trade and imperfect competition', Discussion paper, Graduate Institute of International Studies, Geneva.

Finger, J. M. (1975a), 'A new view of the product cycle theory', *Weltwirtschaftliches Archiv*, 111, pp. 79–99.

Finger, J. M. (1975b), 'Trade overlap and intra-industry trade', *Economic Inquiry*, 13, pp. 581–9.

Fortune, J. N. (1971), 'Some determinants of trade in finished manufactures', *Swedish Journal of Economics*, 73, pp. 311–17.

Giddy, I. H. (1978), 'The demise of the product cycle model in international business theory', *Columbia Journal of World Business*, 13(1), pp. 90–7.

Goodman, B., and Ceyhun, F. (1976), 'US export performance in manufacturing industries: an empirical investigation', *Weltwirtschaftliches Archiv*, 112, pp. 525–55.

Greytak, D., and McHugh, R. (1977), 'Linder's trade thesis: an empirical examination', *Southern Economic Journal*, 43(3), pp. 1386–9.

Grubel, H. G., and Lloyd, P. J. (1975), *Intra-Industry Trade: The Theory and Measurement of International Trade in Differentiated Products*, New York: John Wiley and Sons.

Gruber, W. H., and Vernon, R. (1970), 'The technology factor in a world trade matrix', in R. Vernon (ed.), *The Technology Factor in International Trade*, New York: Columbia University Press, pp. 233–72.

Harbeler, G. (1936), *The Theory of International Trade with its Application to Commercial Policy*, London: William Hodges and Co.

Harkness, J., and Kyle, J. F. (1975), 'Factors influencing United States comparative advantage', *Journal of International Economics*, 5, pp. 153–65.

Hirsch, S. (1967), *Location of Industry and International Competitiveness*, Oxford: Clarendon Press.

Hirsch, S. (1972), 'The United States electronics industry in international trade', in L. T. Wells (ed.), *The Product Life Cycle and International Trade*, Boston: Harvard University Press, pp. 39–52.

Hirsch, S. (1974), 'Capital or technology? Confronting the neo-factor proportions and neo-technology accounts of international trade', *Weltwirtschaftliches Archiv*, 110, pp. 535–63.

Hirsch, S. (1975), 'The product cycle model of international trade – a multi-country cross-section analysis', *Oxford Bulletin of Economics and Statistics*, 37(3), pp. 305–17.

Hoftyzer, J. (1975), 'Empirical verification of Linder's trade thesis: comment', *Southern Economic Journal*, 41(4), pp. 694–8.

Hufbauer, G. C. (1966), *Synthetic Materials and the Theory of International Trade*, London: Duckworth.

Hufbauer, G. C. (1970), 'The impact of national characteristics and technology on the commodity composition of trade in manufactured goods', in R. Vernon (ed.), *The Technology Factor in International Trade*, New York: National Bureau of Economic Research, pp. 145–231.

Hughes, K. S. (1983), 'Exports and innovation: a simultaneous equation model', Economics discussion paper no. 83/141, University of Bristol.

Johnson, H. G. (1964), 'Book review of Linder', *Economica*, 31(1), pp. 86–90.

Katrak, H. (1982), 'Labour skills, R and D and capital requirements in the international trade and investment of the United Kingdom, 1968–78', *National Institute Economic Review*, 101, pp. 38–47.

Katrak, H. (1988), 'R&D, international production and trade: the technological gap theory in a factor endowment model', *The Manchester School of Economic and Social Studies*, 56(3), pp. 205–22.

Keesing, D. B. (1966), 'Labour skills and comparative advantage', *American Economic Review*, 56(2), pp. 249–58.

Kennedy, T. E., and McHugh, R. (1983), 'Taste similarity and trade intensity: a test of the Linder hypothesis for United States exports', *Weltwirtschaftliches Archiv*, 119, pp. 84–96.

Kravis, I. B. (1956), 'Availability and other influences on the commodities composition of trade', *Journal of Political Economy*, 64(2), pp. 143–55.

Krugman, P. R. (1979), 'Increasing returns, monopolistic competition and international trade', *Journal of International Economics*, 9, pp. 469–79.

Lancaster, K. (1969), *Introduction to Modern Microeconomics*, Chicago: Rand McNally.

Leamer, E. E. (1974), 'The commodity composition of international trade in manufactures: an empirical analysis', *Oxford Economic Papers*, 26(3), pp. 350–74.

Leamer, E. E. (1980), 'The Leontief paradox reconsidered', *Journal of Political Economy*, 88(3), pp. 495–503.

Leontief, W. (1954), 'Domestic production and foreign trade: the American capital position re-examined', *Economia Internazionale*, 7(1), pp. 9–45.

Linder, S. B. (1961), *An Essay on Trade and Transformation*, New York: John Wiley and Sons.

MacDougall, G. A. D. (1951), 'British and American exports: a study suggested by the theory of comparative costs, part I', *Economic Journal*, 61, pp. 697–724.

MacDougall, G. A. D. (1952), 'British and American exports: a study suggested by the theory of comparative costs, part II', *Economic Journal*, 62, pp. 487–521.

Magee, S. P. (1977), 'Multinational corporations, the industry technology cycle and development', *Journal of World Trade Law*, 11(4), pp. 297–321.

Mansfield, E., Romeo, A., and Wagner, S. (1979), 'Foreign trade and US research and development', *The Review of Economics and Statistics*, 61, pp. 49–57.

Markusen, J. R. (1986), 'Explaining the volume of trade: an eclectic approach', *American Economic Review*, 76(5), pp. 1002–11.

Morrall, J. F. (1972), *Human Capital, Technology and the Role of the United States in International Trade*, Gainsville: University of Florida Press.

Ohlin, B. G. (1933), *Interregional and International Trade*, Harvard Economic Studies no. 39, Cambridge, Mass.: Harvard University Press.

Poh, L. Y. (1987), 'Product life cycle and export competitiveness of the UK electronics industry (1970–1979)', *The European Journal of Marketing*, 21(7), pp. 326–38.

Posner, M. V. (1961), 'International trade and technical change', *Oxford Economic Papers*, 13(3), pp. 323–41.

Rapp, W. V. (1975), 'The many possible extensions of the product cycle analysis', *Hitotsubashi Journal of Economics*, 16(7), pp. 22–9.

Sailors, J. W., Qureshi, U. A., and Cross, E. M. (1973), 'Empirical verification of Linder's trade thesis', *Southern Economic Journal*, 40(2), pp. 262–8.

Shaked, A., and Sutton, J. (1984), 'Natural oligopolies and international trade', in H. Kierkowski (ed.), *Monopolistic Competition and International Trade*, Oxford: Oxford University Press, pp. 34–50.

Shelburne, R. C. (1987), 'A ratio test of trade intensity and per-capita income similarity', *Weltwirtschaftliches Archiv*, 123, pp. 474–87.

Smith, S. R., White, G. M., Owen, N. C., and Hill, M. R. (1983), 'UK trade in manufacturing: the pattern of specialization during the 1970s', Government Economic Service working paper no. 56, London: HMSO.

Soete, L. L. G. (1981), 'A general test of technological gap trade theory', *Weltwirtschaftliches Archiv*, 117, pp. 638–60.

Stern, R. (1962), 'British and American productivity and comparative costs in international trade', *Oxford Economic Papers*, 14, pp. 275–96.

Stern, R. M., and Maskus, K. E. (1981), 'Determinants of the structure of US foreign trade, 1958–1976', *Journal of International Economics*, 11, pp. 207–24.

Tsurumi, Y. (1972), 'R&D factors and exports of manufactured goods of Japan', in L. T. Wells (ed.), *The Product Life Cycle and International Trade*, Boston: Harvard University Press, pp. 161–89.

Vernon, R. (1966), 'International investment and international trade in the product cycle', *Quarterly Journal of Economics*, 80(2), pp. 190–207.

Vernon, R. (1979), 'The product cycle hypothesis in a new international environment', *Oxford Bulletin of Economics and Statistics*, 41(4), pp. 255–67.

Wells, L. T. (1972), 'Test of a product cycle model of international trade: US exports of consumer variables', in L. T. Wells (ed.), *The Product Life Cycle and International Trade*, Boston: Harvard University Press, pp. 55–79.

Wolter, F. (1977), 'Factor proportions, technology and West German industry's international trade patterns', *Weltwirtschaftliches Archiv*, 113, pp. 250–67.

Index